THE YOUNG LADY'S POCKET LIBRARY, OR PARENTAL MONITOR

With a new Introduction by
Vivien Jones

THOEMMES PRESS

Published in 1995 by
Thoemmes Press
11 Great George Street
Bristol BS1 5RR
England

ISBN 1 85506 382 4

This is a reprint of the 1790 Edition

Publisher's Note

These reprints are taken from original copies of each book. In many cases the condition of those originals is not perfect, the paper, often handmade, having suffered over time and the copy from such things as inconsistent printing pressures resulting in faint text, show-through from one side of a leaf to the other, the filling in of some characters, and the break up of type. The publisher has gone to great lengths to ensure the quality of these reprints but points out that certain characteristics of the original copies will, of necessity, be apparent in reprints thereof.

FOR HER OWN GOOD

A SERIES OF CONDUCT BOOKS

THOEMMES

ACKNOWLEDGEMENTS

I want to thank David Fairer for his invaluable help in following up various references, John Whale for his continuing intellectual support, and Marie Mulvey Roberts and Kate Docker for their patience. This introduction was completed during study leave funded by the Humanities Research Board of the British Academy, and I am grateful for research time both to them, and to the School of English, University of Leeds.

INTRODUCTION

Conduct literature, particularly for young women, was a growth industry during the eighteenth century.[1] 'Industry' is not just an empty metaphor here. This was the period which discovered the book as a consumer item, and which saw a massive expansion in the number and variety of printed texts available to a growing reading public. Within this explosion of print culture, women were quickly identified as an important target group: increasingly, booksellers marketed periodicals, miscellanies, conduct books, and of course novels, for an explicitly female audience. If the sheer numbers of titles published are any indication, conduct books were highly saleable commodities and, unlike novels, they claimed to provide impeccably respectable reading for 'the fair sex'.

The Young Lady's Pocket Library, or Parental Monitor is a clear case of a bookseller cashing in on this market for female advice literature. It offers its readers the bargain of four of the most popular and influential of eighteenth-century conduct books under one cover. The earliest text in the collection is the Marchioness de Lambert's *Advice of a Mother to her Daughter* which was first published in English in 1727, but probably

[1] On the growth in conduct books in the late seventeenth and early eighteenth centuries, see Nancy Armstrong and Leonard Tennenhouse (editors), *The Ideology of Conduct: Essays in Literature and the History of Sexuality* (New York and London: Methuen, 1987), p.10.

written thirty or so years earlier than that; the latest is John Gregory's *A Father's Legacy to His Daughters* of 1774; and *The Young Lady's Parental Monitor* itself, first published in Dublin in 1790, was still available until at least 1808, when a third edition was published by respectable booksellers in Edinburgh and London.[2] Spanning a century, *The Parental Monitor* is thus an important text for modern historians of advice literature and, more generally, of femininity itself.

The feminine ideal which conduct literature endorses is very specific in its social identity and relevance. As I have suggested, the popularity of the form points to women as a significant sub-group within a growing reading public. This growth in literacy (still, of course, very limited in terms of the population as a whole) was both symptom and cause of increased social mobility, as economic expansion extended, blurred and redefined social boundaries. Conduct literature addresses an audience of, almost exclusively young marriageable, women who are either already members of, or who aspire to join, the leisured classes. For a woman, social status and mobility depended almost exclusively on an advantageous marriage. Conduct books are guides to success – and survival. They regulate social and sexual behaviour, teaching women to discipline themselves into acceptable forms of femininity in order to achieve and maintain respectability.

Throughout the eighteenth and into the nineteenth century, the most successful conduct texts were in constant circulation: usually as legitimate reprints; quite frequently in pirated editions; sometimes as plagiarized

[2] The Brotherton Library, Leeds, has a copy of a third edition, printed by George Ramsay for J. Thomson Jun., Edinburgh, and John Murray, London, 1808.

extracts embedded in 'new' texts.[3] At one level, then, *The Parental Monitor* provides useful evidence of the enduring popularity of those individual conduct books which it chooses to include. But this perennial popularity raises more interesting questions about the continuities and the changes within ideals of femininity in the period. *The Parental Monitor* suggests not only that these four texts, written over a period of fifty years, are of continuing relevance to young women at the very end of the century, but also that they are unproblematically compatible with each other. It contributes, in other words, to the assumption that femininity is an unchanging, 'natural' condition which successive generations of conduct writers simply describe.

It is certainly true that these four texts have many premises and preoccupations in common. They collectively produce an image of 'proper' womanhood as chaste, modest, dutiful, and self-effacing. But the image is itself internally contradictory: women are presented as both naturally virtuous, and in particular need of instruction; feminine virtue is celebrated both for its own sake, and because it makes a woman desirable; it is uniquely powerful, yet women are constantly vulnerable. And within this shared conception of acceptable femininity, these texts manifest significant differences of approach and vocabulary. Such differences offer access to the subtle shifts of emphasis

[3] Among the most popular and frequently reprinted conduct books were: Richard Allestree, *The Ladies Calling* (first published 1673; latest edition recorded in the ESTC 1787); and George Savile, Marquis of Halifax, *The Lady's New-Year's Gift: or, Advice to a Daughter* (first published 1688; latest edition recorded in the ESTC 1784). Examples of texts which more or less extensively plagiarize other conduct books are: anonymous, *The Whole Duty of a Woman: Or, an infallible Guide to the Fair Sex* (1737); Wetenhall Wilkes, *A Letter of Genteel and Moral Advice to a Young Lady* (1740), which itself went through at least eight editions.

through which cultural change takes place; they also provide points of contradiction and resistance which give the lie to that implicit and influential claim that femininity is natural, inescapable, and transhistorical.

The four texts in *The Parental Monitor* were certainly written out of very various social and cultural circumstances. Their authors, two women and two men, represent differences not just of gender, but of national identity, rank, education, and religion, as well as of literary and social respectability.

Like many other conduct books, the three prose texts address their authors' own daughters. In doing so, they claim the authority of parenthood, and play – again, in a variety of ways – across the divide between the private sphere of the family and the wider audience invited by publication. John Gregory (1724–1773), professor of medicine at the Universities of Aberdeen and then Edinburgh, came from a highly respected family of Scottish physicians and scientists, and was a prominent figure within the Scottish and English medical and literary establishments. His *A Father's Legacy to his Daughters* (1774) began as a private communication and was made public only posthumously, reinforcing its author's reputation as a man of authority and feeling. For Sarah Pennington (?–1783), the estranged wife of a member of the minor English gentry, writing was a means of surviving financially and of regaining social status after the breakdown of her marriage: *An Unfortunate Mother's Advice to her Absent Daughters* (1761) demands public sympathy for a woman forced into print in order to make contact with her children. In contrast, Anne-Thérèse de Marguenat de Courcelles, Marchioness de Lambert (1647–1733), shunned publicity. She wrote only for the privileged members of the prestigious literary salon which she hosted in early eighteenth-century Paris, circulating her works in manuscript form. When, late in her life, some were published without her consent, *Advice of a Mother to her Daughter* (1727) was immediately translated and assimilated into the English conduct-book tradition.

Fables for the Female Sex (1744), by Edward Moore (1712–1757), is something of a generic oddity within the collection since it is not, strictly, a conduct book at all, but verse satire. It claims authority from poetic tradition, rather than from the prose conventions of instructional literature and moralized personal history. Unlike the authors of the other three texts, Moore depended exclusively on his writing for his livelihood, and the *Fables*' repackaging of a popular verse form for a female audience is shrewdly and unashamedly calculated to appeal to a wide readership. And with considerable success: Moore's *Fables* was reprinted at least once every decade throughout the century – though he himself died in poverty.

Within the common project of offering moral instruction, then, the four texts in *The Parental Monitor* appeal to their readers from a variety of different standpoints. They represent subtle, but significant, distinctions in terms of social rank and respectability, and take up different positions on the question of the respectability of publication itself. I want now to explore these, and other, differences in more detail by discussing each text, and its immediate context, individually. In order to get a sense of historical change, I shall consider the three prose texts in the order of their original publication, rather than following the order in which they appear in *The Parental Monitor*. But because of its generic difference, it will be most useful to follow *The Parental Monitor* in the case of Moore (which was the second of the texts to be published), and to look at the *Fables* at the end.

Anne-Thérèse, Marchioness de Lambert: *Advice of a Mother to her Daughter* (1727)

The *Advice of a Mother to her Daughter* is more concerned to promote female education than to offer instruction in conventional femininity. Indeed, in its stress on intellectual and moral autonomy, and its rejection of the decorous passivity which is generally assumed to please men, it is potentially a very radical text. The *Advice* begins with the challenging assertion that 'the world has in all ages been very negligent in the education of daughters...as if the women were a distinct species' (p. 134). Thus from the start it questions the common assumption that reason was primarily a male characteristic, and claims equality for women as 'rational creatures' – as Mary Wollstonecraft would later put it.[4] For Sarah Pennington, in her *Advice to her Daughters*, those of 'docile tempers' are 'thrice happy' (p. 64). De Lambert, characteristically, does not completely reject 'docility' but argues that, 'By carrying docility too far, you do an injury to your reason' (p. 158). Throughout the text she urges her daughter to 'entertain yourself with your own reason', to 'reverence and stand in awe of yourself', to use 'your own judgment and understanding' (pp. 148, 152, 158), and she regrets the fact that 'we depend too much upon

[4] Mary Wollstonecraft, *A Vindication of the Rights of Woman* (1792), edited by Barbara Taylor (London: Everyman's Library, 1992), p. 3: 'My own sex, I hope, will excuse me, if I treat them like rational creatures, instead of flattering their *fascinating* graces, and viewing them as if they were in a state of perpetual childhood, unable to stand alone.'

the men' (p. 173). Absolutely central to the *Advice*, then, is the belief that, for women as much as for men, 'the greatest science is to know how to be independent' (p. 161).

'Independent' here describes a state of mind. It suggests intellectual and spiritual freedom, rather than the financial security so often referred to when the term was used of a woman in this period. Indeed, mental and worldly wealth are set up as explicit alternatives:

> You must provide yourself some resources against the inquietudes of life, and some equivalent for the goods you had depended on. (p. 161)

Personal history and the wider histories of class and gender lie behind this familiar moral opposition. Part of that history concerns married women's uncertain rights to ownership and inheritance. When the Marquis de Lambert died in 1686, the Marchioness was granted a pension by the king, but she herself had to conduct a long, complex, but in the end successful, lawsuit against her husband's family and on behalf of her children, in order to secure some return for her fortune.[5] In spite of her aristocratic status, then, de Lambert was no stranger to financial dependency. The *Advice* was not published until 1727, but it seems likely that it was written much earlier – possibly during or soon after the lawsuit. Education and the cultivation of

[5] *Nouvelle Biographie Générale* (Paris, 1859). See also her own account in her *Advice of a Mother to her Son* (1727; 2nd edition, 1736), pp. 10–11: 'I might, my Son, in the Order of your Duties, insist on what you owe to me, but I would derive it entirely from your Heart. Consider the Condition in which your Father left me: I had sacrificed all that belonged to me, to raise his Fortune, and I lost my all at his Death. I saw myself alone, destitute of any Support. ...I met with Enemies in my own Family: I had a Law-Suit upon my Hands against potent Adversaries, and my whole Fortune depended on the Event.'

an independent rational self are recommended to her daughter as a vital resource in the face of, even aristocratic, women's uncertain material fortunes.

Rational independence is also offered as an alternative to love, and here, de Lambert can sound frighteningly repressive to the modern reader. In the *Advice*, love is described as 'the most cruel situation a rational person can be in' (p. 168); reason and judgement, the qualities required for 'independence', are opposed to imagination, the mental faculty assumed to fuel irrational passions (pp. 159–60). But it is important to understand the context which produced such apparent denials of female pleasure. The *Advice* is the only text in *The Parental Monitor* written from an aristocratic, rather than a bourgeois, position, and its representation of love and marriage reflects that class base. When John Gregory, writing almost a century later in *A Father's Legacy to his Daughters*, discusses his daughters' independence, it is as a poor alternative to marriage which,

> if entered into from proper motives of esteem and affection, will be the happiest for yourselves, make you most respectable in the eyes of the world, and the most useful members of society. ...But Heaven forbid you should ever relinquish the ease and independence of a single life, to become the slaves of a fool or a tyrant. (p. 44)

For Gregory, marriage is a personal choice, a relationship based on 'esteem and affection', every young woman's ideal of happiness. De Lambert, unlike most conduct writers, is strikingly silent about marriage itself. She refers to it only once, in the context of warnings against the pleasures of the heart:

> When one sees a young person happy enough not to have had her heart touched ... she easily complies, and gives herself naturally to the person designed for her. (p. 147)

Here, the young woman has no choice. She is an object of exchange within the aristocratic kinship system of family alliances and financial transactions, and must submit to the husband 'designed for her', even if he is 'a fool or a tyrant'.

This is very different from Gregory's idealization of marriage as a happy continuum between private affection and public respectability. In a situation where marriage is a dynastic rather than a personal emotional contract, love is a dangerously disruptive force – and particularly so for women, whose reputation depends on modesty and honour. It is perhaps understandable, then, that the *Advice* seems to endorse the subordination of private desires to the social order, and that it concentrates on the dangers of indulging 'the passions' rather than on marriage itself:

> Possess your heart as much as is possible with sentiments for the conduct that you ought to observe; fortify this prejudice of Honour in your mind. (p.139)

In such passages, which rewrite female virtue as intellectual choice, rational 'independence' seems simply to promote an internalized acceptance of the status quo, a willing submission to the dual sexual standard which imprisons women in arranged marriages.

But, as I have already suggested, to reduce the *Advice* simply to this orthodox position would be a mistake. The coexistence of radical and conformist discourses in de Lambert's text can usefully be illustrated by comparing the *Advice* with two contemporary English texts: George Savile, Marquis of Halifax's *The Lady's New-Year's Gift: or, Advice to a Daughter*, first published in 1688; and Mary Astell's proto-feminist tract *A Serious Proposal to the Ladies*, first published in 1694.

One of Halifax's main concerns is to reconcile his daughter to the fact that 'young Women are seldom permitted to make their own *Choice*', by persuading her:

> That the *Institution of Marriage* is too sacred to admit a *Liberty* of *objecting* to it; That the supposition of yours being the weaker *Sex*, having without doubt a good Foundation, maketh it reasonable to subject it to the *Masculine Dominion*....[6]

For Halifax reason supports, rather than challenges, gender inequality and one of the most chilling passages in his *Advice* is that in which he effectively endorses the sexual double standard by suggesting that a woman's role is to ignore her husband's infidelity: 'next to the danger of *committing* the Fault your self, the greatest is that of *seeing* it in your *Husband*'; '*Discretion* and *Silence* will be the most *prevailing Reproof*.'[7]

Like de Lambert, Halifax is an aristocrat, but in de Lambert's text, gender cuts across class. Halifax's advocation of pragmatic passivity is very different from her stress on active independent judgement. Although, like Halifax, de Lambert is concerned with strategies for survival within society, her position is in many ways

[6] Halifax, *The Lady's New-Year's Gift* (6th edition, 1699), pp. 25, 31. Extracts reprinted in Vivien Jones (editor), *Women in the Eighteenth Century: Constructions of Femininity* (London and New York: Routledge, 1990), pp. 18–19.

[7] Halifax, pp. 35, 37 (Jones, p. 20).

much more comparable with that of Mary Astell, who argued in *A Serious Proposal* for the establishment of a female religious community, 'a Retreat from the World for those who desire that advantage'.[8] Astell justifies the plan not just in terms of religious commitment, but on educational grounds: 'one great end of this Institution shall be, to expel that cloud of Ignorance which Custom has involv'd us in.' She also offers it as a refuge where 'Heiresses and Persons of Fortune may be kept secure from the rude attempts of designing Men'.[9] Like de Lambert, Astell starts from the argument that, 'since GOD has given Women as well as Men intelligent Souls, why should they be forbidden to improve them?'[10] Her rationalist retreat has much in common with de Lambert's more secular and internalized vision of independence:

> Secure yourself a retreat and place of refuge in your own breast; you can always return thither, and be sure to find yourself again. When the world is less necessary to you, it will have less power over you. (p. 162)

Astell and de Lambert have a shared philosophical inheritance in the work of late seventeenth-century French theorists, such as Poulain de la Barre and Jacques du Bosc (both of whose work was translated into English), who used Cartesian rationalism, the principle that humanness consists in the capacity for self-conscious thought, to argue for women's intel-

[8] Mary Astell, *A Serious Proposal to the Ladies, For the Advancement of their True and Greatest Interest* (1694; 3rd edition, 1696), p. 40. Also in Jones, p. 202. Reprinted in *Sources of British Feminism*, Routledge/Thoemmes Press, 1993.

[9] Astell, pp. 50, 99 (Jones, pp. 204, 205).

[10] Astell, pp. 52–3.

lectual equality.[11] But, unlike Astell, de Lambert is also clearly steeped in the classical tradition and the work of contemporary French moral philosophers such as La Rochefoucauld and La Bruyère. What is less obvious from the evidence of the *Advice* itself is her allegiance, too, to the conventions of French heroic romance, in which women controlled a sophisticated and aestheticized game of ideal love.[12] In spite of its promotion of rational independence, then, de Lambert's *Advice to a Daughter* offers an account of gender difference which can be more easily assimilated into the English advice tradition than Astell's uncompromising separatism ever could.

The discussion of modesty (pp. 140–43) illustrates my point. De Lambert identifies the 'great virtues' as 'extraordinary valour in the men, and extreme modesty in the women', and emphasizes modesty as the quality which must be 'inseparable' from all the other 'passions' (pp. 140, 143). Her definitions are echoed in Addison and Steele's *Spectator*, the English periodical which was instrumental in shaping an emergent bourgeois identity at the beginning of the eighteenth

[11] [François Poulain de la Barre], *The Woman as Good as the Man* (1677); Jacques du Bosc, *The Excellent Woman* (1692). See Ruth Perry, *The Celebrated Mary Astell: An Early English Feminist* (Chicago and London: University of Chicago Press, 1986), especially pp. 70–73; Hilda Smith, *Reason's Disciples: Seventeenth-Century English Feminists* (Urbana, Chicago, London: University of Illinois Press, 1982), pp. 115–39.

[12] In her *New Reflexions on the Fair Sex* (translated into English by J. Lockman, 1729), de Lambert works much more explicitly within the French heroic romance tradition, celebrating women's special capacity for love and sensibility, and making direct references to the work of, for example, the romance writer Madeleine de Scudéry. For a helpful summary of French heroic romance in the context of early eighteenth-century English narratives by women, see Ros Ballaster, *Seductive Forms: Women's Amatory Fiction from 1684 to 1740* (Oxford: Clarendon Press, 1992), pp. 42–9.

century.[13] In turn, the definition of gendered virtues in both de Lambert and *The Spectator* echoes La Rochefoucauld's *Moral Maxims* (1694), while the discussion of modesty recalls both Seneca and La Bruyère's *Characters* (1702).[14] What we glimpse here, then, is shared influences which link the French aristocratic text with the English moral tradition.

De Lambert's language retains vestiges of heroic romance. In *The Spectator*, the vocabulary is more unequivocally moralistic: 'valour' becomes 'courage'; 'modesty' is narrowed to 'chastity'; the 'passions' ('Truth' and 'Love') in the *Advice* are the 'virtues' in *The Spectator*. In *The Spectator*, heroic ideals and gender identities are rewritten: they are self-consciously domesticated into the bourgeois ideal of marriage which Gregory still endorses sixty years later. Writing pragmatically for her daughter, de Lambert follows a comparable trajectory. As do so many conduct writers, she warns against romance reading (p. 156), and rejects the extra-marital 'passions' which heroic romance might idealize and celebrate. In spite of significant differences of nuance and context, then, de Lambert's *Advice to her Daughter* was read as fitting safely into the conduct literature tradition within which *The Spectator* plays such a significant role.

[13] See Michael G. Ketcham, *Transparent Designs: Reading, Performance and Form in the* Spectator *Papers* (Athens, Georgia: University of Georgia Press, 1985), especially Chapter 4; Kathryn Shevelow, *Women and Print Culture: The Construction of Femininity in the Early Periodical* (London and New York: Routledge, 1989), pp. 93–145.

[14] Cf. *Spectator* 99: 'The great Point of Honour in Men is Courage, and in Women Chastity'; *Spectator* 231: 'Modesty ... sets off every great Talent which a Man can be possessed of. It heightens all the Vertues which it accompanies...'. For references to La Rochefoucauld, etc., see *The Spectator*, editor Donald F. Bond (Oxford: Clarendon Press, 1965), Volume I, p. 416; Volume II, pp. 399–400.

Sarah Pennington, *An Unfortunate Mother's Advice to her Absent Daughters, in a Letter to Miss Pennington* (1761)

Sarah Pennington's *Unfortunate Mother's Advice* is framed by the story of her own marital difficulties, and of her fight to recover her good name after her estrangement from her husband. Indeed, the text itself is a part of that narrative, an act of self-justification which exposes private principles to public scrutiny. The opening of *An Unfortunate Mother's Advice* is thus very different from de Lambert's confident challenge on behalf of women's education. Pennington appeals not to reason, but to sentiment and sympathy, representing herself as tragically caught between the risk of impropriety and her duty as a mother: 'my circumstances are such as lay me under the necessity of either communicating my sentiments to the world, or of concealing them from you' (p. 57). Where de Lambert's conduct book can be identified generically with tracts on women's education and proto-feminist texts, then, Pennington's is closer to that other generic grouping with which conduct literature has close affinities: the periodical and epistolary tradition of moralized narratives.[15]

The Unfortunate Mother's Advice begins and ends with a few sparse autobiographical details (pp. 58–63; 127–9). At the start of the text, Pennington describes herself as a foolish but, she claims, morally blameless, young woman whose 'very high flow of spirits' meant

[15] See, for example: Elizabeth Singer Rowe, *Letters Moral and Entertaining in Prose and Verse*, 3 volumes (1728–32); Samuel Richardson, *Letters written to and for Particular Friends, On the Most Important Occasions* (1741). On women's relationship with the epistolary tradition, see Ruth Perry, *Women, Letters and the Novel* (New York: AMS Press, 1980).

that she 'never broke... into the formal rules of decorum' (pp. 59–60); at the end, she has matured through experience into a living example of the pleasures of retirement, which gives 'more real satisfaction... than the gayest scenes of festive mirth ever afforded me' (p. 127). And without giving any details, she hints that her husband's desire to gain control of her independent fortune lies behind 'many of those appearances which have been urged against me' (p. 61). Both in *An Unfortunate Mother's Advice*, and in her other major publication, *Letters on Different Subjects* (1767), Pennington tantalizes the reader (and her husband) with her power 'to give the world a history of the whole truth'.[16] Indeed, in the preface to the third volume of the *Letters*, she has to justify herself to subscribers who had expected an unexpurgated account of her life. But she chooses the moral high ground, describing how, in spite of extreme and continuing provocation, she has been unable to bring herself to publish memoirs which contain 'so many incidents of a kind which a benevolent heart must shrink with reluctance from the thought of exposing to public view'.[17] Pennington thus implicitly defines her writings against those of the 'scandalous memoirists' – women such as Teresia Constantia Phillips, Laetitia Pilkington and Frances Anne, Viscountess Vane – who became notorious in the period for publishing frank accounts of their transgressive sexual histories.[18] Pennington, in contrast,

[16] *Letters on Different Subjects, in four volumes; Amongst which are interspers'd the Adventures of Alphonso, After the Destruction of Lisbon.* (2nd edition, 1767), volume III, sig. a3v.

[17] *Letters*, vol. III., sig.a4v.

[18] For accounts of these writers, see Janet Todd, *The Sign of Angellica: Women, Writing and Fiction, 1660-1800* (London: Virago, 1989), pp. 128–31; Felicity Nussbaum, 'Heteroclites: The Gender of Character in

presents herself as heroinically maintaining a much more conformist femininity in the face of personal abuse and financial difficulty.

In Pennington's text, then, the power of experience lends authority – and necessity – to a very orthodox account of feminine identity, the main characteristics of which are piety, domesticity, and self-effacement. Where de Lambert's *Advice* recommends independence and scepticism towards received opinions, Pennington uses herself as an example against the mistaken faith that 'the self-approbation arising from conscious virtue' is a sufficient defence for women against 'the public voice' (p. 58). Instead, she urges 'prudence', a term which plays constantly through her text, as necessary for self-preservation in 'a world full of deceit and falsehood' (p. 64). Pennington's daughters are reminded that the 'management of all domestic affairs is certainly the proper business of woman'; and although they should neglect 'no branch of knowledge that your capacity is equal to', self-improvement must be subordinated always to domestic duties, and subject to the humbling recognition that 'all the learning her utmost application can make her mistress of, will be... inferior to that of a school boy' (pp. 76–7).

This 'prudence' involves a strong sense of social hierarchy. On the one hand, for example, Pennington recommends 'decency and cleanliness' of dress such as is 'suitable to your rank and fortune', rather than the 'ill-placed finery' associated with the ostentatious display of the aristocracy (p. 82). On the other, she

the Scandalous Memoirs', in *The New Eighteenth Century: Theory Politics Literature*, edited by Felicity Nussbaum and Laura Brown (New York and London: Methuen, 1987), pp. 144–68; Clare Brant, 'Speaking of Women: Scandal and Law in the Mid-Eighteenth Century', in *Women, Texts and Histories 1575–1760*, edited by Clare Brant and Diane Purkis (London & New York: Routledge, 1992), pp. 242–70.

warns against too great an intimacy with servants 'whose birth, education and early views in life were not superior to a state of servitude' (p. 81). Pennington's ideal woman is thus recognizably a member of the 'middle rank': she fits – much more neatly than de Lambert – into the mould of the bourgeois 'proper lady', the 'new domestic woman' identified by recent feminist commentators on the conduct literature of the period.[19] Nancy Armstrong argues that the ideal bourgeois wife was defined 'in opposition to certain practices attributed to women at both extremes of the social scale', and that the rejection of aristocratic display meant 'the invention of depths in the self', the measurement of femininity in terms of private, internal virtues.[20] Pennington herself emerges from her text as a frustrated example of that ideal figure: she has to fulfil her duty as a mother through the substitute of writing; and her retirement is a solitary version of proper domesticity.

But Pennington's strategic manipulation of the power of print also manifests a less self-effacing version of 'prudence', and a motivation much closer to the 'scandalous memoirists'. In her decorous mixture of conduct literature and autobiography, she uses the identity of the 'proper lady' to secure financial survival as well as social respectability. Sarah Pennington saved her reputation by creating it – albeit within the

[19] On the 'proper lady', see Mary Poovey, *The Proper Lady and the Woman Writer: Ideology as Style in the Works of Mary Wollstonecraft, Mary Shelley, and Jane Austen* (Chicago and London: University of Chicago Press, 1984), especially pp. 3–47. The 'new domestic woman' is discussed in Nancy Armstrong, *Desire and Domestic Fiction: A Political History of the Novel* (New York and Oxford: Oxford University Press, 1987). See particularly 'The Rise of the Domestic Woman', pp. 59–95, also reprinted in Armstrong and Tennenhouse, *The Ideology of Conduct*, pp. 96–141.

[20] Armstrong, *Desire*, pp. 75–6.

powerful constraints of the mid-century's orthodox femininity. The list of subscribers to her *Letters* includes the Queen and numerous members of the aristocracy, and when she died, her obituary in *The Gentleman's Magazine* reproduced the self-image created in her books:

> This lady, whose extraordinary abilities, long since displayed to the world, in her excellent and much-admired writings, which could only be equalled by her piety, charity, and benevolence, united to that patient and unreserved resignation, with which she sustained (through the course of many years) a series of very severe and uncommon afflictions. [*sic*][21]

As in novels, the particularity of Pennington's personal history problematizes the conduct-book paradigm which her text promotes.[22] In *An Unfortunate Mother's Advice*, she acknowledges that her potential as ideal wife was denied in part by her own early failure to match public with private behaviour:

> my private conduct was what the severest prude could not condemn; my public, such as the most finished coquet alone would have ventured upon. (p. 60)

But the real blame lies with her husband. 'Perfectly acquainted with my principles and with my natural disposition' (p. 61), he nevertheless failed to fulfil his side of the new marital contract, preferring material to moral wealth. In her narrative, it is unreformed masculinity which threatens the new feminine ideal.

[21] *Gentleman's Magazine* 53 (1783), p. 978.

[22] On fiction's problematization of conduct-book material, see Carol Houlihan Flynn, 'Defoe's Idea of Conduct: Ideological fictions and fictional reality', in Armstrong and Tennenhouse, *The Ideology of Conduct*, pp. 73–95.

Men, again as in novels, are difficult to read: it can be all too easy to mistake the mere 'Good-Humour' which disguises the domestic tyrant, for 'a truly benevolent disposition' (pp. 98–9); and some of the most painful – but also potentially subversive – passages in *An Unfortunate Mother's Advice* are those in which Pennington offers strategies for coping with a bad husband. They are painful because of their Halifax-like counsel to remain passive in the face of abuse and infidelity (pp. 107, 113), but also because they communicate a level of anxiety which suggests that such abuse is all too possible. Marriage, it would seem, is very likely to be a damage-limitation exercise, staving off 'absolute misery' rather than embodying 'true happiness' (p. 115). The implicit narrative of Pennington's own experience gives such passages a power which threatens to undermine the official moral of her text. Marriage, she asserts, can be 'the highest satisfaction of human life' (p. 116). But:

> so great is the hazard, so disproportioned the chances, that I could almost wish the dangerous die was never to be thrown for any of you. (p. 96)

In spite of her advocacy of 'prudence', then, there are brief moments when Pennington, too, recalls the radical separatism of a Mary Astell.

John Gregory, *A Father's Legacy to his Daughters* (1774)

John Gregory's *A Father's Legacy to his Daughters* has the dubious distinction of having been attacked during the post-revolutionary 1790s both by the radical Mary Wollstonecraft in her *Vindication of the Rights of Woman* (1792), and by Thomas Gisborne, an influential Evangelical conduct writer, in his *Enquiry into the Duties of the Female Sex* (1797). This critical attention at a moment of ideological crisis is a measure of the text's popularity and influence (Wollstonecraft refers to the 'celebrated' *Legacy to his Daughters*).[23] It is also indicative of the *Legacy*'s peculiarly contradictory quality, its tension between the father as 'friend' (p. 45), as the man of feeling, and as the voice of repressive, even predatory, masculinity.

Wollstonecraft, with her usual sharp insight, notes a symptomatic stylistic inconsistency: between an 'easy familiar style' which is 'particularly suited to the tenor of his advice', and 'a degree of concise elegance in many passages that disturbs this sympathy…we pop on the author, when we only expected to meet the – father'. She goes on:

> Besides, having two objects in view, he seldom adhered steadily to either; for wishing to make his daughters amiable, and fearing lest unhappiness should be the only consequence, of instilling sentiments that might draw them out of the track of common life without enabling them to act with consonant independence and dignity, he checks the natural flow of his thoughts, and neither advises one thing nor the other.[24]

Her reading radically disagrees with the less politically astute 'Preface', in which Gregory's editor presents the text as a spontaneous, 'domestic' communication, entirely private and therefore, supposedly, forced to

[23] Wollstonecraft, p. 30. The other text Wollstonecraft uses to epitomize conduct-book discourse is James Fordyce's *Sermons to Young Women* (1766), which Mr Collins tries unsuccessfully to read to the Bennet sisters in Chapter 14 (Book 1) of Jane Austen's *Pride and Prejudice*.

[24] Wollstonecraft, p. 104.

make no 'sacrifices' to the public world, to 'prejudices, to customs, to fashionable opinions' (p. iii). Wollstonecraft is concerned to deconstruct precisely this assumption that private, family relationships are free from political 'prejudices' and 'customs'. Of Gregory, she declares: 'I respect his heart, but entirely disapprove' of his *Legacy*, which she uses to 'show how absurd and tyrannic it is thus to lay down a system of slavery'.[25] Writing in the 1790s, in the immediate aftermath of the French Revolution, Wollstonecraft adopts the terms of revolutionary political analysis – 'tyrannic'; 'slavery' – to expose the injustices in sexual politics.

Like Wollstonecraft, Gisborne objects to Gregory's over-protective suggestions that women should conceal their learning from men (p. 13) and their love from their husbands (p. 35). For Wollstonecraft, such dissimulation precludes the rational friendship – 'the most holy band of society'[26] – which should be the basis of marriage. Gisborne's view of women and of marriage, in contrast, rests on the Pauline doctrine of inequality: a woman's role is to 'learn to place delight in the performance of duty', and, in the words of St Paul, to 'see that she reverence her husband'. To conceal her affection is thus a failure in her duty to 'render herself pleasing to him'. He therefore also deeply disapproves of Gregory's potentially radical view that young women might develop non-sexual friendships with men (p. 30): 'no advice could easily be more repugnant to discretion and common sense'.[27] Gisborne's concern is that Gregory's

[25] Wollstonecraft, pp. 30, 35.

[26] Wollstonecraft, p. 32.

[27] Thomas Gisborne, *An Enquiry into the Duties of the Female Sex* (6th edition, London, 1805), pp. 139, 152, 171, 173n.

ideal of easy social relationships between the sexes might give women too much autonomy rather than too little. His conduct book, published right at the end of the century, points forward to the Victorian 'angel in the house'.

Gregory's persona in the *Legacy* is as important as that of Sarah Pennington in the *Unfortunate Mother's Advice*. He is the mid-eighteenth-century man of sensibility, the domesticated hero who can be traced back to *The Spectator*, and to Richardson's last novel *Sir Charles Grandison*.[28] Compared with Gisborne's stern Evangelicalism, then, Gregory seems to represent a liberal and enlightened version of masculinity. At the beginning of the *Legacy*, he carefully displays his 'honourable' view of women: 'not as domestic drudges, or the slaves of our pleasures, but as our companions and equals'. The terms seem almost Wollstonecraftian – until assumptions about sexual difference begin to undermine the egalitarian implications of 'companions and equals'. Women, it seems, are in fact 'designed to soften our hearts and polish our manners', and their place in society demands 'a certain propriety of conduct' (p. 3). And slightly later in the text, femininity and companionship have become explicitly antithetical: frankness of behaviour, we are told, 'might render you more agreeable as companions, but it would make you less amiable as women' (p. 15).

Wollstonecraft's response to this passage is to expose Gregory's collusion with women's 'degradation': 'this desire of being always women, is the very consciousness

[28] On sensibility generally, and the man of sensibility in particular, see John Mullan, *Sentiment and Sociability: The Language of Feeling in the Eighteenth Century* (Oxford: Clarendon Press, 1988); Janet Todd, *Sensibility: An Introduction* (London and New York: Methuen, 1986).

that degrades the sex'.[29] In spite of his gestures towards equality, Gregory endorses precisely that infantilizing identification of femininity with 'delicacy', with 'softness and sensibility' (pp. 4–5), which Wollstonecraft so devastatingly deconstructs in the *Vindication*: 'to their senses, are women made slaves, because it is by their sensibility that they obtain present power'.[30] 'Delicacy' is the term which constantly recurs in the *Legacy*. The motivation throughout the text is to shelter the fragile bloom of femininity: from the 'chaos' of religious controversy which 'has no good effect on the heart' (p. 6); from reading anything which could stimulate 'sentiments that might perplex you' (p. 22); from 'the first impressions of love' (p. 41). And from itself: Gregory reproduces the classic double bind of sensibility, through which women's highly-tuned sensitivity can flip over at any moment into sensual excess.[31] Women, we are told, are 'peculiarly susceptible of the feelings of [religious] devotion', but they are just as apt to be led into 'a dissipated state of life' (p. 5); and a girl dancing 'with spirit' can too easily be 'thought to discover a spirit she little dreams of' (pp. 23–4). Gregory's tactic here is typical: throughout the *Legacy*, he justifies his protectiveness by offering privileged access to a male gaze which is assumed to have the power of definition.

Again Wollstonecraft comments: 'why, to damp innocent vivacity, is she darkly to be told that men will draw conclusions which she little thinks of? Let the libertine draw what inference he pleases.'[32] Her

[29] Wollstonecraft, p. 107.

[30] Wollstonecraft, p. 66.

[31] See Mullan, pp. 217–24.

[32] Wollstonecraft, p. 31.

'spirited' refusal even to entertain the libertine interpretation exposes Gregory's own anxious collusion with predatory and lascivious masculinity. There is a continuity, rather than the difference Gregory claims, between the man of sensibility and the rake; in Wollstonecraft's rationalist analysis, they have the same effect on women:

> [Women] have, to maintain their power, resigned the natural rights which the exercise of reason might have procured them.... Exalted by their inferiority...they constantly demand homage as women, though experience should teach them that the men who pride themselves upon paying this arbitrary insolent respect to the sex, with the most scrupulous exactness, are most inclined to tyrannize over, and despise the very weakness they cherish.[33]

As a man of sensibility, Gregory ostensibly rejects the double standard in sexual behaviour which the Marquis of Halifax, for example, took for granted in his conduct book of 1688, when he advised his daughter on how to cope with an unfaithful husband. A double standard certainly operates in other areas: in matters of religion (p. 9), learning (p. 13), and conversation (pp. 14–15), for example, Gregory takes it for granted that gender imposes different rules of behaviour. But male sexuality is rewritten in sentimental terms: for Gregory, men, as well as women, are ideally creatures of 'spirit and delicacy' (pp. 28, 37). Indeed, in a reversal of the usual assumption, it is men rather than women who are most susceptible to the individual attachments and emotional extremes of romantic love (pp. 33, 35). Women, we are told, do not have 'much of that sensibility which

[33] Wollstonecraft, p. 59.

disposes to such attachments'; having less choice, they have been 'assigned...a greater flexibility of taste on this subject': they experience 'gratitude' rather than love (pp. 32–3). Perhaps, then, in Gregory, the sexual double standard has not so much disappeared as mutated.

The terms of that mutation are important in plotting the history of sexuality and subjectivity. Dominant definitions of gender identity and of sexual relations have shifted considerably in the period represented by the three prose texts in *The Parental Monitor*. Marriage in Gregory, as I pointed out earlier, is a site of personal happiness rather than mere social and financial convenience; and the influence of Sarah Pennington's 'prudent' feminine ideal (represented in Gregory's case by the deceased wife who haunts his text) has 'improved' and feminized masculinity into a new 'delicacy' of sensibility. The shift can be characterized in class terms as signalling the transition from a traditional aristocratic to a dominantly bourgeois culture; from a culture of public alliances to one of private 'relationships'; from, in Michel Foucault's terms, 'the deployment of alliance' to the 'deployment of sexuality' as the dominant principle in the social organization of sexual relations.[34] In terms of literary genres, it is central to the difference between heroic romance or Restoration comedy and the Richardsonian novel. What is much less clear is what women gained from this 'feminizing' process. It is very difficult to decide

[34] Michel Foucault, *The History of Sexuality. Volume I: An Introduction*, translated by Robert Hurley (Harmondsworth: Penguin, 1981), pp. 106–7. On the shift to a culture of affectivity during the eighteenth century, see also Jean Hagstrum, *Sex and Sensibility: Ideal and Erotic Love from Milton to Mozart* (Chicago and London: University of Chicago Press, 1980); Lawrence Stone, *The Family, Sex and Marriage in England 1500–1800* (Harmondsworth: Penguin, 1979).

whether women experienced greater 'independence' in de Lambert's aristocratic setting of arranged marriages, or as the civilizing influence within Gregory's bourgeois ideal of domestic complementarity.

John Moore, *Fables for the Female Sex* (1744)

The first edition of Moore's *Fables for the Female Sex* made its literary allegiance immediately clear: the title page, typeface and woodcut illustrations exactly replicate the style of John Gay's second volume of *Fables*, published posthumously in 1738. Thus Moore's text claims a place within the literary establishment, and within the tradition of moral satire. Gay was a member of the Scriblerus Club, a friend of Pope and Swift, and his *Fables* were for a long time his most popular work, running eventually to over 350 editions.[35] In producing a version for a female audience, Moore, and his collaborator Henry Brooke, strategically combine two popular forms. One is the beast fable itself, long-established in both classical and vernacular literatures, used by Chaucer and Spenser, and most famously represented by the fables of la Fontaine and 'Aesop'; the other is anti-female satire, again with immediate French and classical precedents in Boileau and Juvenal.[36]

[35] See *John Gay: Poetry and Prose*, edited by Vinton A. Dearing, 2 volumes (Oxford: Clarendon Press, 1974), volume II, p. 619. The first volume of Gay's *Fables* was published in 1727. A facsimile edition of both volumes was published as an Augustan Reprint Society special edition in 1967.

[36] The first thirteen Fables are by Moore; the last three, as their very different style suggests, are by Brooke (1703?–1783), a prolific professional writer, who was also connected to the Pope/Swift/Gay circle. On the beast fable, see *John Gay: Poetry and Prose*, volume II, pp. 620–21; on traditions of anti-female satire, see Felicity Nussbaum, *The Brink of all we Hate: English Satires on Women 1660–1750* (Lexington: University of Kentucky Press, 1984).

Interestingly, from the point of view of advice literature, the connection between the two forms had already been made in *The Spectator*. In *Spectator* 209, Addison playfully translated characterizations of female types, by the classical Greek poet Simonides, which compared them with particular animals. Versions of several of these characterizations recur in Moore.[37] Simonides includes a positive example: the Bee is the type of the 'best Wife that Jupiter can bestow on Man'; 'Her family flourishes and improves by her good management'. Addison uses this representation of an ideal to make an important theoretical point, rejecting the purely negative anti-female satires of Juvenal and Boileau: 'where they have endeavoured to expose the Sex in general, without doing Justice to the valuable Part of it. Such levelling Satyrs are of no use to the world.'[38] In keeping with Addison's reformist position, Moore's *Fables* do not reproduce the kind of damning generalizations about women which, for example, Pope perpetuated in his 'Epistle to a Lady' (1735): 'Most Women have no Characters at all'; 'Ev'ry Woman is at heart a Rake'.[39] Nor, however, do they offer the complex individual portraits which problematize those generalizations in Pope's poem. Instead, they deal in general terms with satiric commonplaces, predictable situations and feminine types, and they promote an ideal femininity very close to that celebrated by Pennington and Gregory. Like *The Spectator* itself, then, but in poetic form, they occupy a position which

[37] Fable XIII, for example, recalls Simonides' account of the swine-like woman: 'A Woman of this Make is a Slutt in her House, and a Glutton at her Table' (*Spectator* 209; Volume II, p. 319).

[38] *The Spectator* 209, p. 320.

[39] Alexander Pope, *Moral Essays*, 'Epistle II: To a Lady', ll. 2, 216.

connects classic moral satire with the more narrowly-directed preoccupations of female advice literature.

Like Pennington and Gregory, the *Fables* work with the affective bourgeois marriage as their ideal: Fable XIV, for example, sets the faithful dove's hymn to the comforts of marriage and the family against the sparrow's empty libertine pleasures: 'Thee, wretch! no lisping babe shall name' (p. 262). And elsewhere, the *Fables* expose the deathly consequences of marriages based on lust or mercenary motives (Fables IV, VI). The grotesque portrait of the wife who neglects her family for learning (Fable XIII) recalls Pennington's more sober advice to put family before self-education (p. 76), and in Fable XV, prudence is personified, lamenting that she is now 'held as one whose form intruded' (p. 308). Several of the *Fables* attack female vanity and display (Fables II, III, X, XV), and the prurient fascination with modesty of dress in Fable X is only a more explicit version of Gregory's warning that men are not necessarily attracted 'by the fullest display of... personal charms' (p. 17): 'The maid, who modestly conceals/Her beauties, while she hides, reveals' (p. 231). Conduct literature is haunted by predatory male sexuality in the form of the rake. Pennington, for example, points to the 'unhappy victims to the ridiculous opinion, "A reformed libertine makes the best husband"' (p. 97). In the *Fables*, those 'unhappy victims' are graphically realized in the Gothic melodrama of Fable VI, where the wolf/rake feeds off his wife's sister-lambs at her own table: 'The crashing bones he grinds for food,/And slakes his thirst with streaming blood' (p. 211).

The *Fables*' satiric techniques position the reader very differently from the implied reader of the other three texts in *The Parental Monitor*. From an individualized authority based on personal experience and parental status, which produces the reader as the innocent in need of instruction, we move to the generalized, but much more precarious, moral authority of the satiric observer. The fable form itself, with its beast parallels and allegorical landscapes, puts contemporary manners and forms of femininity in a timeless context. But the *Fables* have to prove their moral case in aesthetic terms, through the wit and skill with which the connections and parallels are made. They ideally assume a quite sophisticated reader who can pick up on classical allusions, and who can also appreciate the satirical connections being made between sexual politics and, for example, legal abuses or Grub Street (Fables VIII, XIII). The reader is invited to share – but is also given a critical space in which to judge – the poet's analysis of human, or feminine, 'nature'.

References to Grub Street would, of course, be of less immediacy and relevance to readers of *The Parental Monitor* in the 1790s – as would the Cartesian debates of the late-seventeenth century which de Lambert evokes in her text. But that does not mean that the conduct books reprinted in *The Parental Monitor* are therefore safely outside or beyond debate and controversy. *The Parental Monitor* was published in 1790, at a moment when the French Revolution had generated revolutionary activity and fierce political confrontation in Britain. As is so often the case at times of political crisis, definitions of gender and the family came under radical scrutiny in this period, and *The Parental Monitor* could well be read as an intervention on behalf of traditional values. Like every other text, conduct books are written, reprinted – and received – in particular, changing, circumstances. Though the intention might have been conservative, de Lambert's engagement with Cartesian rationalism, for example, could well have taken on newly radical meanings in the revolutionary 90s.

Conduct literature is sometimes presented as a thoroughly efficient disciplinary apparatus, an unambiguous guide to the history of gender identity. Conduct books certainly clearly articulate a dominant and repressive ideology of femininity – a 'system of slavery' in Wollstonecraft's words – and their popularity suggests a wide readership and a pervasive influence. But while we can learn a lot from conduct literature about the cultural production of gender, we need to guard against producing our own, critical, mirror-image of a transhistorical 'proper lady'. In individual examples of the genre, as I have tried to suggest, contingent circumstances alter that ideology in subtle but significant ways. And, again as with any text, conduct literature is subject to the unpredictability of interpretation: how, and alongside what other kinds of writing, it will be read. The implied reader of conduct books is clear enough, but it is very difficult to assess precisely how, and by whom, conduct literature was used, how the 'proper lady' was mediated in lived experience. It is certainly dangerous to assume that its readers were simply passive consumers.

In Jane Austen's *Pride and Prejudice*, the odious Mr Collins tries to read James Fordyce's influential conduct book, *Sermons to Young Women*, to the Bennet sisters.[40] He doesn't get very far: 'Lydia gaped as he opened the volume, and before he had, with very

[40] Jane Austen, *Pride and Prejudice* (1813), Chapter 14 of Book 1.

monotonous solemnity, read three pages, she interrupted him.' Mr Collins is 'much offended', and shocked at his cousins' indifference to instruction. We laugh at his pompous judgement, but we might hope that, for once, his observations at least are accurate: 'I have often observed how little young ladies are interested by books of a serious stamp, though written solely for their benefit.'

Vivien Jones
University of Leeds, 1995

EXPLANATORY NOTES

p. 3. *a little Treatise of mine.* John Gregory, *A Comparative View of the Faculties of Man with those of the Animal World* (1765). The passage referred to reads: 'If we impress their minds with a belief that they were made only to be domestic drudges, and the slaves of our pleasures, we debase their minds, and destroy all generous emulation to excel; whereas, if we use them in a more liberal and generous manner; a decent pride, a conscious dignity, and a sense of their own worth, will naturally induce them to exert themselves to be what they would wish to be thought, and are entitled to be, our companions and friends' (7th edition, 1777, pp. 116–17).

p. 3. *To raise the virtues... human life.* James Thomson, *The Seasons* (1730), 'Autumn', ll. 606–9: 'To raise the virtues, animate the bliss,/Even charm the pains to something more than joy,/And sweeten all the toils of human life:/This be the female dignity and praise.'

p. 19. *Grace was in... and love.* John Milton, *Paradise Lost*, VIII, ll. 488–9.

p. 22. *'But when I reflect... vanity or convenience'.* Untraced, but the comment is a contemporary commonplace which could have come from any number of conduct books or novels.

p. 35. *Thomson's Spring.* In *The Seasons*, 'Spring', ll. 983–1075, Thomson describes the 'charming agonies of love,/Whose misery delights' (ll.1074–5).

p. 67. *Doctor Hoadly's.* Benjamin Hoadly (1676–1761): became Bishop of Winchester in 1734; his prayers were published as part of his complete works. (See also next note.)

pp.70–1. *Bishop Hoadly's... Nelson's Christian Sacrifice.* Hoadly's *Plain Account...* (1735) caused great theological excitement when it was published, since it argues that the sacrament of the Lord's Supper is simply a commemorative rite. Robert Nelson (1656–1715): religious writer and Jacobite sympathizer. His *Great Duty...* was published in 1707.

p. 74ff. *necessary and polite acquisitions.* Pennington recommends the standard female curriculum of the period, as offered at respectable boarding schools for girls.

pp. 86–7. The recommended reading was expanded by Pennington herself in the fifth edition of *An Unfortunate Mother's Advice*, published in 1770, and again by the editor of *The Parental Monitor*. Pennington's revision simply expanded existing categories: sermons; classical moralists (which would be read in translation); periodicals; histories; poetry; and narrative conduct books by Rowe and Moore. It is interesting that, in spite of Pennington's warnings against fiction, the editor of *The Parental Monitor* added several novels to the list, including Charlotte Smith's *Emmeline* (1788), a novel which excited controversy when it was published because of its sympathy for a woman who has an illegitimate child. The surprising omission from the list is Samuel Richardson, whose last novel, *Sir Charles Grandison* (1753–4), particularly, was generally considered a masterpiece of moral fiction. His novels were approved, for example, by James Fordyce in his *Sermons to Young Women* (1766).

p. 88. *The Vicar of Wakefield.* (1766), a comic novel by Oliver Goldsmith, the essayist, playwright, and poet, which follows the fortunes of its innocent and moral hero, Parson Oliver Primrose. The novel deals, among other things, with Primrose's search for his lost daughter and his imprisonment for debt – situations which might have appealed particularly to Sarah Pennington.

p. 90. *Mr Garrick.* David Garrick (1717–79): the most famous of eighteenth-century actors. When Pennington wrote, he was manager of the Drury Lane theatre, and at the height of his fame.

p. 116. *Oeconomy.* The term 'economy' shifted during the eighteenth century from a primarily domestic application to its modern specialist definition. The first definition in Samuel Johnson's *Dictionary of the English Language* (1755) is: 'The management of a family; the government of a household.'

p. 134. *entails.* An entail is any settlement which restricts the terms by which an estate can be bequeathed in subsequent generations. A frequent common law arrangement was the entail 'in fee tail male' (the situation of Mr Bennet's estate in Jane Austen's *Pride and Prejudice*), which ensured that only males could inherit.

p. 140. *Agrippina…says Tacitus.* Agrippina: granddaughter of Augustus and wife of the Emperor

Germanicus who died in AD 19. Publius Cornelius Tacitus (c. AD 55–117): historian of the Roman Empire.

p. 140. *nice.* In the now almost obsolete sense of 'particular, precise, strict, careful, in regard to some special thing' (*OED*, definition 7b). It was during the eighteenth century, that 'nice' began to take on its modern usage, loosely referring to something pleasing. In Jane Austen's *Northanger Abbey*, for example, Henry Tilney criticizes Catherine Morland for using 'nice' as an imprecise term of approbation (Chapter 14).

p. 145. *the Graces.* In Greek mythology, minor goddesses, usually three in number, who personify loveliness or grace.

p. 147. *the spleen.* 'Excessive dejection or depression of spirits; gloominess and irritability; moroseness; melancholia' (*OED*, definition 8c). One of Anne Finch, Countess of Winchilsea's, most famous poems was 'The Spleen. A Pindaric Poem' (1701). Cf. also the Cave of Spleen in Canto IV of Pope's *The Rape of the Lock* (1714).

p. 151. *Montagne.* Michel Eyquem de Montaigne (1533–92): French essayist. His *Essays* (1588) are sceptical meditations on a vast range of subjects.

p. 152. *Seneca.* Lucius Annaeus Seneca (c. 4 BC – AD 65): Roman writer and Stoic philosopher, best known for his *Dialogues*, moral treatises and letters, and tragedies. His *Letters to Lucilius* offer guidance in Stoicism.

p. 154. *Curiosity*. De Lambert here challenges the common view, that curiosity was a dangerous tendency in women. Cf. the contemporary French writer on education François de Salignac de la Mothe-Fénélon in his *Treatise on the Education of Daughters* (1687): 'In regard to Girls, some exclaim, "why make them learned? curiosity renders them vain and conceited: it is sufficient if they be one day able to govern their families, and implicitly obey their husbands!"' (1805 translation, in Jones, p. 102).

p. 155. *Cicero, Pliny*. Marcus Tullius Cicero (106–43 BC): Roman orator, statesman and deist philosopher, whose writings were taken as a model of prose style during the Renaissance and the eighteenth century. Pliny 'the Younger' (c. 61–c. 113): Roman writer, best known for his ten books of letters on a wide range of subjects.

p. 156. *Corneille*. Pierre Corneille (1606–84), French poetic dramatist, best known for his tragedies, some of which explore the classic heroic conflict between duty, honour and passion.

p. 159. *Seneca and Epictetus*. Seneca: see above, note to p. 152. Epictetus (c. AD 60–140): Greek Stoic philosopher. The two are linked here as representatives of Stoicism, which stressed detachment from and independence of the material world.

p. 162. *Pliny*. See above, note to p. 155.

p. 164. *Horace*. Quintus Horatius Flaccus (65–8 BC): Roman poet, author of the *Satires* and *Epistles*, who had a pervasive influence on later poets in the classical tradition.

p. 165. *M. de la Rochefoucault.* François, Duc de la Rochefoucauld (1613–80): French moralist, best known for his *Refléxions ou sentences et maximes morales* (1665), an analysis of human motivation.

p. 169. *St. Augustine.* St. Augustine of Hippo (345–430): the reference here is to the *Confessions*, the account of his conversion to Christianity.

p. 178. *Caesar ... an example of it.* Gaius Julius Caesar (c. 102–44 BC). This incident, from the Civil War against Pompey in 49 BC, exactly parallels Antony's treatment of Enobarbus in Shakespeare's *Antony and Cleopatra* (Act IV, Scene 5).

p. 202. *Silenus ... Plutus.* Figures from Greek mythology. Silenus, a satyr, here represents lust; Plutus was a personification of wealth.

p. 205. *Appollo ... Phoebus.* Phoebus Apollo: in Roman mythology, the god of music and prophecy.

p. 215. *Appelles.* Apelles: known as the greatest painter of the ancient world. He worked for Alexander the Great in the fourth century BC.

p. 223. *Romish.* Roman law.

p. 224. *Hardwick.* Philip Yorke, first Earl of Hardwicke (1690–1764): as attorney-general, he prosecuted Curll for libel in 1727 (see next note); he became Lord Chancellor in 1737, and was associated with reform of the legal system.

p. 246. *Blackmore ... Curl.* Sir Richard Blackmore (d. 1729): physician to Queen Anne and author of some very long heroic poems. Edmund Curll (1675–1747): bookseller and pamphleteer. Both figures were attacked by Pope in *The Dunciad* (1728; 1742). (See also next note.)

p. 247. *Cibber... Henley.* Colly Cibber (1671–1757), playwright and hero of the 1742 edition of *The Dunciad*; John Henley (1692–1756), known as 'Orator Henley', also features in the poem.

p. 248. *thy talents scan... meant for man.* Cf. Pope, *An Essay on Man* (1733), ii. 1–2: 'Know then thyself, presume not God to scan/The proper study of mankind is man.'

p. 268. *Sabaea.* Ancient name for the Yemen.

p. 271. *Hesperia.* A (mythical) western land.

p. 281. *Sirens... Ulysses on the main.* In ancient myth, the sirens were female figures who lured sailors to their death on the rocks by their singing. Ulysses, in Homer's *Odyssey*, escaped them by filling his sailors' ears with wax and lashing himself to the ship's mast. Ausonia is a poetic name for Italy.

p. 281. *Hermes.* In Greek mythology, the messenger of the Gods, represented with wings on his sandals.

p. 282. *Medusa.* In Greek mythology, one of the snake-headed gorgons who turned to stone anything that met their gaze. Frequently used as a type of destructive femininity.

p. 283. *Barca.* The desert coast of North Africa.

p. 285. *Midas.* Semi-legendary king who was granted the power to turn all he touched to gold.

p. 285. *Niobe.* In Greek mythology, mother of seven sons and seven daughters who were killed by Apollo and Artemis when she boasted of her childbearing.

Niobe wept for them until she was turned into a column of stone, from which her tears continued to flow.

p. 297. *a new Promethean plan.* In Greek mythology, Prometheus made mankind out of clay.

p. 298. *Ducalion.* Deucalion: in Greek mythology, son of Prometheus. When Zeus destroyed mankind in a flood, Deucalion escaped and created a new race by throwing stones over his shoulder.

p. 301. *curl'd in tresses kiss the gale.* This passage clearly echoes Pope's portrait of Belinda at her dressing-table, attended by her sylphs, in Canto II of *The Rape of the Lock.*

p. 303. *Sampson's pillars.* In the Old Testament of the Bible, Samson, an Israelite hero renowned for his strength, destroyed the Philistines by pulling down the pillars of the palace in which they were feasting. His suicidal triumph represented his recovery from his seduction by Delilah, who cut off his hair, the source of his strength.

p. 307. *Hypsipyle... Catherine.* Heroines and female martyrs. *Hypsipyle*: in Greek mythology, daughter of Thoas, king of Lemnos, who saved her father when the women of the island, from jealousy, decided to kill all the men; *Portia*: wife of Marcus Brutus, one of Julius Caesar's assassins, who wounded herself to prove she was to be trusted with information about the conspiracy; *Penelope*: a type of the faithful woman, the wife of Odysseus (Ulysses) who waited faithfully for twenty years for her husband's return from the Trojan War; *Daphne*: a type of chastity, in Greek mythology she was changed, at her own request, into a laurel tree when pursued by Apollo; *Laodamia*: in Greek mythology, she committed suicide when her husband Protesilaus was killed in Troy. *Lucretia*: wife of Tarquinius Collatinus, she committed suicide after being raped by Sextus, the son of Tarquin, king of Rome; *Catherine*: St Catherine of Alexandria, Christian martyr, persecuted by the emperor Maxentius, saved by angels from torture and death on the wheel, and finally beheaded.

p. 308. *Cornelia*. A type of the accomplished and dedicated mother, she was the mother of 'the Gracchi', Roman tribunes. Asked to display her jewels, she produced her two sons.

Works Consulted

WORKS BY AUTHORS OF THE TEXTS IN *The Parental Monitor*

Gregory, John, *A Father's Legacy to his Daughters*, London and Edinburgh, 1774.

__________, *A Comparative View of the Faculties of Man with those of the Animal World* [1765], 7th edition, London, 1777.

Lambert, Anne-Thérèse, Marchioness de, *Advice of a Mother to her Son and Daughter*, translated by Mr Tho. Carte [1727], 2nd edition, London, 1736.

__________, *New Reflexions on the Fair Sex. Written originally in French by the celebrated Marchioness de Lambert,* translated into English by J. Lockman, London, 1729.

Moore, Edward, *Fables for the Female Sex*, London, 1744.

__________, *The Poetical Works of Edward Moore*, London, 1797.

Pennington, Sarah, *An Unfortunate Mother's Advice to her Absent Daughters*, 1st edition, London, 1761; 4th edition, London, 1767; 5th edition, London, 1770; 6th edition, London, 1773.

__________, *Letters on Different Subjects, in four volumes; Amongst which are interspers'd the*

Adventures of Alphonso, After the Destruction of Lisbon. 2nd edition, London, 1767.

The Young Lady's Pocket Library, or Parental Monitor [1790], 3rd edition, Edinburgh and London, 1808.

OTHER REFERENCES

Allestree, Richard, *The Ladies Calling* [1673], in *The Works of the Learned and Pious Author of the Whole Duty of Man*, Second Part, Oxford and London, 1695.

Armstrong, Nancy, *Desire and Domestic Fiction: A Political History of the Novel*, New York and Oxford: Oxford University Press, 1987.

____________, and Leonard Tennenhouse (editors), *The Ideology of Conduct: Essays in Literature and the History of Sexuality*, New York and London: Methuen, 1987.

Astell, Mary, *A Serious Proposal to the Ladies, For the Advancement of their True and Greatest Interest* [1694], 3rd edition, 1696. Reprinted in *Sources of British Feminism*, Routledge/Thoemmes Press, 1993.

Austen, Jane, *Pride and Prejudice*, London, 1813.

Ballaster, Ros, *Seductive Forms: Women's Amatory Fiction from 1684 to 1740*, Oxford: Clarendon Press, 1992.

Brant, Clare, 'Speaking of Women: Scandal and Law in the Mid-Eighteenth Century', in *Women, Texts and Histories 1575–1760*, edited by Clare Brant and Diane Purkis, London and New York: Routledge, 1992, pp. 242–70.

Flynn, Carol Houlihan, 'Defoe's Idea of Conduct: Ideological fictions and fictional reality', in Armstrong and Tennenhouse, pp. 73–95.

Fordyce, James, *Sermons to Young Women*, 2 volumes, London, 1766.

Foucault, Michel, *The History of Sexuality. Volume I: An Introduction*, translated by Robert Hurley, Harmondsworth: Penguin, 1981.

Gay, John, *Fables* [1727, 1738], edited by Vinton A. Dearing, Los Angeles: Augustan Reprint Society, 1967.

____________, *John Gay: Poetry and Prose*, edited by Vinton A. Dearing, 2 volumes, Oxford: Clarendon Press, 1974.

The Gentleman's Magazine, volume 53, 1783.

Gisborne, Thomas, *An Enquiry into the Duties of the Female Sex* [1797], 6th edition, London, 1805.

Hagstrum, Jean, *Sex and Sensibility: Ideal and Erotic Love from Milton to Mozart*, Chicago and London: University of Chicago Press, 1980.

Halifax, George Savile, Marquis of, *The Lady's New-Year's Gift: or, Advice to a Daughter* [1688], 6th edition, London, 1699.

Jones, Vivien (editor), *Women in the Eighteenth Century: Constructions of Femininity*, London and New York: Routledge, 1990.

Ketcham, Michael G., *Transparent Designs: Reading, Performance and Form in the* Spectator *Papers*, Athens Georgia: University of Georgia Press, 1985.

Mullan, John, *Sentiment and Sociability: The Language of Feeling in the Eighteenth Century*, Oxford: Clarendon Press, 1988.

Nussbaum, Felicity, *The Brink of all We Hate: English Satires on Women 1660–1750*, Lexington: University of Kentucky Press, 1984.

____________, 'Heteroclites: The Gender of Character in the Scandalous Memoirs', in *The New Eighteenth Century: Theory Politics Literature*, edited by Felicity Nussbaum and Laura Brown, New York and London: Methuen, 1987, pp. 144–68.

Perry, Ruth, *Women, Letters and the Novel*, New York: AMS Press, 1980.

____________, *The Celebrated Mary Astell: An Early English Feminist*, Chicago and London: University of Chicago Press, 1986.

Poovey, Mary, *The Proper Lady and the Woman Writer: Ideology as Style in the Works of Mary Wollstonecraft, Mary Shelley, and Jane Austen*, Chicago and London: University of Chicago Press, 1984.

Pope, Alexander, *The Poems of Alexander Pope*, edited by John Butt, London: Methuen, 1963.

Richardson, Samuel, *Letters written to and for Particular Friends, On the Most Important Occasions*, London and Bath, 1741; reprinted as *Familiar Letters on Important Occasions*, edited by Brian W. Downs, London: Routledge, 1928.

Rowe, Elizabeth Singer, *Letters Moral and Entertaining in Prose and Verse* [1728–32], 3 volumes, 3rd edition, London, 1735.

Shevelow, Kathryn, *Women and Print Culture: The Construction of Femininity in the Early Periodical*, London and New York: Routledge, 1989.

Smith, Hilda, *Reason's Disciples: Seventeenth-Century English Feminists*, Urbana, Chicago, London: University of Illinois Press, 1982.

The Spectator, edited by Donald F. Bond, 5 volumes, Oxford: Clarendon Press, 1965.

Stone, Lawrence, *The Family, Sex and Marriage in England 1500–1800*, Harmondsworth: Penguin, 1979.

Todd, Janet, (editor), *A Dictionary of British and American Women Writers 1660–1800*, London: Methuen, 1984.

___________, *Sensibility: An Introduction*, London and New York: Methuen, 1986.

___________, *The Sign of Angellica: Women, Writing and Fiction, 1660–1800*, London, Virago, 1989.

The Whole Duty of a Woman: Or, an infallible Guide to the Fair Sex. Containing, Rules, Directions, and Observations, for their Conduct and Behaviour through all Ages and Circumstances of Life, as Virgins, Wives or Widows, London, 1737.

Wilkes, Rev. Mr Wetenhall, *A Letter of Genteel and Moral Advice to a Young Lady* [1740], 8th edition, London, 1766.

Wollstonecraft, Mary, *A Vindication of the Rights of Woman* [1792], edited by Barbara Taylor, London: Everyman's Library, 1992.

THE

YOUNG LADY'S

POCKET LIBRARY, OR

PARENTAL MONITOR;

CONTAINING,

I.

DR. GREGORY'S,
FATHER'S LEGACY TO HIS DAUGHTERS.

II.

LADY PENNINGTON'S,
UNFORTUNATE MOTHER'S ADVICE TO HER DAUGHTERS.

III.

MARCHIONESS DE LAMBERT'S.
ADVICE OF A MOTHER TO HER DAUGHTER.

IV.

MOORE'S,
FABLES FOR THE FEMALE SEX.

"——— Every moral charm,
"That leads in ſweet captivity the mind
"To virtue."———

THOMSON.

——DUBLIN;——

PRINTED BY GRAISBERRY AND CAMPBELL,

FOR JOHN ARCHER, NO. 80, DAME-STREET.

1790.

A

FATHER'S LEGACY

TO

HIS DAUGHTERS.

BY THE LATE

DR. GREGORY,

OF EDINBURGH.

"—— Be each paſſion gratify'd,
"That tends to happineſs or eaſe."

CARTWRIGHT.

DUBLIN;

PRINTED BY GRAISBERRY AND CAMPBELL,

FOR JOHN ARCHER, NO. 80, DAME-STREET.

1790.

THE

CONTENTS.

PREFACE.

THAT the ſubſequent Letters were written by a tender father, in a declining ſtate of health, for the inſtruction of his daughters, and not intended for the Public, is a circumſtance which will recommend them to every one who conſiders them in the light of admonition and advice. In ſuch domeſtic intercourſe, no ſacrifices are made to prejudices, to cuſtoms, to faſhionable opinions.

Paternal love, paternal care, ſpeak their genuine ſentiments, undiſguiſed and unreſtrained. A father's zeal for his daughter's improvement, in whatever can make a woman amiable, with a father's quick apprehenſion of the dangers that too often ariſe, even from the attainment of that very point, ſuggeſt his admonitions, and render him attentive to a thouſand little graces and little decorums, which would eſcape the niceſt moraliſt who ſhould undertake the ſubject on unintereſted ſpeculation. Every faculty is on the alarm when the objects of ſuch tender affection are concerned.

In the writer of theſe Letters paternal tenderneſs and vigilance were doubled, as he was at that time ſole parent; death having before deprived the young ladies of their excellent mother. His own precarious ſtate of health inſpired him with the moſt tender ſolicitude for their future welfare; and though he might have concluded, that the impreſſions made by his inſtructions and uniform example could never be effaced from the memory of his children, yet his anxiety for their orphan condition ſuggeſted to him this method of continuing to them thoſe advantages.

The Editor is encouraged to offer this Treatiſe to the Public, by the very favourable reception which the reſt of his father's works have met with. The Comparative View of the State of Man and other Animals, and the Eſſay on the Office and Duties of a Phyſician, have been very generally read; and, if he is not deceived by the partiality of his friends, he has reaſon to believe they have met with general approbation.

In ſome of thoſe tracts, the Author's object was to improve the taſte and underſtanding of his reader; in others, to mend his heart; in others, to point out to him the proper uſe of philoſophy, by ſhewing its application to the duties of common life. In all his writings his chief view was the good of his fellow-creatures; and as thoſe among his friends, in whoſe taſte and judgment he moſt confided, think the publication of this ſmall work will contribute to that general deſign, and at the ſame time do honour to his memory, the Editor can no longer hesitate to comply with their advice in communicating it to the Public.

A

FATHER'S LEGACY

TO

HIS DAUGHTERS.

MY DEAR GIRLS,

YOU had the misfortune to be deprived of your mother at a time of life when you were insensible of your loss, and could receive little benefit either from her instruction or her example. Before this comes to your hands, you will likewise have lost your father.

I have had many melancholy reflections on the forlorn and helpless situation you must be in, if it should please God to remove me from you, before you arrive at that period of life when you will be able to think and act for yourselves. I know mankind too well; I know their falsehood, their dissipation, their coldness to all the duties of friendship and humanity.

I know the little attention paid to helpleſs infancy. You will meet with few friends diſintereſted enough to do you good offices, when you are incapable of making them any return, by contributing to their intereſt or their pleaſure, or even to the gratification of their vanity.

I have been ſupported under the gloom naturally ariſing from theſe reflections, by a reliance on the goodneſs of that Providence which has hitherto preſerved you, and given me the moſt pleaſing proſpect of the goodneſs of your diſpoſitions; and by the ſecret hope that your mother's virtues will entail a bleſſing on her children.

The anxiety I have for your happineſs, has made me reſolve to throw together my ſentiments relating to your future conduct in life. If I live for ſome years, you will receive them with much greater advantage, ſuited to your different geniuſes and diſpoſitions. If I die ſooner, you muſt receive them in this very imperfect manner,—the laſt proof of my affection.

You will all remember your father's fondneſs, when perhaps every other circumſtance relating to him is forgotten. This remembrance, I hope, will induce you to give a ſerious attention to the advices I am now going to leave with you. I can requeſt this attention with the greater confidence, as my ſentiments on the moſt intereſting points that regard life and manners, were entirely correſpondent to your mother's, whoſe judgment and taſte I truſted much more than my own.

You muſt expect that the advices which I ſhall give you will be very imperfect, as there are many nameleſs delicacies in female manners, of which none but a woman can judge. You will have one advantage by attending to what I am going to leave with you; you will hear, at leaſt for once in your lives, the genuine ſentiments of a man who has no intereſt in flattering or deceiving you. I ſhall throw my reflections together without any ſtudied order, and ſhall only, to avoid confuſion, range them under a few general heads.

You will ſee, in a little Treatiſe of mine juſt publiſhed, in what an honourable point of view I have conſidered your ſex; not as domeſtic drudges, or the ſlaves of our pleaſures, but as our companions and equals; as deſigned to ſoften our hearts and poliſh our manners; and as Thomſon finely ſays,

> To raiſe the virtues, animate the bliſs,
> And ſweeten all the toils of human life.

I ſhall not repeat what I have there ſaid on this ſubject, and ſhall only obſerve, that from the view I have given of your natural character and place in ſociety, there ariſes a certain propriety of conduct peculiar to your ſex. It is this peculiar propriety of female manners of which I intend to give you my ſentiments, without touching on thoſe general rules of conduct by which men and women are equally bound.

While I. explain to you that ſyſtem of conduct which I think will tend moſt to your honour and happineſs, I ſhall, at the ſame time, endeavour to point out thoſe virtues and accompliſhments which render you moſt reſpectable and moſt amiable in the eyes of my own ſex.

RELIGION.

THOUGH the duties of religion, ſtrictly ſpeaking, are equally binding on both ſexes, yet certain differences in their natural character and education, render ſome vices in your ſex particularly odious. The natural hardneſs of our hearts, and ſtrength of our paſſions, inflamed by the uncontrouled licence we are too often indulged with in our youth, are apt to render our manners more diſſolute, and make us leſs ſuſceptible of the finer feelings of the heart. Your ſuperior delicacy, your modeſty, and the uſual ſeverity of your education, preſerve you, in a great meaſure, from any temptation to thoſe vices to which we are moſt ſubjected. The natural ſoftneſs and ſenſibility of your diſpoſitions particularly fit you for the practice of thoſe duties where the heart is chiefly concerned. And this, along with the natural warmth of your imagination, renders you peculiarly ſuſceptible of the feelings of devotion.

There are many circumſtances in your ſituation that peculiarly require the ſupports of religion to enable you to act in them with ſpirit and propriety. Your whole life is often a life of ſuffering. You cannot plunge into buſineſs, or diſſipate yourſelves in pleaſure and riot, as men too often do, when under the preſſure of misfortunes. You muſt bear your ſorrows in ſilence, unknown and unpitied. You muſt often put on a face of ſerenity and cheerfulneſs, when your hearts are torn with anguiſh, or ſinking in deſpair. Then your only reſource is in the conſolations of religion. It is chiefly owing to theſe, that you bear domeſtic misfortunes better than we do.

But you are ſometimes in very different circumſtances, that equally require the reſtraints of religion. The natural vivacity, and perhaps the natural vanity of your ſex, is very apt to lead you into a diſſipated ſtate of life that deceives you under the appearance of innocent pleaſure; but which in reality waſtes your ſpirits, impairs your health, weakens all the ſuperior faculties of your minds, and often ſullies your reputations. Religion, by checking this diſſipation, and rage for pleaſure, enables you to draw more happineſs, even from thoſe very ſources of amuſement, which, when too frequently applied to, are often productive of ſatiety and diſguſt.

Religion is rather a matter of ſentiment than reaſoning. The important and intereſting articles of faith are ſufficiently plain. Fix your attention on theſe, and do not meddle with controverſy. If you get into that, you plunge into a chaos, from which you will never be able to extricate yourſelves. It ſpoils the temper, and, I ſuſpect, has no good effect on the heart.

Avoid all books and all converſations that tend to ſhake your faith on thoſe great points of religion which ſhould ſerve to regulate your conduct, and on which your hopes of future and eternal happineſs depend.

Never indulge yourſelves in ridicule on religious ſubjects, nor give countenance to it in others by ſeeming diverted with what they ſay. This, to people of good-breeding, will be a ſufficient check.

I wiſh to go no further than the Scriptures for your religious opinions. Embrace thoſe you find clearly revealed. Never perplex yourſelves about ſuch as you do not underſtand, but treat them with ſilent and becoming reverence. I would adviſe you to read only ſuch religious books as are addreſſed to the heart, ſuch as inſpire pious and devout affections, ſuch as are proper to direct you in your conduct, and not ſuch as tend to entangle you in the endleſs maze of opinions and ſyſtems.

Be punctual in the ſtated performance of your private devotions, morning and evening. If you have any ſenſibility or imagination, this will eſtabliſh ſuch an intercourſe between you and the Supreme Being, as will be of infinite conſequence to you in life. It will communicate an habitual cheerfulneſs to your tempers, give a firmneſs and ſteadineſs to your virtue, and enable you to go through all the viciſſitudes of human life with propriety and dignity.

I wiſh you to be regular in your attendance on public worſhip, and in receiving the communion. Allow nothing to interrupt your public or private devotions, except the performance of ſome active duty in life, to which they ſhould always give place. In your behaviour at public worſhip obſerve an exemplary attention and gravity.

That extreme ſtrictneſs which I recommend to you in theſe duties, will be conſidered by many of your acquaintance as a ſuperſtitious attachment to forms; but in the advices I give you on this and other ſubjects, I have an eye to the ſpirit and manners of the age. There is a levity and diſſipation in the preſent manners, a coldneſs and liſtleſſneſs in whatever relates to religion which cannot fail to infect you, unleſs you purpoſely cultivate in your minds a contrary bias, and make the devotional taſte habitual.

Avoid all grimace and oſtentation in your religious duties. They are the uſual cloaks of hypocriſy; at leaſt they ſhew a weak and vain mind.

Do not make religion a ſubject of common converſation in mixed companies. When it is introduced, rather ſeem to decline it. At the ſame time, never ſuffer any perſon to inſult you by any fooliſh ribaldry on your religious opinions, but ſhew the ſame reſentment you would naturally do on being offered any other perſonal inſult. But the ſureſt way to avoid this, is by a modeſt reſerve on the ſubject, and by uſing no freedom with others about their religious ſentiments.

Cultivate an enlarged charity for all mankind, however they may differ from you in their religious opions. That difference may probably ariſe from cauſes in which you had no ſhare, and from which you can derive no merit.

Shew your regard to religion by a diſtinguiſhing reſpect to all its miniſters, of whatever perſuaſion, who do not by their lives diſhonour their profeſſion; but never allow them the direction of your conſciences, leſt they taint you with the narrow ſpirit of their party.

The beſt effect of your religion will be a diffuſive humanity to all in diſtreſs. Set apart a certain proportion of your income as ſacred to charitable purpoſes. But in this, as well as in the practice of every other duty, carefully avoid oſtentation. Vanity is always defeating her own purpoſes. Fame is one of the natural rewards of virtue. Do not purſue her, and ſhe will follow you.

Do not confine your charity to giving money. You may have many opportunities of ſhewing a tender and compaſſionate ſpirit where your money is not wanted. There is a falſe and unnatural refinement in ſenſibility, which makes ſome people ſhun the ſight of every object in diſtreſs. Never indulge this, eſpecially where your friends or acquaintances are concerned. Let the days of their misfortunes, when the world forgets or avoids them, be the ſeaſon for you to exerciſe your humanity and friendſhip. The ſight of human miſery ſoftens the heart, and makes it better: it checks the pride of health and proſperity, and the diſtreſs it occaſions is amply compenſated by the conſciouſneſs of doing your duty, and by the ſecret endearment which nature has annexed to all our ſympathetic ſorrows

Women are greatly deceived, when they think they recommend themſelves to our ſex by their indifference about religion. Even thoſe men who are themſelves unbelievers, diſlike infidelity in you. Every man who knows human nature, connects a religious taſte in your ſex with ſoftneſs and ſenſibility of heart; at leaſt we always conſider the want of it as a proof of that hard and maſculine ſpirit, which of all your faults we diſlike the moſt. Beſides, men conſider your religion as one of their principal ſecurities for that female virtue in which they are moſt intereſted. If a gentleman pretends an attachment to any of you, and endeavours to ſhake your religious principles, be aſſured he is either a fool, or has deſigns on you which he dares not openly avow.

You will probably wonder at my having educated you in a church different from my own. The reaſon was plainly this: I looked on the differences between our churches to be of no real importance, and that a preference of one to the other was a mere matter of taſte. Your mother was educated in the Church of England, and had an attachment to it, and I had a prejudice in favour of every thing ſhe liked. It never was her deſire that you ſhould be baptiſed by a clergyman of the Church of England, or be educated in that Church. On the contrary, the delicacy of her regard to the ſmalleſt circumſtance that could affect me in the eye of the world, made her anxiouſly inſiſt it might be otherwiſe. But I could not yield to her in that kind of generoſity. When I loſt her, I became ſtill more determined to educate you in that Church, as I feel a ſecret pleaſure in doing every thing that appears to me to expreſs my affection and veneration for her memory. I draw but a very faint and imperfect picture of what your mother was, while I endeavour to point out what you should be*

CONDUCT AND BEHAVIOUR.

ONE of the chief beauties in a female character, is that modest reserve, that retiring delicacy, which avoids the public eye, and is disconcerted even at the gaze of admiration.—I do not wish you to be insensible to applause; if you were, you must become, if not worse, at least less amiable women: but you may be dazzled by that admiration which yet rejoices your hearts.

When a girl ceases to blush, she has lost the most powerful charm of beauty. That extreme sensibility which it indicates, may be a weakness and incumbrance in our sex, as I have too often felt; but in yours it is peculiarly engaging. Pedants, who think themselves philosophers, ask why a woman should

* The reader will remember, that such observations as respect equally both the sexes, are all along as much as possibly avoided.

blufh when fhe is confcious of no crime? It is a fufficient anfwer, that Nature has made you to blufh when you are guilty of no fault, and has forced us to love you becaufe you do fo.—Blufhing is fo far from being neceffarily an attendant on guilt, that it is the ufual companion of innocence.

This modefty, which I think fo effential in your fex, will naturally difpofe you to be rather filent in company, efpecially in a large one.—People of fenfe and difcernment will never miftake fuch filence for dullnefs. One may take a fhare in converfation without uttering a fyllable. The expreffion in the countenance fhews it, and this never efcapes an obferving eye.

I fhould be glad that you had an eafy dignity in your behaviour at public places, but not that confident eafe, that unabafhed countenance, which feems to fet the company at defiance. If, while a gentleman is fpeaking to you, one of fuperior rank addreffes you, do not let your eager attention and vifible preference betray the flutter of your heart: let your pride on this occafion preferve you from that meannefs into which your vanity would fink you. Confider that you expofe yourfelves to the ridicule of the company, and affront one gentleman only to fwell the triumph of another, who perhaps thinks he does you honour in fpeaking to you.

Converſe with men even of the firſt rank with that dignified modeſty which may prevent the approach of the moſt diſtant familiarity, and conſequently prevent them from feeling themſelves your ſuperiors.

Wit is the moſt dangerous talent you can poſſeſs. It muſt be guarded with great diſcretion and good nature, otherwiſe it will create you many enemies. Wit is perfectly conſiſtent with ſoftneſs and delicacy; yet they are ſeldom found united. Wit is ſo flattering to vanity, that they who poſſeſs it become intoxicated, and loſe all ſelf-command.

Humour is a different quality. It will make your company much ſolicited; but be cautious how you indulge it It is often a great enemy to delicacy, and a ſtill greater one to dignity of character. It may ſometimes gain you applauſe, but will never procure you reſpect.

Be even cautious of diſplaying your good ſenſe. It will be thought you aſſume a ſuperiority over the reſt of the company. But if you happen to have any learning, keep it a profound ſecret, eſpecially from the men, who generally look with a jealous and malignant eye on a woman of great parts, and a cultivated underſtanding.

A man of real genius and candour is far ſuperior to this meanneſs; but ſuch a one will ſeldom fall in your way; and if by accident he ſhould, do not be anxious to ſhew the full extent of your knowlege.

If he has any opportunities of ſeeing you, he will ſoon diſcover it himſelf; and if you have any advanvantages of perſon or manner, and keep your own ſecret, he will probably give you credit for a great deal more than you poſſeſs. The great art of pleasing in converſation conſiſts in making the company pleaſed with themſelves. You will more readily hear them talk yourſelves into their good graces.

Beware of detraction, eſpecially where your own ſex are concerned. You are generally accuſed of being particularly addicted to this vice—I think, unjuſtly. Men are fully as guilty of it when their intereſts interfere. As your intereſts more frequently claſh, and as your feelings are quicker than ours, your temptations to it are more frequent: for this reaſon be particularly tender of the reputation of your own ſex, eſpecially when they happen to rival you in our regard. We look on this as the ſtrongeſt proof of dignity and true greatneſs of mind.

Shew a compaſſionate ſympathy to unfortunate woman eſpecially to thoſe who are rendered ſo by the villany of men. Indulge a ſecret pleaſure, I may ſay pride, in being the friends and refuge of the unhappy, but without the vanity of ſhewing it.

Conſider every ſpecies of indelicacy in converſation, as ſhameful in itſelf, and as highly diſguſting to us. All double entendre is of this ſort. The diſſoluteneſs of men's education allows them to be diverted with a kind of wit, which yet they have delicacy enough to be ſhocked at, when it comes from your mouths, or even when you hear it without pain and contempt.—Virgin purity is of that delicate nature, that it cannot bear certain things without contamination. It is always in your power to avoid theſe. No man but a brute or a fool, will inſult a woman with converſation which he ſees gives her pain; nor will he dare to do it, if ſhe reſent the injury with a becoming ſpirit. There is a dignity in conſcious virtue which is able to awe the moſt ſhameleſs and abandoned of men.

You will be reproached perhaps with prudery. By prudery is uſually meant an affectation of delicacy: Now I do not wiſh you to affect delicacy; I wiſh you to poſſeſs it: at any rate it is better to run the riſk of being thought ridiculous than diſguſting.

The men will complain of your reſerve. They will aſſure you that a franker behaviour would, make you more amiable. But, truſt me, they are not ſincere when they tell you ſo. I acknowledge, that on ſome occaſions it might render you more agreeable as companions, but it would make you leſs amiable as women—an important diſtinction, which many of your ſex are not aware of. After all, I wiſh you to have great eaſe and openneſs in your converſation; I only point out ſome conſiderations which ought to regulate your behaviour in that reſpect.

Have a ſacred regard to truth. Lying is a mean and deſpicable vice. I have known ſome women of excellent parts, who were ſo much addicted to it, that they could not be truſted in the relation of any ſtory, eſpecially if it contained any thing of the marvellous, or if they themſelves were the heroines of the tale. This weakneſs did not proceed from a bad heart, but was merely the effect of vanity, or an unbridled imagination. I do not mean to cenſure that lively embelliſhment of a humorous ſtory, which is only intended to promote innocent mirth.

There is a certain gentleneſs of ſpirit and manners extremely engaging in your ſex; not that indiſcriminate attention, that unmeaning ſimper, which ſmiles on all alike. This ariſes either from an affectation of ſoftneſs, or from perfect inſipidity.

There is a ſpecies of refinement in luxury, juſt beginning to prevail among the gentlemen of this country, to which our ladies are yet as great ſtrangers as any women upon earth; I hope, for the honour of the ſex, they may ever continue ſo; I mean, the luxury of eating. It is a deſpicable ſelfiſh vice in men, but in your ſex it is beyond expreſſion indelicate and diſguſting.

Every one who remembers a few years back, is ſenſible of a very ſtriking change in the attention and reſpect formerly paid by the gentlemen to the ladies; their drawing-rooms are deſerted, and after dinner and ſupper the gentlemen are impatient till they retire. How they came to loſe this reſpect, which nature and politeneſs ſo well entitle them to, I ſhall not here particularly inquire. The revolutions of manners in any country depend on cauſes very various and complicated. I ſhall only obſerve, that the behaviour of the ladies in the laſt age was very reſerved and ſtately. It would now be reckoned ridiculouſly ſtiff and formal. Whatever it was, it had certainly the effect of making them more reſpected.

A fine woman, like other fine things in nature, has her proper point of view, from which ſhe may be ſeen to moſt advantage. To fix this point requires great judgment, and an intimate knowledge of the human heart. By the preſent mode of female manners, the ladies ſeem to expect that they ſhall regain their aſcendency over us, by the fulleſt diſplay of their perſonal charms, by being always in our eye at public places, by converſing with us with the ſame unreſerved freedom as we do with one another; in ſhort, by reſembling us as nearly as they poſſibly can.—But a little time and experience will ſhow the folly of this expectation and conduct.

The power of a fine woman over the hearts of men, of men of the fineſt parts, is even beyond what ſhe conceives. They are ſenſible of the pleaſing illuſion, but they cannot, nor do they wiſh to diſſolve it. But if ſhe is determined to diſpel the charm, it certainly is in her power; ſhe may ſoon reduce the angel to a very ordinary girl.

There is a native dignity in ingenuous modeſty to be expected in your ſex, which is your natural protection from the familiarities of the men, and which you ſhould feel previous to the reflection that it is your intereſt to keep yourſelves ſacred from all perſonal freedoms. The many nameleſs charms and endearments of beauty ſhould be reſerved to bleſs the arms of the happy man to whom you give your heart, but who, if he has the leaſt delicacy, will deſpiſe them if he knows that they have been proſtituted to fifty men before him. The ſentiment, that a woman may allow all innocent freedoms, provided her virtue is ſecure, is both groſsly indelicate and dangerous, and has proved fatal to many of your ſex.

Let me now recommend to your attention that elegance, which is not ſo much a quality itſelf, as the high poliſh of every other. It is what diffuſes an ineffable grace over every look, every motion, every ſentence you utter; it gives that charm to beauty, without which it generally fails to pleaſe. It is partly a perſonal quality, in which reſpect it is the gift of nature; but I ſpeak of it principally as a quality of the mind. In a word, it is the perfection of taſte in life and manners;—every virtue and every excellency in their moſt graceful and amiable forms.

You may perhaps think that I want to throw every ſpark of nature out of your compoſition, and to make you entirely artificial. Far from it. I wiſh you to poſſeſs the moſt perfect ſimplicity of heart and manners. I think you may poſſeſs dignity without pride, affability without meanneſs, and ſimple elegance without affectation. Milton had my idea, when he ſays of Eve,

> Grace was in all her ſteps, Heaven in her eye,
> In every geſture dignity and love.

AMUSEMENTS.

EVERY period of life has amuſements which are natural and proper to it. You may indulge the variety of your taſtes in theſe, while you keep within the bounds of that propriety which is ſuitable to your ſex.

Some amuſements are conducive to health, as various kinds of exerciſe; ſome are connected with qualities really uſeful, as different kinds of women's work, and all the domeſtic concerns of a family; ſome are elegant accompliſhments, as dreſs, dancing, muſic, and drawing. Such books as improve yonr underſtanding, enlarge your knowledge, and cultivate your taſte, may be conſidered in a higher point of view than mere amuſements. There are a variety of others, which are neither uſeful nor ornamental, ſuch as play of different kinds.

I would particularly recommend to you thoſe exerciſes that oblige you to be much abroad in the open air, ſuch as walking and riding on horſeback. This will give vigour to your conſtitutions, and a bloom to your complexions. If you accuſtom yourſelves to go abroad always in chairs and carriages, you will ſoon become ſo enervated, as to be unable to go out of doors without them. They are like moſt articles of luxury, uſeful and agreeable when judiciouſly uſed; but when made habitual, they become both inſipid and pernicious.

An attention to your health is a duty you owe to yourſelves and to your friends. Bad health ſeldom fails to have an influence on the ſpirits and temper. The fineſt geniuſes, the moſt delicate minds, have very frequently a correſpondent delicacy of bodily conſtitution, which they are too apt to neglect. Their luxury lies in reading and late hours, equal enemies to health and beauty.

But though good health be one of the greateſt bleſſings of life, never make a boaſt of it, but enjoy it in grateful ſilence. We ſo naturally aſſociate the idea of female ſoftneſs and delicacy with a correſpondent delicacy of conſtitution, that when a woman ſpeaks of her great ſtrength, her extraordinary appetite, her ability to bear exceſſive fatigue, we recoil at a deſcription in a way ſhe is little aware of.

The intention of your being taught needle-work, knitting, and ſuch like, is not on account of the intrinſic value of all you can do with your hands, which is trifling, but to enable you to judge more perfectly of that kind of work, and to direct the execution of it in others. Another principal end is to enable you to fill up, in a tolerably agreeable way, ſome of the many ſolitary hours you muſt neceſſarily paſs at home. It is a great article in the happineſs of life, to have your pleaſures as independent of others as poſſible. By continually gadding abroad in ſearch of amuſement, you loſe the reſpect of all your acquaintances, whom you oppreſs with thoſe viſits, which, by a more diſcreet management, might have been courted.

The domeſtic œconomy of a family is entirely a woman's province, and furniſhes a variety of ſubjects for the exertion both of good ſenſe and good taſte. If you ever come to have the charge of a family, it ought to engage much of your time and attention; nor can you be excuſed from this by any extent of fortune, though with a narrow one the ruin that follows the neglect of it may be more immediate.

I am at the greateſt loſs what to adviſe you in regard to books. There is no impropriety in your reading hiſtory, or cultivating any art or ſcience to which genius or accident lead you. The whole volume of Nature lies open to your eye, and furniſhes an infinite variety of entertainment. If I was ſure that Nature had given you ſuch ſtrong principles of taſte and ſentiment as would remain with you, and influence your future conduct, with the utmoſt pleaſure would I endeavour to direct your reading in ſuch a way as might form that taſte to the utmoſt perfection of truth and elegance. "But when I reflect how eaſy it is to warm a girl's imagination, and how difficult deeply and permanently to affect her heart; how readily ſhe enters into every refinement of ſentiment, and how eaſily ſhe can ſacrifice them to vanity or convenience;" I think I may very probably do you an injury by artificially creating a taſte, which, if Nature never gave it you, would only ſerve to embarraſs your future conduct. I do not want to *make* you any thing: I want to know what Nature has made you, and to perfect you on her plan. I do not wiſh you to have ſentiments that might perplex you; I wiſh you to have ſentiments that may uniformly and ſteadily guide you, and ſuch as your hearts ſo thoroughly approve, that you would not forego them for any conſideration this world could offer.

Dreſs is an important article in female life. The love of dreſs is natural to you, and therefore it is proper and reaſonable. Good ſenſe will regulate your expence in it, and good taſte will direct you to dreſs in ſuch a way as to conceal any blemiſhes, and ſet off your beauties, if you have any, to the greateſt advantage. But much delicacy and judgement are required in the application of this rule. A fine woman ſhews her charms to moſt advantage, when ſhe ſeems moſt to conceal them. The fineſt boſom in nature is not ſo fine as what imagination forms. The moſt perfect elegance of dreſs appears always the moſt eaſy, and the leaſt ſtudied.

Do not confine your attention to dreſs to your public appearances. Accuſtom yourſelves to an habitual neatneſs, ſo that in the moſt careleſs undreſs, in your moſt unguarded hours, you may have no reaſon to be aſhamed of your appearance. You will not eaſily believe how much we conſider your dreſs as expreſſive of your characters. Vanity, levity, ſlovenlineſs, folly, appear through it. An elegant ſimplicity is an equal proof of taſte and delicacy.

In dancing, the principal points you are to attend to are eaſe and grace. I would have you to dance with ſpirit; but never allow yourſelves to be ſo far tranſported with mirth, as to forget the delicacy of your ſex. Many a girl dancing in the gaiety and innocence of her heart, is thought to discover a spirit she little dreams of.

I know no entertainment that gives such pleasure to any person of sentiment or humour, as the theatre. But I am sorry to say there are few English comedies a lady can see, without a shock to delicacy. You will not readily suspect the comments gentlemen make on your behaviour on such occasions. Men are often best acquainted with the most worthless of your sex, and from them too readily form their judgement of the rest. A virtuous girl often hears very indelicate things with a countenance no-wise embarrassed, because in truth she does not understand them. Yet this is, most ungenerously, ascribed to that command of features, and that ready presence of mind, which you are thought to possess in a degree far beyond us; or, by still more malignant observers, it is ascribed to hardened effrontery.

Sometimes a girl laughs with all the simplicity of unsuspecting innocence, for no other reason but being infected with other people's laughing: she is then believed to know more than she should do. If she does happen to understand an improper thing, she suffers a very complicated distress, she feels her modesty hurt in the most sensible manner, and at the same time is ashamed of appearing conscious of the injury. The only way to avoid these inconveniencies, is never to go to a play that is particularly offensive to delicacy.

Tragedy ſubjects you to no ſuch diſtreſs.—Its ſorrows will ſoften and ennoble your hearts.

I need ſay little about gaming, the ladies in this country being as yet almoſt ſtrangers to it. It is a ruinous and incurable vice; and as it leads to all the ſelfiſh and turbulent paſſions, is peculiarly odious in your ſex. I have no objection to your playing a little at any kind of game, as a variety in your amuſements, provided that what you can poſſibly loſe is ſuch a trifle as can neither intereſt you, nor hurt you.

In this, as well as in all important points of conduct, ſhew a determined reſolution and ſteadineſs. This is not in the leaſt inconſiſtent with that ſoftneſs and gentleneſs ſo amiable in your ſex. On the contrary, it gives that ſpirit to a mild and ſweet diſpoſition, without which it is apt to degenerate into inſipidity. It makes you reſpectable in your own eyes, and dignifies you in ours.

FRIENDSHIP, LOVE. MARRIAGE.

THE luxury and diſſipation that prevails in genteel life, as it corrupts the heart in many reſpects, ſo renders it incapable of warm, ſincere, and ſteady friendſhip. A happy choice of friends will be of the utmoſt conſequence to you, as they may aſſiſt you by their advice and good offices. But the immediate gratification which friendſhip affords to a warm, open, and ingenuous heart, is of itſelf a ſufficient motive to court it.

In the choice of your friends, have your principal regard to goodneſs of heart and fidelity. If they alſo poſſeſs taſte and genius, that will ſtill make them more agreeable and uſeful companions. You have particular reaſon to place confidence in thoſe who have ſhewn affection for you in your early days, when you were incapable of making them any return. This is an obligation for which you cannot be too grateful. When you read this, you will naturally think of your mother's friend, to whom you owe ſo much.

If you have the good fortune to meet with any who deſerve the name of friends, unboſom yourſelf to them with the moſt unſuſpicious confidence. It is one of the world's maxims, never to truſt any perſon with a ſecret, the diſcovery of which could give you any pain; but it is the maxim of a little mind and a cold heart, unleſs where it is the effect of frequent diſappointments and bad uſage. An open temper, if reſtrained but by tolerable prudence, will make you, on the whole, much happier than a reſerved ſuſpicious one, although you may ſometimes ſuffer by it. Coldneſs and diſtruſt are but the too certain conſequences of age and experience; but they are unpleaſant feelings, and need not be anticipated before their time.

But however open you may be in talking of your affairs, never diſcloſe the ſecrets of one friend to another. Theſe are ſecret depoſits, which do not belong to you, nor have you any right to make uſe of them.

There is another caſe, in which I ſuſpect it is proper to be ſecret, not ſo much from motives of prudence, as delicacy; I mean in love matters. Though a woman has no reaſon to be aſhamed of an attachment to a man of merit, yet Nature, whoſe authority is ſuperior to philoſophy, has annexed a ſenſe of ſhame to it. It is even long before a woman of delicacy dares avow to her own heart that ſhe loves; and when all the ſubterfuges of ingenuity to conceal it from herſelf fail, ſhe feels a violence done both to her pride and to her modeſty. This, I ſhould imagine, muſt always be the caſe where ſhe is not ſure of a return to her attachment.

In ſuch a ſituation, to lay the heart open to any perſon whatever, does not appear to me conſiſtent with the perfection of female delicacy. But perhaps I am in the wrong. At the ſame time I muſt tell you, that, in point of prudence, it concerns you to attend well to the conſequences of ſuch a diſcovery.

These secrets, however important in your own estimation, may appear very trifling to your friend, who possibly will not enter into your feelings, but may rather consider them as a subject of pleasantry. For this reason love secrets are of all others the worst kept. But the consequences to you may be very serious, as no man of spirit and delicacy ever valued a heart much hackneyed in the ways of love.

If, therefore, you must have a friend to pour out your heart to, be sure of her honour and secrecy. Let her not be a married woman, especially if she lives happily with her husband. There are certain unguarded moments, in which such a woman, though the best and worthiest of her sex, may let hints escape, which at other times, or to any other person than her husband, she would be incapable of; nor will a husband in this case feel himself under the same obligation of secrecy and honour, as if you had put your confidence originally in himself, especially on a subject which the world is apt to treat so lightly.

If all other circumstances are equal, there are obvious advantages in your making friends of one another. The ties of blood, and your being so much united in one common interest, form an additional bond of union to your friendship. If your brothers should have the good fortune to have hearts susceptible of friendship, to possess truth, honour, sense, and delicacy of sentiment, they are the fittest and most unexceptionable confidants. By placing confidence in them, you will receive every advantage which you could hope for from the friendſhip of men, without any of the inconveniencies that attend ſuch connexions with our ſex.

Beware of making confidants of your ſervants. Dignity not properly underſtood very readily degenerates into pride, which enters into no friendſhip, becauſe it cannot bear an equal, and is ſo fond of flattery as to graſp at it even from ſervants and dependants. The moſt intimate confidants, therefore, of proud people, are valets-de-chambre and waiting-women. Shew the utmoſt humanity to your ſervants; make their ſituation as comfortable to them as poſſible: but if you make them your confidants, you ſpoil them, and debaſe yourſelves.

Never allow any perſon, under the pretended ſanction of friendſhip, to be ſo familiar as to loſe a proper reſpect to you. Never allow them to teaze you on any ſubject that is diſagreeable, or where you have once taken your reſolution. Many will tell you, that this reſerve is inconſiſtent with the freedom which friendſhip allows: but a certain reſpect is as neceſſary in friendſhip as in love. Without it you may be liked as a child, but you will never be beloved as an equal.

The temper and diſpoſition of the heart in your ſex make you enter more readily and warmly into friendſhips than men. Your natural propenſity to it is ſo ſtrong, that you often run into intimacies which you ſoon have ſufficient cauſe to repent of; and this makes your friendſhips ſo very fluctuating.

Another great obſtacle to the ſincerity as well as ſteadineſs of your friendſhips, is the great claſhing of your intereſts in the purſuits of love, ambition, or vanity. For theſe reaſons, it would appear at firſt view more eligible for you to contract your friendſhips with the men. Among other obvious advantages of an eaſy intercourſe between the two ſexes, it occaſions an emulation and exertion in each to excel and be agreeable: hence their reſpective excellencies are mutually communicated and blended. As their intereſts in no degree interfere, there can be no foundation for jealouſy, or ſuſpicion of rivalſhip. The friendſhip of a man for a woman is always blended with tenderneſs, which he never feels for one of his own ſex, even where love is in no degree concerned. Beſides, we are conſcious of a natural title you have to our protection aud good offices, and therefore we feel an additional obligation of honour to ſerve you, and to obſerve an inviolable ſecrecy, whenever you confide in us.

But apply theſe obſervations with great caution. Thouſands of women of the beſt hearts and fineſt parts have been ruined by men who approach them under the ſpecious name of friendſhip. But ſuppoſing a man to have the moſt undoubted honour, yet his friendſhip to a woman is ſo near a-kin to love, that if ſhe be very agreeable in her perſon, ſhe will probably very ſoon find a lover, where ſhe only wiſhed to meet a friend. Let me here, however, warn you againſt that weakneſs ſo common among vain women, the imagination that every man who takes particular notice of you is a lover. Nothing can expoſe you more to ridicule than the taking up a man on the ſuſpicion of being your lover, who perhaps never once thought of you in that view, and giving yourſelves thoſe airs ſo common among all ſilly women on ſuch occaſions.

There is a kind of unmeaning gallantry much practiſed by ſome men, which, if you have any diſcernment, you will find really very harmleſs. Men of this ſort will attend you to public places, and be uſeful to you by a number of little obſervances, which thoſe of a ſuperior claſs do not ſo well underſtand, or have not leiſure to regard, or perhaps are too proud to ſubmit to. Look on the compliments of ſuch men as words of courſe, which they repeat to every agreeable woman of their acquaintance. There is a familiarity they are apt to aſſume, which a proper dignity in your behaviour will be eaſily able to check.

There is a different ſpecies of men whom you may like as agreeable companions, men of worth, taſte, and genius, whoſe converſation, in ſome reſpects, may be ſuperior to what you generally meet with among your own ſex. It will be fooliſh in you to deprive yourſelves of an uſeful and agreeable acquaintance, merely becauſe idle people ſay he is your lover. Such a man may like your company, without having any deſign on your perſon.

People whoſe ſentiments, and particularly whoſe taſtes correſpond, naturally like to aſſociate together, although neither of them have the moſt diſtant view of any further connection. But as this ſimilarity of minds often gives riſe to a more tender attachment than friendſhip, it will be prudent to keep a watchful eye over yourſelves, leſt your hearts become too far engaged before you are aware of it. At the ſame time, I do not think that your ſex, at leaſt in this part of the world, have much of that ſenſibility which diſpoſes to ſuch attachments. What is commonly called love among you is rather gratitude, and a partiality to the man who prefers you to the reſt of your ſex; and ſuch a man you often marry, with little of either perſonal eſteem or affection. Indeed, without an unuſual ſhare of natural ſenſibility, and very peculiar good fortune, a woman in this country has very little probability of marrying for love.

It is a maxim laid down among you, and a very prudent one it is. That love is not to begin on your part, but is entirely to be the conſequence of our attachment to you. Now, ſuppoſing a woman to have ſenſe and taſte, ſhe will not find many men to whom ſhe can poſſibly be ſuppoſed to bear any conſiderable ſhare of eſteem. Among theſe few it is very great chance if any of them diſtinguiſhes her particularly. Love, at leaſt with us, is exceedingly capricious, and will not always fix where reaſon ſays it ſhould. But ſuppoſing one of them ſhould become particularly attached to her, it is ſtill extremely improbable that he ſhould be the man in the world her heart moſt approved of.

As, therefore, Nature has not given you that unlimited range in your choice which we enjoy, ſhe has wiſely and benevolently aſſigned to you a greater flexibility of taſte on this ſubject. Some agreeable qualities recommend a gentleman to your common good liking and friendſhip. In the courſe of his acquaintance, he contracts an attachment to you. When you perceive it, it excites your gratitude: this gratitude riſes into a preference, and this preference perhaps at laſt advances to ſome degree of attachment, eſpecially if it meets with croſſes and difficulties; for theſe, and a ſtate of ſuſpence, are very great incitements to attachment, and are the food of love in both ſexes. If attachment was not excited in your ſex in this manner, there is not one of a million of you that could ever marry with any degree of love.

A man of taſte and delicacy marries a woman becauſe he loves her more than any other. A woman of equal taſte and delicacy marries him becauſe ſhe eſteems him, and becauſe he gives her that preference. But if a man unfortunately becomes attached to a woman whoſe heart is ſecretly pre-engaged, his attachment, inſtead of obtaining a ſuitable return, is particularly offenſive; and if he perſiſts to teaze her, he makes himſelf equally the object of her ſcorn and averſion.

The effects of love among men are diverſified by their different tempers. An artful man may counterfeit every one of them ſo eaſily as to impoſe on a young girl of an open, generous, and feeling heart, if ſhe is not extremely on her guard. The fineſt parts in ſuch a girl may not always prove ſufficient for her ſecurity. The dark and crooked paths of cunning are unſearchable and inconceivable to an honourable and elevated mind.

The following, I apprehend, are the moſt genuine effects of an honourable paſſion among the men, and the moſt difficult to counterfeit. A man of delicacy often betrays his paſſion by his too great anxiety to conceal it, eſpecially if he has little hopes of ſucceſs. True love, in all its ſtages, ſeeks concealment, and never expects ſucceſs. It renders a man not only reſpectful, but timid to the higheſt degree in his behaviour to the woman he loves. To conceal the awe he ſtands in of her, he may ſometimes affect pleaſantry, but it ſits aukwardly on him, and he quickly relapſes into ſerioufneſs, if not into dullneſs. He magnifies all her real perfections in his imagination, and is either blind to her failings, or converts them into beauties. Like a perſon conſcious of guilt, he is jealous that every eye obſerves his; and to avoid this, he ſhuns all the little obſervances of common gallantry.

His heart and his character will be improved in every reſpect by his attachment. His manners will become more gentle, and his converſation more agreeable; but diffidence and embarraſſment will always make him appear to diſadvantage in the company of his miſtreſs. If the faſcination continue long, it will totally depreſs his ſpirit, and extinguiſh every active, vigorous, and manly principle of his mind. You will find this ſubject beautifully and pathetically painted in Thomſon's Spring.

When you obſerve in a gentleman's behaviour theſe marks which I have deſcribed above, reflect ſeriouſly what you are to do. If his attachment is agreeable to you, I leave you to do as nature, good ſenſe, and delicacy ſhall direct you. If you love him, let me adviſe you never to diſcover to him the full extent of your love, no, not although you marry him. That ſufficiently ſhews your preference, which is all he is intitled to know. If he has delicacy, he will aſk for no ſtronger proof of affection for your ſake; if he has ſenſe, he will not aſk it for his own. This is an unpleaſant truth, but it is my duty to let you know it. Violent love cannot ſubſiſt, at leaſt cannot be expreſſed, for any time together on both ſides; otherwiſe the certain conſequence, however concealed, is ſatiety and diſguſt. Nature in this caſe has laid the reſerve on you.

If you ſee evident proofs of a gentleman's attachment, and are determined to ſhut your heart againſt him, as yon ever hope to be uſed with generoſity by the perſon who ſhall engage your own heart, treat him honourably and humanely. Do not let him linger in a miſerable ſuſpenſe, but be anxious to let him know your ſentiments with regard to him.

However people's hearts may deceive them, there is ſcarcely a perſon that can love for any time without at leaſt ſome diſtant hope of ſucceſs. If you really wiſh to undeceive a lover, you may do it in a variety of ways. There is a certain ſpecies of eaſy familiarity in your behaviour which may ſatisfy him, if he has any diſcernment left, that he has nothing to hope for. But perhaps your particular temper may not admit of this: you may eaſily ſhew that you want to avoid his company; but if he is a man whoſe friendſhip you wiſh to preſerve, you may not chuſe this method, becauſe then you loſe him in every capacity. You may get a common friend to explain matters to him, or fall on many other devices, if you are ſeriouſly anxious to put him out of ſuſpenſe.

But if you are resolved against every such method, at least do not shun opportunities of letting him explain himself. If you do this, you act barbarously and unjustly. If he brings you to an explanation, give him a polite, but resolute and decisive answer. In whatever way you convey your sentiments to him, if he is a man of spirit and delicacy, he will give you no fnrther trouble, nor apply to your friends for their intercession. This last is a method of courtship which every man of spirit will disdain. He will never whine nor sue for your pity: That would mortify him almost as much as your scorn. In short, you may possibly break such a heart, but you can never bend it. Great pride always accompanies delicacy, however concealed under the appearance of the utmost gentleness and modesty, and is the passion of all others the most difficult to conquer.

There is a case where a woman may coquette justifiably to the utmost verge which her conscience will allow. It is where a gentleman purposely declines to make his addresses, till such time as he thinks himself perfectly sure of her consent. This at bottom is intended to force a woman to give up the undoubted privilege of her sex, the privilege of refusing; it is intended to force her to explain herself, in effect, before the gentleman deigns to do it, and by this means to oblige her to violate the modesty and delicacy of her sex, and to invert the clearest order of nature. All this ſacrifice is propoſed to be made merely to gratify a moſt deſpicable vanity in a man who would degrade the very woman whom he wiſhes to make his wife.

It is of great importance to diſtinguiſh whether a gentleman, who has the appearance of being your lover, delays to ſpeak explicitly, from the motive I have mentioned, or from a diffidence inſeparable from true attachment. In the one caſe, you can ſcarcely uſe him too ill; in the other, you ought to uſe him with great kindneſs: and the greateſt kindneſs you can ſhew him, if you are determined not to liſten to his addreſſes, is to let him know it as ſoon as poſſible.

I know the many excuſes with which women endeavour to juſtify themſelves to the world, and to their own conſciences, when they act otherwiſe. Sometimes they plead ignorance, or at leaſt uncertainty, of the gentleman's real ſentiments. That may ſometimes be the caſe. Sometimes they plead the decorum of their ſex, which enjoins an equal behaviour to all men, and forbids them to conſider any man as a lover till he has directly told them ſo. Perhaps few women carry their ideas of female delicacy and decorum ſo far as I do. But I muſt ſay, you are not intitled to plead the obligation of theſe virtues, in oppoſition to the ſuperior ones of gratitude, juſtice and humanity. The man is intitled to all these, who prefers you to the rest of your sex, and perhaps whose greatest weakness is this very preference. The truth of the matter is, vanity, and the love of admiration, is so prevailing a passion among you, that you may be considered to make a very great sacrifice whenever you give up a lover, till every art of coquetry fails to keep him, or till he forces you to an explanation. You can be fond of the love, when you are indifferent to, or even when you despise the lover.

But the deepest and most artful coquetry is employed by women of superior taste and sense, to engage and fix the heart of a man whom the world and whom they themselves esteem, although they are firmly determined never to marry him. But his conversation amuses them, and his attachment is the highest gratification to their vanity: nay, they can sometimes be gratified with the utter ruin of his fortune, fame and happiness. God forbid I should ever think so of all your sex! I know many of them have principles, have generosity and dignity of soul that elevate them above the worthless vanity I have been speaking of.

Such a woman, I am persuaded, may always convert a lover, if she cannot give him her affections, into a warm and steady friend, provided he is a man of sense, resolution and candour. If she explains herself with a generous openness and freedom, he muſt feel the ſtroke as a man; but he will likewiſe bear it as a man: what he ſuffers, he will ſuffer in ſilence. Every ſentiment of eſteem will remain; but love, though it requires very little food, and is eaſily ſurfeited with too much, yet it requires ſome. He will view her in the light of a married woman; and though paſſion ſubſides, yet a man of a candid and generous heart always retains a tenderneſs for a woman he has once loved, and who has uſed him well, beyond what he feels for any other of her ſex.

If he has not confided his own ſecret to any body, he has an undoubted title to aſk you not to divulge it. If a woman chuſes to truſt any of her companions with her own unfortunate attachments, ſhe may, as it is her own affair alone; but if ſhe has any generoſity or gratitude, ſhe will not betray a ſecret which does not belong to her.

Male coquetry is much more inexcuſable than female, as well as more pernicious; but it is rare in this country. Very few men will give themſelves the trouble to gain or retain any woman's affections, unleſs they have views on them either of an honourable or diſhonourable kind. Men employed in the purſuits of buſineſs, ambition or pleaſure, will not give themſelves the trouble to engage a woman's affections, merely from the vanity of conqueſt, and of triumphing over the heart of an innocent and defenceleſs girl. Beſides, people never value much what is entirely in their power. A man of parts, ſentiment and addreſs, if he lays aſide all regard to truth and humanity, may engage the hearts of fifty women at the ſame time, and may likewiſe conduct his coquetry with ſo much art, as to put it out of the power of any of them to ſpecify a ſingle expreſſion that could be ſaid to be directly expreſſive of love.

This ambiguity of behaviour, this art of keeping one in ſuſpenſe, is the great ſecret of coquetry in both ſexes. It is the more cruel in us, becauſe we can carry it to what length we pleaſe, and continue it as long as we pleaſe, without your being ſo much as at liberty to complain or expoſtulate; whereas we can break our chain, and force you to explain, whenever we become impatient of our ſituation.

I have inſiſted the more particularly on this ſubject of courtſhip, becauſe it may moſt readily happen to you at that early period of life when you can have little experience or knowledge of the world; when your paſſions are warm, and your judgments not arrived at ſuch full maturity as to be able to correct them. I wiſh you to poſſeſs ſuch high principles of honour and generoſity as will render you incapable of deceiving, and at the ſame time to poſſeſs that acute diſcernment which may ſecure you againſt being deceived.

A woman, in this country, may eaſily prevent the firſt impreſſions of love; and every motive of prudence and delicacy ſhould make her guard her heart againſt them, till ſuch time as ſhe has received the moſt convincing proofs of the attachment of a man of ſuch merit, as will juſtify a reciprocal regard. Your hearts indeed may be ſhut inflexibly and permanently againſt all the merit a man can poſſeſs. That may be your misfortune, but cannot be your fault. In ſuch a ſituation, you would be equally unjuſt to yourſelf and your lover, if you gave him your hand when your heart revolted againſt him. But miſerable will be your fate, if you allow an attachment to ſteal on you before you are ſure of a return; or, what is infinitely worſe, where there are wanting thoſe qualities which alone can enſure happineſs in a married ſtate.

I know nothing that renders a woman more deſpicable, than her thinking it eſſential to happineſs to be married. Beſides the groſs indelicacy of the ſentiment, it is a falſe one, as thouſands of women have experienced. But if it was true, the belief that it is ſo, and the conſequent impatience to be married, is the moſt effectual way to prevent it.

You muſt not think from this that I do not wiſh you to marry; on the contrary, I am of opinion, that you may attain a ſuperior degree of happineſs in a married ſtate, to what you can poſſibly find in any other. I know the forlorn and unprotected ſituation of an old maid, the chagrin and peeviſhneſs which are apt to infect their tempers, and the great difficulty of making a tranſition, with dignity and cheerfulneſs, from the period of youth, beauty, admiration and reſpect, into the calm, ſilent, unnoticed retreat of declining years.

I ſee ſome unmarried women, of active, vigorous minds, and great vivacity of ſpirits, degrading themſelves; ſometimes by entering into a diſſipated courſe of life, unſuitable to their years, and expoſing themſelves to the ridicule of girls, who might have been their grand-children; ſometimes by oppreſſing their acquaintances by impertinent intruſions into their private affairs; and ſometimes by being the propagators of ſcandal and defamation. All this is owing to an exuberant activity of ſpirit, which, if it had found employment at home, would have rendered them reſpectable and uſeful members of ſociety.

I ſee other women, in the ſame ſituation, gentle, modeſt, bleſſed with ſenſe, taſte, delicacy, and every milder feminine virtue of the heart, but of weak ſpirits, baſhful, and timid: I ſee ſuch women ſinking into obſcurity and inſignificance, and gradually loſing every elegant accompliſhment; for this evident reaſon, that they are not united to a partner who has ſenſe, and worth, and taſte, to know their value; one who is able to draw forth their concealed qualities, and ſhew them to advantage; who can give that ſupport to their feeble ſpirits which they ſtand ſo much in need of; and who, by his affection and tenderneſs, might make ſuch a woman happy in exerting every talent, and accompliſhing herſelf in every elegant art that could contribute to his amuſement.

In ſhort, I am of opinion, that a married ſtate, if entered into from proper moti es of eſteem and affection, will be the happieſt for yourſelves, make you moſt reſpectable in the eyes of the world, and the moſt uſeful members of ſociety: but I confeſs I am not enough of a Patriot to wiſh you to marry for the good of the public;—I wiſh you to marry for no other reaſon but to make yourſelves happier. When I am ſo particular in my advices about your conduct, I own my heart beats with the fond hope of making you worthy the attachment of men who will deſerve you, and be ſenſible of your merit. But Heaven forbid you ſhould ever relinquiſh the eaſe and independence of a ſingle life, to become the ſlaves of a fool or a tyrant's caprice.

As theſe have always been my ſentiments, I ſhall do you but juſtice, when I leave you in ſuch independent circumſtances as may lay you under no temptation to do from neceſſity what you would never do from choice. This will likewiſe ſave you from that cruel mortification to a woman of ſpirit, the ſuſpicion that a gentleman thinks he does you an honour or a favour when he aſks you for his wife.

If I live till you arrive at that age when you ſhall be capable to judge for yourſelves, and do not ſtrangely alter my ſentiments, I ſhall act towards you in a very different manner from what moſt parents do. My opinion has always been, that when that period arrives, the parental authority ceaſes.

I hope I ſhall always treat you with that affection and eaſy confidence which may diſpoſe you to look on me as your friend; in that capacity alone I ſhall think myſelf intitled to give you my opinion; in the doing of which, I ſhould think myſelf highly criminal, if I did not to the utmoſt of my power endeavour to diveſt myſelf of all perſonal vanity, and all prejudices in favour of my particular taſte. If you did not chuſe to follow my advice, I ſhould not on that account ceaſe to love you as my children: though my right to your obedience was expired, yet I ſhould think nothing could releaſe me from the ties of nature and humanity.

You may perhaps imagine, that the reſerved behaviour which I recommend to you, and your appearing ſeldom at public places, muſt cut off all opportunities of your being acquainted with gentlemen; I am very far from intending this. I adviſe you to no reſerve, but what will render you more reſpected and beloved by our ſex. I do not think public places ſuited to make people acquainted together: they can only be diſtinguiſhed there by their looks and external behaviour; but it is in private companies alone where you can expect eaſy and agreeable converſation, which I ſhould never wiſh you to decline. If you do not allow gentlemen to become acquainted with you, you can never expect to marry with attachment on either ſide—Love is very ſeldom produced at firſt ſight, at leaſt it muſt have, in that caſe, a very unjuſtifiable foundation. True love is founded on eſteem, in a correſpondence of taſtes and ſentiments, and ſteals on the heart imperceptibly.

There is one advice I ſhall leave you, to which I beg your particular attention:—Before your affections come to be in the leaſt engaged to any man, examine your tempers, your taſtes, and your hearts, very ſeverely, and ſettle in your own minds, what are the requiſites to your happineſs in a married ſtate; and, as it is almoſt impoſſible that you ſhould get every thing you wiſh, come to a ſteady determination what you are to conſider as eſſential, and what may be ſacrificed.

If you have hearts diſpoſed by nature for love and friendſhip, and poſſeſs thoſe feelings which enable you to enter into all the refinements and delicacies of theſe attachments, conſider well, for Heaven's ſake, and as you value your future happineſs, before you give them any indulgence. If you have the misfortune (for a very great misfortune it commonly is to your ſex) to have ſuch a temper and ſuch ſentiments deeply rooted in you, if you have ſpirit and reſolution to reſiſt the ſolicitations of vanity, the perſecution of friends (for you will have loſt the only friend that would never perſecute you), and can ſupport the proſpect of the many inconveniences attending the ſtate of an old maid, which I formerly pointed out, then you may indulge yourſelves in that kind of ſentimental reading and converſation which is moſt correſpondent to your feelings.

But if you find on a ſtrict ſelf-examination that marriage is abſolutely eſſential to your happineſs, keep the ſecret inviolable in your own boſoms, for the reaſons I formerly mentioned: but ſhun as you would do the moſt fatal poiſon, all that ſpecies of reading and converſation which warms the imagination, which engages and ſoftens the heart, and raiſes the taſte above the level of common life; if you do otherwiſe, conſider the terrible conflict of paſſions this may afterwards raiſe in your breaſts.

If this refinement once takes deep root in your minds, and you do not obey its dictates, but marry from vulgar and mercenary views, you may never be able to eradicate it entirely, and then it will embitter all your married days. Inſtead of meeting with ſenſe, delicacy, tenderneſs, a lover, a friend, an equal companion, in a huſband, you may be tired with inſipidity and dulneſs; ſhocked with indelicacy, or mortified by indifference. You will find none to compaſſionate, or even underſtand your ſufferings; for your huſbands may not uſe you cruelly, and may give you as much money for your clothes, perſonal expence, and domeſtic neceſſaries, as is ſuitable to their fortunes. The world would therefore look on you as unreaſonable women, and that did not deſerve to be happy, if you were not ſo. To avoid theſe complicated evils, if you are determined at all events to marry, I would adviſe you to make all your reading and amuſements of ſuch a kind, as do not affect the heart nor the imagination, except in the way of wit or humour.

I have no view by theſe advices to lead your taſtes; I only want to perſuade you of the neceſſity of knowing your own minds, which, though ſeemingly very eaſy, is what your ſex ſeldom attain on many important occaſions in life, but particularly on this of which I am ſpeaking. There is not a quality I more anxiouſly wiſh you to poſſeſs, than that collective deciſive ſpirit, which reſts on itſelf, which enables you to ſee where your true happineſs lies, and to purſue it with the moſt determined reſolution. In matters of buſineſs, follow the advice of thoſe who know them better than yourſelves, and in whoſe integrity you can confide; but in matters of taſte that depend on your own feelings, conſult no one friend whatever, but conſult your own hearts.

If a gentleman makes his addreſſes to you, or gives you reaſon to believe he will do ſo, before you allow your affections to be engaged, endeavou, in the moſt prudent and ſecret manner, to procure from your friends every neceſſary piece of information concerning him; ſuch as his character for ſenſe, his morals, his temper, fortune, and family; whether it is diſtinguiſhed for parts and worth, or for folly, knavery, and loathſome hereditary diſeaſes. When your friends inform you of theſe, they have fulfilled their duty. If they go farther, they have not that deference for you which a becoming dignity on your part would effectually command.

Whatever your views are in marrying, take every poſſible precaution to prevent their being diſappointed. If fortune, and the pleaſures it brings, are your aim, it is not ſufficient that the ſettlements of a jointure and children's proviſions be ample, and properly ſecured; it is neceſſary that you ſhould enjoy the fortune during your own life. The principal ſecurity you can have for this will depend on your marrying a good-natured, generous man, who deſpiſes money, and who will let you live where you can beſt enjoy that pleaſure, that pomp and parade of life, for which you married him.

From what I have ſaid, you will eaſily ſee that I could never pretend to adviſe whom you ſhould marry; but I can with great confidence adviſe whom you ſhould not marry.

Avoid a companion that may entail any hereditary diſeaſe on your poſterity, particularly (that moſt dreadful of all human calamities) madneſs. It is the height of imprudence to run into ſuch a danger, and, in my opinion, highly criminal.

Do not marry a fool; he is the moſt intractable of all animals; he is led by his paſſions and caprices, and is incapable of hearing the voice of reaſon. It may probably too, hurt your vanity to have huſbands for whom you have reaſon to bluſh and tremble every time they open their lips in company. But the worſt circumſtance that attends a fool, is his conſtant jealouſly of his wife being thought to govern him. This renders it impoſſible to lead him, and he is continually doing abſurd and diſagreeable things, for no other reaſon but to ſhew he dares do them.

A rake is always a ſuſpicious huſband, becauſe he has only known the moſt worthleſs of your ſex. He likewiſe entails the worſt diſeaſes on his wife and children, if he has the misfortune to have any.

If you have a ſenſe of religion yourſelves, do not think of huſbands who have none. If they have tolerable underſtandings, they will be glad that you have religion, for their own ſakes, and for the ſake of their families; but it will ſink you in their eſteem. If they are weak men, they will be continually teazing and ſhocking you about your principles.—If you have children, you will ſuffer the moſt bitter diſtreſs, in ſeeing all your endeavours to form their minds to virtue and piety, all your endeavours to ſecure their present and eternal happineſs, fruſtrated and turned into ridicule.

As I look on your choice of a huſband to be of the greateſt conſequence to your happineſs, I hope you will make it with the utmoſt circumſpection. Do not give way to a ſudden ſally of paſſion. and dignify it with the name of love.—Genuine love is not founded in caprice; it is founded in nature, on honourable views, on virtue, on ſimilarity of taſtes and ſympathy of ſouls.

If you have theſe ſentiments, you will never marry any one, when you are not in that ſituation, in point of fortune, which is neceſſary to the happineſs of either of you. What that competency may be, can only be determined by your own taſtes. It would be ungenerous in you to take advantage of a lover's attachment, to plunge him into diſtreſs; and if he has any honour, no perſonal gratification will ever tempt him to enter into any connection which will render you unhappy. If you have as much between you as to ſatisfy all your demands, it is ſufficient.

I ſhall conclude with endeavouring to remove a difficulty which muſt naturally occur to any woman of reflection on the ſubject of marriage. What is to become of all thoſe refinements of delicacy, that dignity of manners, which checked all familiarities, and ſuſpended deſire in reſpectful and awful admiration? In anſwer to this, I ſhall only obſerve, that if motives of intereſt or vanity have had any ſhare in your reſolutions to marry, none of theſe chimerical notions will give you any pain; nay, they will very quickly appear as ridiculous in your own eyes, as they probably always did in the eyes of your huſbands. They have been ſentiments which have floated in your imaginations, but have never reached your hearts. But if theſe ſentiments have been truly genuine, and if you have had the ſingular happy fate to attach thoſe who underſtand them, you have no reaſon to be afraid.

Marriage, indeed, will at once diſpel the enchantment raiſed by external beauty; but the virtues and graces that firſt warmed the heart, that reſerve and delicacy which always left the lover ſomething further to wiſh, and often made him doubtful of your ſenſibility or attachment, may and ought ever to remain. The tumult of paſſion will neceſſarily ſubſide; but it will be ſucceeded by an endearment, that effects the heart in a more equal, more ſenſible, and tender manner. But I muſt check myſelf, and not indulge in deſcriptions that may miſlead you, and that too ſenſibly awake the remembrance of my happier days, which, perhaps, it were better for me to forget for ever.

I have thus given you my opinion on ſome of the moſt important articles of your future life, chiefly calculated for that period when you are juſt entering the world. I have endeavoured to avoid ſome peculiarities of opinion, which, from their contradiction to the general practice of the world, I might reaſonably have ſuſpected were not ſo well founded. But, in writing to you, I am afraid my heart has been too full, and too warmly intereſted, to allow me to keep this reſolution. This may have produced ſome embarraſſments and ſome ſeeming contradictions. What I have written has been the amuſement of ſome ſolitary hours, and has ſerved to divert ſome melancholy reflections.—I am conſcious I undertook a taſk to which I was very unequal; but I have diſcharged a part of my duty.—You will at leaſt be pleaſed with it, as the laſt mark of your father's love and attention.

the world.—I have endeavoured to avoid those peculiarities of opinion which, from their contradiction to the general practice of the world, I might reasonably have suspected were not so well founded.—But, in writing to you, I am afraid my heart has been too full, and too warmly interested, to allow me to keep this resolution.—This may have produced some embarrassments, and some seeming contradictions.—What I have written has been the amusement of some solitary hours, and has served to divert some melancholy reflections.—I am conscious I undertook a task to which I was very unequal; but I have discharged a part of my duty.—You will at least be pleased with it, as the last mark of your father's love and attention.

AN UNFORTUNATE MOTHER'S ADVICE TO HER ABSENT DAUGHTERS, IN A LETTER TO MISS PENNINGTON.

BY THE LATE
LADY PENNINGTON.

——DUBLIN;——

PRINTED BY GRAISBERRY AND CAMPBELL,
FOR JOHN ARCHER, NO. 80, DAME-STREET.

1790.

AN

UNFORTUNATE MOTHER'S

A D V I C E

TO HER

A B S E N T D A U G H T E R S.

MY DRAR JENNY,

WAS there any probability that a letter from me would be permitted to reach *your hand alone*, I ſhould not have choſen this leaſt eligible method of writing to you. The public is no way concerned in family affairs, and ought not to be made a party in them; but my circumſtances are ſuch as lay me under the neceſſity of either communicating my ſentiments to the world, or of concealing them *from you:* the latter would, I think, be the breach of an indiſpenſable duty, which obliges me to waive the impropriety of the former.

A long train of events, of a moſt extraordinary nature, conſpired to remove you very early from the tender care of an affectionate mother. You were too young to be able to form any right judgment of her conduct; and ſince that time it is very probable that it has been repreſented to you in a moſt unfavourable light. The general prejudice againſt me I never gave myſelf the uſeleſs trouble of any endeavour to remove. I do not mean to infer from hence that the opinion of others is of no material conſequence; on the contrary, I would adviſe you always to remember, that, next to the conſciouſneſs of acting right, the public voice ſhould be regarded; and to endeavour by a prudent behaviour, even in the moſt trifling inſtances, to ſecure it in your favour. The being educated in a different opinion, was a misfortune to *me*. I was indeed early and wiſely taught, that virtue was the one thing neceſſary, and that without it no happineſs could be expected either in this, or in any future ſtate of exiſtence; but, with this good principle, a miſtaken one was at the ſame time inculcated, namely, That the ſelf-approbation ariſing from conſcious virtue was alone ſufficient; and, That the cenſures of an ill-natured world, ever ready to calumniate, when not founded on truth, were beneath the concern of a perſon whoſe actions were guided by the ſuperior motive of obedience to the will of Heaven.

This notion, ſtrongly imbibed before reaſon had gained ſufficient ſtrength to diſcover its fallacy, was the cauſe of an inconſiderate conduct in my ſubſequent life, which marked my character with a diſadvantageous impreſſion. To you I ſhall ſpeak with the moſt unreſerved ſincerity, not concealing a fault which you may profit by the knowledge of; and therefore I freely own, that in my younger years, ſatisfied with keeping ſtrictly within the bounds of virtue, I took a fooliſh pleaſure in exceeding thoſe of prudence, and was ridiculouſly vain of indulging a latitude of behaviour; into which others of my age were afraid of launching: but then, in juſtice to myſelf, I muſt at the ſame time declare, that this freedom was only taken in public company; and ſo extremely cautious was I of doing any thing which appeared to me a juſt ground for cenſure, that I call Heaven to witneſs, your father was the firſt man whom I ever made any private aſſignation with, or even met in a room alone; nor did I take that liberty with him till the moſt ſolemn mutual engagement, the matrimonial ceremony, had bound us to each other. My behaviour then, he has frequently ſince acknowledged, fully convinced him I was not only innocent of any criminal act, but of every vicious thought; and that the outward freedom of my deportment proceeded merely from a great gaiety of temper, and from a very high flow of ſpirits, never broke (if the expreſſion may be allowed) into the formal rules of decorum. To ſum up the whole in a few words, my private conduct was what the ſevereſt prude could not condemn; my public, ſuch as the moſt finiſhed coquet alone would have ventured upon: the latter only could be known to the world, and conſequently, from thence muſt their opinion be taken. You will therefore eaſily be ſenſible, that it would not be favourable to me; on the contrary it gave a general prejudice againſt me: and this has been ſince made uſe of as an argument to gain credit to the malicious falſhoods laid to my charge. For this reaſon, convinced by long experience that the greater part of mankind are ſo apt to receive, and ſo willing to retain a bad impreſſion of others, that, when it is once eſtabliſhed, there is hardly a poſſibility of removing it through life; I have, for ſome years paſt, ſilently acquieſced in the diſpenſations of Providence, without attempting any juſtification of myſelf; and, being conſcious that the infamous aſperſions caſt on my character were not founded on truth, I have ſat down content with the certainty of an open and perfect acquittal of all vicious diſpoſitions, or criminal conduct, at that great day, when all things ſhall appear as they really are, and when both our actions, and the moſt ſecret motives for them, will be made manifeſt to men and angels.

Had your father been amongſt the number of thoſe who were deceived by appearances, I ſhould have thought it my duty to leave no method uneſſay'd to clear myſelf in his opinion; but that was not the caſe. He knows that many of thoſe appearances which have been urged againſt me, I was forced to ſubmit to, not only from his direction, but by his abſolute command; which, contrary to reaſon and to my own intereſt, I was, for more than twelve years, weak enough implicitly to obey; and that others, even ſince our ſeparation, were occaſioned by ſome particular inſtances of his behaviour, which rendered it impoſſible for me to act with ſafety in any other manner. To *him* I appeal for the truth of this aſſertion, who is conſcious of the meaning that may hereafter be explained to you. Perfectly acquainted with my principles and with my natural diſpoſition, his heart, I am convinced, never here condemned me. Being greatly incenſed that my father's will gave to me an independent fortune; which will he imagined I was acceſſary to, or at leaſt that I could have prevented; he was thereby laid open to the arts of deſigning men, who, having their own intereſt ſolely in view, worked him up into a deſire of revenge, and from thence, upon probable circumſtances, into a public accuſation; though that public accuſation was ſupported only by the ſingle teſtimony of a perſon, whoſe known falſehood had made him a thouſand times declare that he would not credit her oath in the moſt trifling incident: yet, when he was diſappointed of the additional evidence he might have been flattered with the hope of obtaining, it was too late to recede. This I ſincerely believe to be the truth of the caſe, though I too well know his *tenacious* temper to expect a preſent juſtification; but, whenever he ſhall arrive on the verge of eternity, if Reaſon holds her place at that awful moment, and if Religion has then any power on his heart, I make no doubt, he will at that time acquit me to his children; and with truth he muſt then confeſs, that no part of my behaviour to him ever deſerved the treatment I have met with.

Sorry am I to be under the neceſſity of pointing out faults in the conduct of another, which are, perhaps, long ſince repented of, and ought in that caſe to be as much forgotten as they are moſt truly forgiven. Heaven knows, that, ſo far from retaining any degree of reſentment in my heart, the perſon breathes not whom I wiſh to hurt, or to whom I would not this moment render every ſervice in my power. The injuries which I have ſuſtained, had I no children, ſhould contentedly be buried in ſilence till the great day of retribution; but, in juſtice to you, to them, and to myſelf, it is incumbent on me, as far as poſſible, to efface the falſe impreſſions, which, by ſuch ſilence, might be fixed on your mind, and on thoſe of your brothers and ſiſters, whom I include with you. To this end, it will be neceſſary to enter into a circumſtantial hiſtory of near fifteen years, full of incidents of a nature ſo uncommon as to be ſcarcely credible. This, I am convinced, will effectually clear me, in your opinions, of the imputations I now lie under, and it will prove, almoſt to a demonſtration, the true cauſe of thoſe proceedings againſt me that were couched under pretended motives, as injurious to my reputation as they were falſe in themſelves.

But this muſt be deferred ſome time longer. You are all yet too young to enter into things of this kind, or to judge properly of them. When a few years ſhall, by ripening your underſtandings, remove this objection, you ſhall be informed of the whole truth, moſt impartially and without diſguiſe. 'Till then ſuſpend your belief of all that may have reached your ears with regard to me, and wait the knowledge of thoſe facts, which my future letters will reveal for your information.

Thus much I thought it neceſſary to premiſe concerning myſelf, tho' foreign to the deſign of *this epiſtle*, which is only to remind you that you have ſtill an affectionate mother, who is anxious for your welfare, and deſirous of giving you ſome advice with regard to your conduct in life. I would lay down a few precepts for you, which, if attended to, will ſupply, as far as it is in my power to ſupply, the deprivation of a conſtant and tender maternal care. The addreſs is *to you* in particular, your ſiſters being yet too young to receive it, but my intention is for the equal ſervice of you all.

You are juſt entering, my dear girl, into a world full of deceit and falſhood, where few perſons or things appear in their true character. Vice hides her deformity with the borrowed garb of virtue; and, though diſcernible to an intelligent and careful obſerver, by the unbecoming awkwardneſs of her deportment under it, ſhe paſſes on thouſands undetected. Every preſent pleaſure uſurps the name of happineſs, and as ſuch deceives the unwary purſuer. Thus one general maſk diſguiſes the whole face of things, and it reqnires a long experience, and a penetrating judgment, to diſcover the truth. Thrice happy they, whoſe docile tempers improve from the inſtructions of maturer age, and who thereby attain ſome degree of this neceſſary knowledge, while it may be uſeful in directing their conduct!

The turn which your mind may now take, will fix the happineſs or miſery of your future life; and I am too nearly concerned for your welfare, not to be moſt ſolicitouſly anxious that you may be early led into ſo juſt a way of thinking as will be productive to you of a prudent, rational behaviour, and which will ſecure to you a laſting felicity. You were old enough before our ſeparation, to convince me that

Heaven had not denied you a good natural understanding. This, if properly cultivated, will ſet you above that trifling diſpoſition, too common among the female world, which makes youth ridiculous, maturity inſignificant, and old age contemptible. It is therefore needleſs to enlarge on that head, ſince good ſenſe is there the beſt adviſer; and, without it, all admonitions or directions on the ſubject would be as fruitleſs as to lay down rules for the conduct or for the actions of an ideot.

There is no room to doubt but that ſufficient care will be taken to give you a polite education; but a religious one is ſtill of greater conſequence. Neceſſary as the former is for your making a proper figure in the world, and for your being well accepted in it, the latter is yet more ſo to ſecure to you the approbation of the greateſt and beſt of Beings; on whoſe favour depends your everlaſting happineſs. Let therefore your duty to God be ever the firſt and principal object of your care. As your Creator and Governor, he claims adoration and obedience; as your father and friend, he demands ſubmiſſive duty and affection. Remember that from this common Parent of the univerſe you received your life; that to His general providence you owe the continuance of it; and to his bounty you are indebted for all the health, eaſe, advantages, or enjoyments, which help to make that life agreeable. A ſenſe of benefits received naturally inſpires a grateful diſpoſition, with a deſire of making ſuitable returns. All that can here be made, for innumerable favours every moment beſtowed, is a thankful acknowledgement, and a willing obedience. In theſe be never wanting. Make it an invariable rule to begin and end the day with a ſolemn addreſs to the Deity, I mean not by this, what is commonly, with too much propriety, called *ſaying of prayers*, namely, a cuſtomary repetition of a few good words, without either devotion or attention; than which nothing is more inexcuſable and affrontive to the Deity; it is the homage of the heart that can alone be accepted by him. Expreſſions of our abſolute dependence on, and of our entire reſignation to him; thankſgivings for the mercies already received; petitions for thoſe bleſſings it is fit for us to pray for; and interceſſions for all our fellow-creatures, compoſe the principal parts of this duty; which may be comprized in a very few words, or may be more enlarged upon, as the circumſtances of time and diſpoſition may render moſt ſuitable; for it is not the length, but the ſincerity and attention of our prayers that will make them efficacious. A good heart, joined to a tolerable underſtanding, will ſeldom be at a loſs for proper words with which to clothe theſe ſentiments; and all perſons, being beſt acquainted with their own particular circumſtances, may reaſonably be ſuppoſed beſt qualified for adapting their petitions and acknowledgements to them; but for thoſe who are of a different opinion, there are many excellent forms of prayer already compoſed. Among theſe, none that I know of, are equal to Doctor Hoadly's, the late Biſhop of Wincheſter, which I recommend to your peruſal and uſe. In the preface to them, you will find better inſtructions on this head than I am capable of giving, and to theſe I refer you.

It is acknowledged that our petitions cannot in any degree alter the intention of a Being, who is in himſelf invariable, and without a poſſibility of change; all that can be expected from them is, that, by bettering ourſelves, they will render us more proper objects of His favourable regard; and this muſt neceſſarily be the reſult of a ſerious, regular, and conſtant diſcharge of this branch of our duty; for it is ſcarcely poſſible to offer up our ſincere and fervent devotions to Heaven every morning and evening, without leaving on our minds ſuch uſeful impreſſions as will naturally diſpoſe us to a ready and cheerful obedience, and will inſpire a filial fear of offending, the beſt ſecurity virtue can have. As you value your own happineſs, let not the force of bad examples ever lead you into an habitual diſuſe of ſecret prayer; nor let an unpardonable negligence ſo far prevail on you, as to make you reſt ſatisfied with a formal, cuſtomary, inattentive repetition of ſome well-choſen words: let your heart and attention always go with your lips, and experience will ſoon convince you, that this permiſſion of addreſſing the Supreme Being is the moſt valuable prerogative of human nature; the chief, nay the only ſupport under all the diſtreſſes and calamities to which this ſtate of ſin and miſery is liable; the higheſt rational ſatisfaction the mind is capable of on this ſide the grave; and the beſt preparative for everlaſting happineſs beyond it. This is a duty ever in your own power, and therefore you only will be culpable by the omiſſion of it.

Public worſhip may not allways be ſo, but whenever it is, do not wilfully neglect the ſervice of the church, at leaſt on Sundays; and let your behaviour there be adapted to the ſolemnity of the place, and to the intention of the meeting. Regard neither the actions nor the dreſs of others: let not your eyes rove in ſearch of acquaintance, but in the time of divine ſervice avoid, as much as poſſible, all complimental civilities, of which there art too great an intercourſe, in moſt of our churches. Remember that your only buſineſs there is to pay a ſolemn act of devotion to Almighty God, and let every part of your conduct be ſuitable to this great end. If you hear a good ſermon, treaſure it in your memory, that you may reap all the benefit it was capable of imparting; if you ſhould hear but an indifferent one, ſome good things muſt be in it; retain thoſe, and let the remainder be buried in oblivion. Ridicule not the preacher, who no doubt has done his beſt, and who is rather the object of pity than of contempt, for having been placed in a ſituation of life, to which his talents were not equal; he may perhaps be a good man, though he is not a great orator.

I would alſo recommend to you the early and frequent participation of the Communion, or what is commonly called Receiving the Sacrament, as the indiſpenſible duty of every chriſtian. There is no inſtitution of our religion more ſimple, plain, and intelligible than this, as delivered to us by our Saviour; and moſt of the elaborate treatiſes written on the ſubject have ſerved only to puzzle and to diſturb weak minds, by throwing the dark veil of ſuperſtition and of human invention over a plain poſitive command, given by him in ſo explicit a manner as to be eaſily comprehended by the meaneſt capacity, and which is doubtleſs in the power of all his ſincere followers to pay an acceptable obedience to. Nothing has more contributed to the neglect of this duty, than the numerous well-meaning books that have been written to enjoin a month's or a week's preparation, as previouſly neceſſary to the due performance of it; by theſe means filling the minds of many with needleſs terror, putting it even out of the power of ſome to receive it at all, and inducing great numbers to reſt ſatisfied with doing it only once or twice a year, on ſome high feſtival; whereas it was certainly the conſtant cuſtom of the apoſtles and primitive chriſtians on every Sunday; and it ought to be received by us as often as it is adminiſtered in the church we frequent, which in moſt places is but once in a month. Nor do I think it excuſable, at any time, to turn our backs upon the table we ſee prepared for that purpoſe, on pretence of not being fit to partake worthily of it. The beſt, the only true preparation for this, and for every other part of religious duty, is a good and virtuous life, by which the mind is conſtantly kept in ſuch a devotional frame, as to require but a little recollection to be ſuited to any particular act of worſhip or of obedience that may occaſionally offer: and without a good and virtuous life, there cannot be a greater or more fatal miſtake than to ſuppoſe that a few days or weeks ſpent in humiliation and prayer will render us at all the more acceptable to the Deity, or that we ſhould be thereby better fitted for any one inſtance of that duty which we muſt univerſally pay, to be either approved by him, or to be advantageous to ourſelves: I would not therefore adviſe you to read any of thoſe weekly preparatives, which are too apt to lead the mind into error, by teaching it to reſt in a mere ſhadow of piety, wherein there is nothing rationally ſatiſfactory. The beſt books which I have ever met with on this ſubject, are Biſhop HOADLY's *Plain Account of the Nature and End of the Sacrament of the Lord's Supper*, and NELSON's *Great Duty of*

it

frequenting the Christian Sacrifice. To the former are annexed the prayers which I before mentioned: these are well worth your attentive perusal; the design of the institution is therein fully explained, agreeable both to scripture and to reason; stript of that veil of mystery which has been industriously thrown over it by designing or by mistaking men; and it is there laid as plainly open to every capacity as it was at first left us by our great Master. Read *these books* with due attention: you will there find every necessary instruction concerning the right, and every reasonable inducement to the constant and to the conscientious performance of it.

The sincere practice of religious duties naturally leads to the proper discharge of the social, which may be all comprehended in that one great general rule of *doing unto others as you would they should do unto you;* but of these more particularly hereafter.— I shall first give you my advice concerning EMPLOYMENT, it being of great moment to set out in life in such a method as may be useful to yourself and beneficial to others.

Time is invaluable, its loss is irretrievable! The remembrance of having made an ill use of it must be one of the sharpest tortures to those who are on the brink of eternity! and what can yield a more unpleasing retrospect than whole years idled away in an irrational insignificant manner, examples of which are continually before our eyes! Look on every day as a blank ſheet of paper put into your hands to be filled up; remember the characters will remain to endleſs ages, and that they never can be expunged; be careful therefore not to write any thing but what you may read with pleaſure a thouſand years after. I would not be underſtood in a ſenſe ſo ſtrict as might debar you from any innocent amuſement, ſuitable to your age, and agreeable to your inclination. Diverſions, properly regulated, are not only allowable, they are abſolutely neceſſary to youth, and are never criminal but when taken to exceſs; that is, when they engroſs the whole thought, when they are made the chief buſineſs of life: they then give a diſtaſte to every valuable employment, and, by a ſort of infatuation, leave the mind in a ſtate of reſtleſs impatience from the concluſion of one 'till the commencement of another. This is the unfortunate diſpoſition of many; guard moſt carefully againſt it, for nothing can be attended with more pernicious conſequences. A little obſervation will convince you, that there is not, amongſt the human ſpecies, a ſet of more miſerable beings than thoſe who cannot live out of a conſtant ſucceſſion of diverſions. Theſe people have no comprehenſion of the more ſatisfacry pleaſure to be found in retirement: thought is inſupportable, and conſequently ſolitude muſt be intolerable to them; they are a burthen to themſelves, and a peſt to their acquaintance, by vainly ſeeking for happineſs in company, where they are ſeldom acceptable: I ſay vainly, for true happineſs exiſts only in the mind, nothing foreign can give it. The utmoſt to be attained by what is called a gay life, is a ſhort forgetfulneſs of miſery, to be felt with accumulated anguiſh in every interval of reflection. This reſtleſs temper is frequently the product of a too eager purſuit of pleaſure in the early part of life, to the neglect of thoſe valuable improvements which would lay the foundation of a more ſolid and permanent felicity. Youth is the ſeaſon for diverſions, but it is alſo the ſeaſon for acquiring knowledge, for fixing uſeful habits, and for laying in a ſtock of ſuch well-choſen materials, as may grow into a ſerene happineſs, which will encreaſe with every added year of life, and will bloom in the fulleſt perfection in the decline of it. The great art of education conſiſts in aſſigning to each its proper place, in ſuch a manner that the one ſhall never become irkſome by intrenching on the other.—Our ſeparation having taken from me the pleaſing taſk of endeavouring, to the beſt of my ability, to ſuit them occaſionally, as might be moſt conducive both to your profit and pleaſure, it only remains for me to give you general rules, which indeed accidents may make it neceſſary ſometimes to vary; thoſe however muſt be left to your own diſcretion, and I am convinced you have a ſufficient ſhare of underſtanding to be very capable of making advantageouſly ſuch caſual regulations to yourſelf, if the inclination is not wanting.

It is an excellent method to appropriate the morning wholly to improvement; the afternoon may then be allowed to diverſions. Under this laſt head, I place company, books of the amuſing kind, and entertaining productions of the needle, as well as plays, balls, cards, &c. which more commonly go by the name of diverſions: the afternoon, and evening till ſupper, may by theſe be employed with innocence and propriety; but let not one of them ever be ſuffered to intrude on the former part of the day, which ſhould be always devoted to more uſeful employments. One half hour, or more, either before or immediately after breakfaſt, I would have you conſtantly give to the attentive peruſal of ſome rationally pious author, or to ſome part of the New Teſtament, with which, and indeed with the whole Scripture, you ought to make yourſelf perfectly acquainted, as the baſis on which your religion is founded. From this practice you will reap more real benefit than can be ſuppoſed by thoſe who have never made the experiment. The other hours may be divided amongſt thoſe neceſſary and polite acquiſitions which are ſuitable to your ſex, age, and to your rank in life.—Study *your own language* thoroughly, that you may ſpeak correctly, and write grammatically: do not content yourſelf with the common uſe of words, which cuſtom has taught you from the cradle, but learn from whence they are derived, and what are their proper ſignifications.—*French* you ought to be as well acquainted with as with *Engliſh*, and *Italian* might, without much difficulty, be added.—Acquire a good knowledge of hiſtory; that of your own country firſt, then of the other European nations: read them not with a view to amuſe, but to improve your mind; and to that end make reflections on what you have read, which may be uſeful to yourſelf, and will render your converſation agreeable to others.—Learn ſo much of *Geography* as to form a juſt idea of the ſituation of places, mentioned in any author; and this will make hiſtory more entertaining to you.

It is neceſſary for you to be perfect in *the firſt four rules of Arithmetic:* more you can never have occaſion for, and the mind ſhould not be burthened with needleſs application.—*Muſic* and *Drawing* are accompliſhments well worth the trouble of attaining, if your inclination and genius lead to either: if not, do not attempt them; for it will be only much time and great labour unprofitably thrown away; it being next to impoſſible to arrive at any degree of perfection in thoſe arts, by the dint of perſeverance only, if a good ear and a native genius be wanting.—The ſtudy of *Natural Philoſophy*, you will find both pleaſing and inſtructive; pleaſing, from the continual new diſcoveries to be made of the innumerably various beauties of nature, a moſt agreeable gratification of that deſire of knowledge wiſely implanted in the human mind; and highly inſtructive, as thoſe diſcoveries lead to the contemplation of the great Author of Nature, whoſe wiſdom and goodneſs ſo conſpicuouſly ſhine through all His works, that it is impoſſible to reflect ſeriouſly on them, without admiration and gratitude.

Theſe, my dear, are but a few of thoſe mental improvements I would recommend to you. Indeed there is no branch of knowledge that your capacity is equal to, and which you have an opportunity of acquiring, that, I think, ought to be neglected. It has been objected againſt all female learning, beyond that of houſehold œconomy, that it tends only to fill the minds of the ſex with a conceited vanity, which ſets them above their proper buſineſs; occaſions an indifference to, if not a total neglect of, their family affairs; and ſerves only to render them uſeleſs wives, and impertinent companions. It muſt be confeſſed, that ſome reading ladies have given but too much cauſe for this objection; and could it be proved to hold good throughout the ſex, it would certainly be right to confine their improvements within the narrow limits of the nurſery, of the kitchen, and the confectionary: but, I believe, it will, upon examination, be found, that ſuch ill conſequences proceed chiefly from too great an imbecility of mind to be capable of much enlargement, or from a mere affectation of knowledge, void of all reality. Vanity is never the reſult of underſtanding. A ſenſible woman will ſoon be convinced, that all the learning her utmoſt application can make her miſtreſs of, will be from the difference of education, in many points, inferior to that of a ſchool boy: this reflection will keep her always humble, and will be an effectual check to that loquacity which renders ſome women ſuch inſupportable companions.

The management of all domeſtic affairs is certainly the proper buſineſs of woman; and, unfaſhionably ruſtic as ſuch an aſſertion may be thought, it is not beneath the dignity of any lady, however high her rank, to know *how* to educate her children, to govern her ſervants; how to order an elegant table with œconomy, and to manage her whole family with prudence, regularity and method. If in theſe ſhe is defective, whatever may be her attainments in any other kinds of knowledge, ſhe will act out of character; and, by not moving in her proper ſphere, ſhe will become rather the object of ridicule than of approbation. But I believe it may with truth be affirmed, that the neglect of theſe domeſtic concerns has much more frequently proceeded from an exorbitant love of diverſions, from a ridiculous fondneſs for dreſs and gallantry, or from a miſtaken pride, that has placed ſuch duties in a ſervile light, from whence they have been conſidered as ſit only for the employment of dependents, and below the attention of a fine lady, than from too great an attachment to mental improvements; yet, from whatſoever cauſe ſuch a neglect proceeds, it is equally unjuſtifiable. If any thing can be urged in vindication of a cuſtom unknown to our anceſtors, which the prevalence of faſhion has made ſo general amongſt the modern ladies; I mean, that of committing to the care and diſcretionary power of different ſervants, the ſole management of family affairs; nothing certainly can be alledged in defence of ſuch an ignorance, in things of this nature, as renders a lady incapable of giving proper directions on all occaſions; an ignorance, which, in ever ſo exalted a ſtation, will render her contemptible, even to thoſe ſervants on whoſe underſtanding and fidelity ſhe, in fact, becomes dependent for the regularity of her houſe, for the propriety, elegance, and frugality of her table; which laſt article is ſeldom regarded by ſuch ſort of people, who too frequently impoſe on thoſe by whom they are thus implicitly truſted. Make yourſelf, therefore, ſo thoroughly acquainted with the moſt proper method of conducting a family, and with the neceſſary expence which every article, in proportion to their number, will occaſion, that you may come to a reaſonable certainty of not being materially deceived, without the ridiculous drudgery of following your ſervants continually, and meanly peeping into every obſcure corner of your houſe: nor is this at all difficult to attain, as it requires nothing more than an attentive obſervation.

It is of late, in moſt great families, become too much the cuſtom to be long upon the books of every tradeſman they employ. To aſſign a reaſon for this is foreign to my purpoſe; but I am certain it would, in general, be better both for themſelves, and for the people they deal with, never to be on them at all; and what difficulty or inconvenience can ariſe, in a well regulated family, from commiſſioning the ſteward or houſe-keeper to pay for every thing at the time when it is brought in? This obſolete practice, though in itſelf very laudable, is not at preſent, and perhaps never may be again, authoriſed by faſhion; however, let it be a rule with you to contract as few debts as poſſible: moſt things are to be purchaſed both better in their kind, and at a lower price, by paying for them at the time of purchaſing. But if, to avoid the ſuppoſed trouble of frequent trifling diſburſements, you chuſe to have the leſſer articles thrown together in a bill, let a note of the quantity and price be brought with every ſuch parcel: file theſe notes, compare them with the bill when delivered in, and let ſuch bills be regularly paid every quarter: for it is not reaſonable to expect that a tradeſman ſhould give longer credit, without making up the intereſt of his money by an advanced price on what he ſells: and be aſſured, if you find it inconvenient to pay at the end of three months, that inconvenience muſt ariſe from living at too great an expence, and will conſequently increaſe in ſix months, and grow ſtill greater at the end of the year. By making ſhort payments, you will become the ſooner ſenſible of ſuch a miſtake, and you will find it at firſt more eaſy to retrench any ſupernumeries than after having been long habituated to them.

If your houſe is ſuperintended by an houſe-keeper, and your ſervants are accountable to her, let your houſekeeper be accountable to yourſelf, and let her be entirely governed by your directions. Carefully examine her bills, and ſuffer no extravagancies or unneceſſary articles to paſs unnoticed. Let theſe bills be brought to you every morning; what they contain will then be eaſily recollected without burthening your memory; and your accounts being ſhort will be adjuſted with leſs trouble and with more exactneſs. Should you at any time have an upper ſervant, whoſe family and education were ſuperior to that ſtate of ſubjection to which ſucceeding misfortunes may have reduced her, ſhe ought to be treated with peculiar indulgence: if ſhe has underſtanding enough to be converſible, and humility enough always to keep her proper diſtance, leſſen, as much as poſſible, every painful remembrance of former proſpects, by looking on her as an humble friend, and making her an occaſional companion. But never deſcend to converſe with thoſe whoſe birth, education and early views in life were not ſuperior to a ſtate of ſervitude: their minds being in general ſuited to their ſtation, they are apt to be intoxicated by any degree of familiarity, and to become uſeleſs and impertinent. The habit which very many ladies have contracted of talking to and conſulting with their women, has ſo ſpoiled that ſet of ſervants, that few of them are to be met with, who do not commence their ſervice by giving their unaſked opinion of your perſon, dreſs, or management, artfully conveyed in the too generally accepted vehicle of flattery; and, if they are allowed in this, they will next proceed to offer their advice on any occaſion that may happen to diſcompoſe or ruffle your temper: check therefore the firſt appearance of ſuch impertinence, by a reprimand ſufficiently ſevere to prevent a repetition of it.

Give your orders in a plain diſtinct manner, with good-nature joined to a ſteadineſs that will ſhew they muſt be punctually obeyed. Treat all your domeſtics with ſuch mildneſs and affability, that you may be ſerved rather out of affection than fear. Let them live happily under you. Give them leiſure for their own buſineſs, time for innocent recreation, and more eſpecially for attending the public ſervice of the church, to be inſtructed in their duty to God; without which you have no right to expect the diſcharge of that owing to yourſelf. When wrong, tell them calmly of their faults; if they amend not after two or three ſuch rebukes, diſmiſs them; but never deſcend to paſſion and ſcolding, which is inconſiſtent with a good underſtanding, and beneath the dignity of a gentlewoman.

Be very exact in your hours, without which there can be no order in your family, I mean thoſe of riſing, eating, &c. Require from your ſervants punctuality in theſe, and never be yourſelf the cauſe of breaking through the rules you have laid down, by deferring breakfaſt, putting back the dinner, or letting it grow cold on the table, to wait your dreſſing; a cuſtom by which many ladies introduce confuſion, and bring their orders into neglect. Be always dreſſed at leaſt half an hour before dinner. Having mentioned this important article, I muſt be allowed a little digreſſion on the ſubject.

Whatever time is taken up in dreſs beyond what is neceſſary to decency and cleanlineſs, may be looked upon, to ſay no worſe, as a vacuum in life. By decency, I mean ſuch a habit as is ſuitable to your rank and fortune: an ill-placed finery, inconſiſtent with either, is not ornamental but ridiculous. A compliance with faſhion, ſo far as to avoid the affectation of ſingularity, is neceſſary; but to run into the extreme of faſhions, more eſpecially thoſe which are inconvenient, is the certain proof of a weak mind. Have a better opinion of yourſelf than to ſuppoſe you can receive any additional merit from the adventitious ornaments of dreſs. Leave the ſtudy of the toilet to thoſe who are adapted to it; I mean that inſignificant ſet of females, whoſe whole life, from the cradle to the coffin, is but a varied ſcene of trifling, and whoſe intellectuals fit them not for any thing beyond it. Such as theſe may be allowed to paſs whole mornings at their looking-glaſs, in the important buſineſs of ſuiting a ſet of ribbands, adjuſting a few curls, or determining the poſition of a patch; one, perhaps, of their moſt innocent ways of idling. But let as ſmall a portion of your time as poſſible be taken up in dreſſing. Be always perfectly clean and neat, both in your perſon and clothes; equally ſo when alone, as in company. Look upon all beyond this as immaterial in itſelf, any further than as the different ranks of mankind have made ſome diſtinction in habit generally eſteemed neceſſary; and remember, that it is never the dreſs, however ſumptuous, which reflects dignity and honour on the perſon: it is the rank and merit of the perſon that gives conſequence to the dreſs. But to return:—

It is your own ſteadineſs and example of regularity that alone can preſerve uninterrupted order in your family. If, by forgetfulneſs or inattention, you at any time ſuffer your commands to be diſobeyed with impunity, your ſervants will grow upon ſuch neglect into a habit of careleſſneſs, till repeated faults, of which this is properly the ſource, rouſe you into anger, which an even hand would never have made neceſſary. Be not whimſical or capricious in your likings: approve with judgment, and condemn with reaſon; that acting right may be as certainly the means of obtaining your favour, as the contrary of incurring your diſpleaſure.

From what has been ſaid you will ſee, that in order to the proper diſcharge of your domeſtic duties, it is abſolutely neceſſary for you to have a perfect knowledge of every branch of houſehold œconomy, without which you can neither correct what is wrong, approve what is right, nor give directions with propriety. It is the want of this knowledge that reduces many a fine lady's family to a ſtate of the utmoſt confuſion and diſorder, on the ſudden removal of a managing ſervant, till the place is ſupplied by a ſucceſſor of equal ability. How much out of character, how ridiculous muſt a miſtreſs of a family appear, who is entirely incapable of giving practical orders on ſuch an occaſion. Let that never be *your* caſe! Remember, my dear, this is the only proper temporal buſineſs aſſigned you by Providence, and in a thing ſo indiſpenſably needful, ſo eaſily attained, where ſo little ſtudy or application is neceſſary to arrive at the moſt commendable degree of it, the want even of perfection is almoſt inexcuſable. Make yourſelf miſtreſs of the theory, that you may be able the more readily to reduce it into practice; and when you have a family to command, let the care of it always employ your principal attention, and let every part of it be ſubjected to your own inſpection. If you riſe early, a cuſtom I hope you have not left off ſince you was with me, if you waſte no unneceſſary time in dreſſing, and if you conduct your houſe in a regular method, you will find many vacant hours unfilled by this material buſineſs; and no objection can be made to your employing thoſe in ſuch improvements of the mind, as are moſt ſuitable to your genius and inclination. I believe no man of underſtanding will think that, under ſuch regulations, a woman will either make a leſs agreeable companion, a leſs uſeful wife, a leſs careful mother, or a worſe miſtreſs of a family, for all the additional knowledge her induſtry and application can acquire.

The morning being always thus advantageouſly engaged, the latter part of the day, as I before ſaid, may be given to relaxation and amuſement. Some of theſe hours may be very agreeably and uſefully employed by entertaining books; a few of which, in the Engliſh language I will mention to you, as a ſpecimen of the kind I would recommend to your peruſal; and I ſhall include ſome others, religious and inſtructive.

Maſon on Self Knowledge
Œconomy of Human Life
Seneca's Morals
Epictetus Morals
Cicero's Offices
Collier's Antoninus
Hoadly's
Seed's
Sherlock's } Sermons
Sterne's
Fordyce's
Rollin's Belles Lettres
Nature Diſplay'd
The Spectator
The Guardian
The Female Spectator
The Rambler
The Idler
The Adventurer
The World
Cicero's Familiar Letters
Pliny's Letters

Fitzoſborne's Letters
Telemachus
The Vicar of Wakefield
Guthrie's Geographical Grammar
Potter's Antiquities of Greece
Rollin's Ancient Hiſtory
Kennett's Antiquities of Rome
Hooke's Roman Hiſtory
Hume's Hiſtory of England
Robertſon's Works
Milton's Poetical Works
Pope's Works
——— Homer
Thomſon's Works
Young's Works
Mrs. Rowe's Works
Langhorne's Works
Moore's Fables for the Female Sex
Tales of the Genii
Dodſley's Collection of Poems

☞ To the above Liſt the Editor of this volume begs leave to add the following books, moſt of which have appeared ſince Lady P.'s Letter was firſt printed:

Blair's
Franklin's
White's } Sermons
Walker's
Weſt on the Reſurrection
Lord Lyttleton on the Converſion of St. Paul
Miſs Talbot's Reflections and Eſſays
Dr. Watts on the Improvement of the Mind

Mrs. Chapone's Letters and Miſcellanies
The Mirror, 2 vols.
The Lounger, 3 vols
The Obſerver, 4 vols.
Hayley's Triumphs of Temper
Raſſelas, Prince of Abyſſinia
Female Reader
Speaker, 2 vols.
Mrs. Trimmer's Works

Works of Madame De Genlis
Marchioness de Lambert's Works, 2 vols.
Miss Burney's Evelina, 2 vols. and Cecilia, 3 vols.
Mrs. Smith's Emmeline, 2 vols.
General Biographical Dictionary, 12 vols. 8vo.
Shakespeare's Plays
Johnson's Poets, 75 vols. with their Lives
Miss More' Poems, and Prose Pieces
Ethelinde, 3 vols.
Miss Bodler's Essay, &c.
Elegant Extracts, in Prose and Verse, 2 vols.

From these you may form a judgment of that sort of reading which will be both useful and entertaining to you. I have named only those *Practical Sermons*, which, I thought, would more directly influence your conduct in life—*Our rule of faith* should be taken from the scripture alone, which we must understand for ourselves; therefore the controverted opinions of others serve in general rather to puzzle than to improve the mind.

Of *Novels and Romances*, very few are worth the trouble of reading: some of them perhaps do contain a few goods morals, but they are not worth the finding where so much rubbish is intermixed. Their moral parts indeed are like small diamonds amongst mountains of dirt and trash, which, after you have found them, are too inconsiderable to answer the pains of coming at; yet, ridiculous as these fictitious tales generally are, they are so artfully managed as to excite an idle curiosity to see the conclusion, by which means the reader is drawn on, through a tiresome length of foolish adventures, from which neither knowledge, pleaſure, or profit, ſeldom can accrue, to the common cataſtrophe of a wedding. The moſt I have met with of theſe writings, to ſay no worſe, it is little better than the loſs of time to peruſe. But ſome of them have more pernicious conſequences. By drawing characters that never exiſt in life, by repreſenting perſons and things in a falſe and extravagant light, and by a ſeries of improbable cauſes bringing on impoſſible events, they are apt to give a romantic turn to the mind, which is often productive of great errors in judgment, and of fatal miſtakes in conduct. Of this I have ſeen frequent inſtances, and therefore adviſe you ſcarce ever to meddle with any of them.

In juſtice however to a late ingenious author, this Letter muſt not be reprinted, without my acknowledging that, ſince the laſt edition was publiſhed, I have accidentally met with one exception to my general rule, namely, *The Vicar of Wakefield*. That novel is equally entertaining and inſtructive, without being liable to any of the objections that occaſioned the above reſtriction. This poſſibly may not be the only unexceptionable piece of the kind, but as I have not met with any other, amongſt a number I have peruſed, a ſingle inſtance does not alter my opinion of that ſort of writing; and I ſtill think, the chance is perhaps a thouſand to one againſt the probability of obtaining the ſmalleſt degree of advantage from the reading any of them, as well as that very few are to be found from which much injury may not be received.

WORKS OF THE NEEDLE that employ the fancy, may, if they ſuit your inclination, be ſometimes a pretty amuſement; but let this employment never extend to large pieces, beyond what can be accompliſhed by yourſelf without aſſiſtance. There is not a greater extravagance, under the ſpecious name of good houſewifery, than the furniſhing of houſes in this manner. Whole apartments have been ſeen thus ornamented by the ſuppoſed work of a lady, who, perhaps, never ſhaded two leaves in the artificial foreſt, but has paid four times its value to the ſeveral people employed in bringing it to perfection. The expence of theſe tedious pieces of work I ſpeak of experimentally, having, many years paſt, undertaken one them, which, when finiſhed, was not worth fifteen pounds; and by a computation ſince made, it did not coſt leſs than fifty, in the hire and maintenance of the people employed in it. This indeed was at the age of ſeventeen, when the thoughtleſs inexperience of youth could alone excuſe ſuch a piece of folly.—*Embroideries in gold, ſilver, or ſhades of ſilk*, come within a narrower compaſs. Works of that kind which may, without calling in expenſive aſſiſtance, or tiring the fancy, be finiſhed in a ſummer, will be a well-choſen change of amuſement, and may, as there are three of you, be made much more agreeable, by one alternately reading aloud, while the other two are thus employed.—All kinds of what is called *plain-work*, though no very polite accomplishment, you must be so well versed in, as to be able to cut out, make, or mend your own linen. Some fathers, and some husbands, chuse to have their daughters and their wives thus attired in the labour of their own hands, and, from a mistaken notion, believe this to be the great criterion of frugal œconomy. Where that happens to be the inclination or opinion of either, it ought always to be readily complied with: but, exclusive of such a motive, I see no other that makes the practical part necessary to any lady; excepting, indeed, where there is such a narrowness of fortune as admits not conveniently the keeping a servant, to whom such exercises of the needle much more properly appertain.

The Theatre, which, by the indefatigable labour of the inimitable Mr. Garrick, has been brought to very great perfection, will afford you an equally rational and improving entertainment. Your judgment will not now be called in question, your understanding affronted, nor will your modesty be offended by the indecent ribaldry of those authors, who, to their defect in wit, have added the want of good sense and of good manners. Faults of this kind, which, from a blameful compliance with a corrupted taste, have ſometimes crept into the works of good writers, are by his prudent direction generally rectified or omitted on the ſtage. You may now ſee many of the beſt plays performed in the beſt manner. Do not, however, go to any that you have not before heard the character of; be preſent only at thoſe which are approved by perſons of underſtanding and virtue, as calculated to anſwer the proper ends of the theatre, namely, that of conveying inſtruction in the moſt pleaſing method. Attend to the ſentiment, apply the moral, and then you cannot, I think, paſs an evening in a more uſeful, or in a more entertaining diverſion.

DANCING may alſo take its turn as a healthful exerciſe, as it is generally ſuitable to the taſte and gaiety of young minds.

PART of the hours appropriated to relaxation muſt of neceſſity be leſs agreeably taken up in the paying and receiving viſits of mere ceremony and civility; a tribute, by cuſtom authorized, by good manners enjoined. In *theſe*, when the converſation is only inſignificant, join in it with an apparent ſatisfaction. Talk of the elegance of a birth-day ſuit, the pattern of a lace, the judicious aſſortment of jewels, the cut of a ruffle, or the ſet of a ſleeve, with an unaffected eaſe; not according to the rank they hold in your eſtimation, but proportioned to the conſequence they may be of in the opinion of thoſe you are converſing with. The great art of pleaſing is to appear pleaſed with others; ſuffer not then an ill-bred abſence of thought, or a contemptuous ſneer, ever to betray a conſcious ſuperiority of underſtanding, always productive of ill-nature and diſlike. Suit yourſelf to the capacity and to the taſte of your company, when that taſte is confined to harmleſs trifles; but where it is ſo far depraved as to delight in cruel ſarcaſms on the abſent, to be pleaſed with diſcovering the blemiſhes in a good character, or in repeating the greater faults of a bad one, religion and humanity in that caſe forbid the leaſt degree of aſſent. If you have not any knowledge of the perſons thus unhappily ſacrificed to envy or to malice, and conſequently are ignorant as to the truth or falſhood of ſuch aſperſions, always ſuſpect them to be ill grounded, or, at leaſt, greatly exaggerated. Shew your diſapprobation by a ſilent gravity, and by taking the firſt opportunity to change the ſubject. But where any acquaintance with the character in queſtion gives room for defending it, let not an ill-timed complaiſance prevail over juſtice: vindicate injured innocence with all the freedom and warmth of an unreſtrained benevolence; and where the faults of the guilty will admit of palliation, urge all that truth can allow in mitigation of error. From this method, beſides the pleaſure ariſing from the conſciouſneſs of a ſtrict conformity to the great rule of *doing as you would be done* ly, you will alſo reap to yourſelf the benefit of being leſs frequently peſtered with themes ever painful to a humane diſpoſition. If, unfortunately, you have ſome acquaintance whoſe malevolence of heart no ſentiment of virtue, no check of good-manners, can reſtrain from theſe malicious ſallies of ill-nature, to them let your viſits be made as ſeldom, and as ſhort, as decency will permit; there being neither benefit nor ſatisfaction to be found in ſuch company, amongſt whom only cards may be introduced with any advantage. On this account, it will be proper for you to know how to play at the games moſt in uſe, becauſe it is an argument of great folly to engage in any thing without doing it well; but this is a diverſion which I hope you will have no fondneſs for, as it is in itſelf, to ſay no worſe, a very inſignificant amuſement.

With perſons for whom you can have no eſteem, good-breeding may oblige you to keep up an intercourſe of ceremonious viſits, but politeneſs enjoins not the length or frequency of them. Here inclination may be followed without a breach of civility: there is no tax upon intimacy but from choice; and that choice ſhould ever be founded on merit, the certainty whereof you cannot be too careful in previouſly examining. Great caution is neceſſary not to be deceived by ſpecious appearances. A plauſible behaviour often, upon a ſuperficial knowledge, creates a prepoſſeſſion in favour of particulars, who, upon a nearer view, may be found to have no claim to eſteem. The forming a precipitate judgment ſometimes leads into an unwary intimacy, which it may prove abſolutely neceſſary to break off; and yet that breach may be attended with innumerable inconveniences; nay, perhaps, with very material and laſting ill conſequences: prudence, therefore, here enjoins the greateſt circumſpection.

Few people are capable of friendſhip, and ſtill fewer have all the qualifications one would chuſe in a friend. The fundamental point is a virtuous diſpoſition; but to that ſhould be added a good underſtanding, a ſolid judgment, ſweetneſs of temper, ſteadineſs of mind, freedom of behaviour, and ſincerity of heart. Seldom as theſe are to be found united, never make a boſom friend of any one greatly deficient in either. Be ſlow in contracting friendſhip, and invariably conſtant in maintaining it. Expect not many friends, but think yourſelf happy, if, through life, you meet with one or two who deſerve that name, and have all the requiſites for the valuable relation. This may juſtly be deemed the higheſt bleſſing of mortality. Uninterrupted health has the general voice; but, in my opinion, ſuch an intercourſe of friendſhip as much deſerves the preference, as the mental pleaſures, both in nature and degree, exceed the corporeal. The weakneſſes, the pains of the body may be inexpreſſibly alleviated by the converſation of a perſon, by affection endeared, by reaſon approved; whoſe tender ſympathy partakes your afflictions, and ſhares your enjoyments; who is ſteady in the correction, but mild in the reproof of your faults; like a guardian angel, ever watchful to warn you of unforeſeen danger, and, by timely admonitions, to prevent the miſtakes incident to human frailty and to ſelf-partiality: this is the true office of friendſhip. With ſuch a friend, no ſtate of life can be abſolutely unhappy; but, deſtitute of ſome ſuch connection, Heaven has ſo formed our natures for this intimate ſociety, that amidſt the affluence of fortune, and in the flow of uninterrupted health, there will be an aching void in the ſolitary breaſt, which can never otherwiſe know a plenitude of happineſs.

Should the Supreme Diſpoſer of all events beſtow on you this ſuperlative gift, to ſuch a friend let your heart be ever unreſervedly open. Conceal no ſecret thought, diſguiſe no latent weakneſs, but bare your boſom to the faithful probe of honeſt friendſhip, and ſhrink not if it ſmarts beneath the touch; nor with tenacious pride diſlike the perſon who freely dares to condemn ſome favourite foible; but, ever open to conviction, hear with attention, and receive with gratitude, the kind reproof that flows from tenderneſs. When ſenſible of a fault, be ingenuous in the confeſſion—be ſincere and ſteady in the correction of it.

Happy is her lot, who in a husband finds this invaluable friend! Yet so great is the hazard, so disproportioned the chances, that I could almost wish the dangerous die was never to be thrown for any of you: but as probably it may, let me conjure ye all, my dear girls, if ever any of you take this most important step in life, to proceed with the utmost care and with deliberate circumspection. Fortune and Family it is the sole province of your father to direct in: he certainly has always an undoubted right to a negative voice, though not to a compulsive one. As a child is very justifiable in the refusal of her hand, even to the absolute command of a father, where her heart cannot go with it, so is she extremely culpable in giving it contrary to his approbation. Here I must take shame to myself; and for this unpardonable fault, I do justly acknowledge that the subsequent ill consequences of a most unhappy marriage were the proper punishment. This, and every other error in my own conduct, I do, and shall, with the utmost candour, lay open to you; sincerely praying that you may reap the benefit of my experience, and that you may avoid those rocks, which, either by carelessness, or sometimes, alas, by too much caution, I have split against! But to return:—

The chief point to be regarded in the choice of *a companion for life*, is a really virtuous principle, an unaffected goodness of heart. Without this, you will be continually ſhocked by indecency, and pained by impiety. So numerous have been the unhappy victims to the ridiculous opinion, "*A reformed libertine makes the beſt huſband,*" that, did not experience daily evince the contrary, one would believe it impoſſible for a girl who has a tolerable degree of common underſtanding to be made the dupe of ſo erroneous a poſition, which has not the leaſt ſhadow of reaſon for its foundation, and which a ſmall ſhare of obſervation will prove to be falſe in fact. A man who has been long converſant with the worſt ſort of women, is very apt to contract a bad opinion of, and a contempt for, the ſex in general. Incapable of eſteeming any, he is ſuſpicious of all, jealous without cauſe, angry without provocation, and his own diſturbed imagination is a continual ſource of ill humour. To this is frequently joined a bad habit of body, the natural conſequence of an irregular life, which gives an additional ſourneſs to the temper. What rational proſpect of happineſs can there be with ſuch a companion? And that this is the general character of thoſe who are called reformed rakes, obſervation will certify—But, admit there may be ſome exceptions, it is a hazard upon which no conſiderate woman would venture the peace of her whole future life. The vanity of thoſe girls who believe themſelves capable of working miracles of this kind, and who give up their perſons to men of libertine principles, upon the wild expectation of reclaiming them, justly deserves the disappointment which it will generally meet with; for, believe me, a wife is, of all persons, the least likely to succeed in such an attempt. Be it your care to find that virtue in a lover which you must never hope to form in a husband. Good-sense and good-nature are almost equally requisite. If the former is wanting, it will be next to impossible for you to esteem the person of whose behaviour you may have cause to be ashamed; and mutual esteem is as necessary to happiness in the married state as mutual affection: without the latter, every day will bring with it some fresh cause of vexation; 'till repeated quarrels produce a coldness, which will settle into an irreconcileable aversion, and you will become not only each other's torment, but the object of contempt to your family and to your acquaintance.

This quality of Good-Nature is, of all others, the most difficult to be ascertained, on account of the general mistake of blending it with Good-Humour, as if they were in themselves the same; whereas, in fact, no two principles of action are more essentially different. And this may require some explanation. —By Good-Nature I mean, that true benevolence which partakes the felicity of all mankind; which promotes the satisfaction of every individual within the reach of its ability; which relieves the distressed, comforts the afflicted, diffuses blessings, and communicates happineſs, as far as its ſphere of action can extend; and which, in the private ſcenes of life, will ſhine conſpicuous in the dutiful ſon, the affectionate huſband, the indulgent father, the faithful friend, and the compaſſionate maſter both to man and beaſt: whilſt Good-Humour is nothing more than a cheerful, pleaſing deportment, ariſing either from a natural gaiety of mind, or from an affectation of popularity, joined to an affability of behaviour, the reſult of good-breeding, and a ready compliance with the taſte of every company. This kind of mere good-humour is, by far, the moſt ſtriking quality; 'tis frequently miſtaken for, and complimented with, the ſuperior name of real good-nature. A man by this ſpecious appearance has often acquired that appellation, who, in all the actions of his private life, has been a moroſe, cruel, revengeful, ſullen, haughty tyrant. Let them put on the cap whoſe temples fit the galling wreath! On the contrary, a man of a truly benevolent diſpoſition, and formed to promote the happineſs of all round him, may ſometimes, perhaps from an ill habit of body an accidental vexation, or from a commendable openneſs of heart above the meanneſs of diſguiſe, be guilty of little ſallies of peeviſhneſs, or of ill-humour, which, carrying the appearance of ill-nature, may be unjuſtly thought to proceed from it, by perſons who are unacquainted with his true character, and who take ill-humour and ill-nature to be ſynonimous terms, though in reality they bear not the leaſt analogy to each other. In order to the forming a right judgment, it is abſolutely neceſſary to obſerve this diſtinction, which will effectually ſecure you from the dangerous error of taking the ſhadow for the ſubſtance; an irretrievable miſtake, pregnant with innumerable conſequent evils!

From what has been ſaid it plainly appears, that the criterion of this amiable virtue is not to be taken from the general opinion; mere good-humour being, to all intents and purpoſes, ſufficient in this particular to eſtabliſh the public voice in favour of a man utterly devoid of every humane and benevolent affection of heart. It is only from the leſs conſpicuous ſcenes of life, the more retired ſphere of action, from the artleſs tenor of domeſtic conduct, that the real character can with any certainty be drawn. Theſe undiſguiſed proclaim the man; but, as they ſhun the glare of light, nor court the noiſe of popular applauſe, they paſs unnoticed, and are ſeldom known 'till after an intimate acquaintance. The beſt method, therefore, to avoid the deception in this caſe, is to lay no ſtreſs on outward appearances, which are too often fallacious, but to take the rule of judging from the ſimple, unpoliſhed ſentiments of thoſe, whoſe dependent connections give them an undeniable certainty; who not only ſee, but hourly feel the good or bad effects of that diſpoſition to which they are ſubjected.

By this I mean, that if a man is equally refpected, efteemed, and beloved by his tenants, by his dependents and domeftics; from the fubftantial farmer to the laborious peafant; from the proud fteward to the fubmiffive wretch, who, thankful for employment, humbly obeys the menial tribe; you may juftly conclude he has that true good-nature, that real benevolence, which delights in communicating felicity, and enjoys the fatisfaction it diffufes. But if by thefe he is defpifed and hated, ferved merely from a principle of fear, devoid of affection—which is very eafily difcoverable—whatever may be his public character, however favourable the general opinion, be affured, that his difpofition is fuch as can never be productive of domeftic happinefs.—I have been the more particular on this head, as it is one of the moft effential qualifications to be regarded, and of all others the moft liable to be miftaken.

Never be prevailed with, my dear, to give your hand to a perfon defective in thefe material points. Secure of virtue, of good-nature, and underftanding in a hufband, you may be fecure of happinefs. Without the two former, it is unattainable: without the latter, in a tolerable degree, it muft be very imperfect.

Remember, however, that infallibility is not the property of man, or you may entail difappointment on yourfelf, by expecting what is never to be found.

The beſt men are ſometimes inconſiſtent with themſelves. They are liable to be hurried by ſudden ſtarts of paſſion into expreſſions and actions which their cooler reaſon will condemn. They may have ſome oddities of behaviour, ſome peculiarities of temper; they may be ſubject to accidental ill-humour, or to whimſical complaints: blemiſhes of this kind often ſhade the brighteſt character, but they are never deſtructive of mutual felicity, unleſs when they are made ſo by an improper reſentment, or by an ill-judged oppoſition. Reaſon can never be heard by paſſion; the offer of it tends only to enflame the more. When cooled, and in his uſual temper, the man of underſtanding, if he has been wrong, will ſuggeſt to himſelf all that could be urged againſt him: the man of good-nature will, unupbraided, own his error: immediate contradiction is, therefore, wholly unſerviceable, and highly imprudent; an after repetition equally unneceſſary and injudicious. Any peculiarities in the temper or behaviour ought to be properly repreſented in the tendereſt and in the moſt friendly manner, and if the repreſentation of them is made diſcreetly, it will generally be well taken: but if they are ſo habitual as not eaſily to be altered, ſtrike not too often upon the unharmonious ſtring; rather let them paſs as unobſerved: ſuch a chearful compliance will better cement your union; and they may be made eaſy to yourſelf, by reflecting on the ſuperior good qualities by which theſe trifling faults are ſo greatly over-balanced.—You muſt remember, my dear, theſe rules are laid down, on the ſuppoſition of your being united to a perſon who poſſeſſes the three eſſential qualifications for happineſs before-mentioned. In this caſe, no farther direction is neceſſary, but that you ſtrictly perform the duty of a wife, namely, to love, to honour, and obey. The two firſt articles are a tribute ſo indiſpenſibly due to merit, that they muſt be paid by inclination; and they naturally lead to the performance of the laſt, which will not only be an eaſy, but a pleaſing taſk, ſince nothing can ever be enjoined by ſuch a perſon that is in itſelf improper, and few things will, that can with any reaſon be diſagreeable to you.

Here ſhould this ſubject end, were it not more than poſſible for you, after all that has been urged, to be led by ſome inferior motive to the neglect of the primary caution; and that, either from an opinion too haſtily entertained, from an unaccountable partiality, or from the powerful prevalence of perſuaſion, you may be unfortunately induced to give your hand to a man whoſe bad heart and moroſe temper, concealed by a well practiſed diſſimulation, may render every flattering hope of happineſs abortive.—May Heaven, in mercy, guard you from this fatal error! Such a companion is the worſt of all temporal ills; a deadly potion, that imbitters every ſocial ſcene of life, damps every rising joy, and banishes that chearful temper which alone can give a true relish to the blessings of mortality. Most sincerely do I pray that this may never be your lot! and I hope your prudent circumspection will be sufficient to guard you from the danger. But the bare possibility of the event makes it not unnecessary to lay down a few rules for the maintaining some degree of ease, under such a deprivation of happiness. This is by far the most difficult part of my present undertaking; it is hard to advise here, and still harder to practise the advice: the subject also is too extensive to be minutely treated within the compass of *a letter*, which must confine me to the most material points only; in these I shall give you the best directions in my power, very ardently wishing that you may never have occasion to make use of them.

The being united to a man of irreligious principles makes it impossible to discharge a great part of the proper duty of a wife. To name but one instance, obedience will be rendered impracticable by frequent injunctions inconsistent with and contrary to the higher obligations of morality. This is not supposition, but is founded upon facts, which I have too often seen and can attest. Where this happens, the reasons for non-compliance ought to be offered in a plain, strong, good-natured manner; there is at least the chance of success from being heard; but should those reasons be rejected, or the hearing of them be refused, and silence on the ſubject enjoined—which is moſt probable, few people caring to hear what they know to be right, when determined not to appear convinced by it—obey the injunction, and urge not the argument farther: keep, however, ſteady to your principles, and ſuffer neither perſuaſion not threats to prevail on you to act contrary to them. All commands repugnant to the laws of chriſtianity, it is your indiſpenſible duty to diſobey; all requeſts that are inconſiſtent with prudence, or incompatible with the rank and character which you ought to maintain in life, it is your intereſt to refuſe. A compliance with the former would be criminal; a conſent to the latter highly indiſcreet; and it might thereby ſubject you to general cenſure: for a man capable of requiring from his wife what he knows to be in itſelf wrong, is equally capable of throwing the whole blame of ſuch miſconduct on her; and of afterwards upbraiding her for a behaviour to which he will, upon the ſame principle, diſown that he has been acceſſary. Many ſimilar inſtances have come within the compaſs of my own obſervation. In things of a leſs material nature, that are neither criminal in themſelves nor pernicious in their conſequences, always acquieſce, if inſiſted on, however diſagreeable they may be to your own temper and inclination. Such a compliance will evidently prove that your refuſal, in the other caſes, proceeds not from a ſpirit of contradiction, but merely from a juſt regard to that ſuperior duty, which can never be infringed with impunity. Paſſion may reſent, but reaſon muſt approve this conduct; and therefore it is the moſt likely method, in time, to make a favourable impreſſion. But, if you ſhould fail of ſuch ſucceſs, you will at leaſt enjoy that ſatisfactory ſelf-approbation, which is the inſeparable attendant of a truly religious and rational deportment.

Should the painful taſk of dealing with a moroſe tyrannical temper be aſſigned you, there is little more to be recommended than a patient ſubmiſſion to an evil which admits not of a remedy. Ill-nature is increaſed, obſtinacy confirmed, by oppoſition: the leſs ſuch a temper is contradicted, the more ſupportable will it be to thoſe who are under its baneful influence. When all endeavours to pleaſe are ineffectual, and when a man ſeems determined to find fault with every thing, as if his chief pleaſure conſiſted in tormenting thoſe about him, it requires a more than common degree of patience and reſolution to forbear uttering reproaches, which ſuch a behaviour may be juſtly allowed to deſerve: yet it is abſolutely neceſſary to the maintaining any tolerable degree of eaſe, not only to reſtrain all expreſſions of reſentment, but to withhold even thoſe diſdainful looks which are apt to accompany a contemptuous ſilence; and they both equally tend only to encreaſe the malady. This infernal delight in giving pain is moſt unwearied in the ſearch of matter for its gratification, and can either find, or unaccountably can form it, in almoſt all the occurrences of life; but, when ſuffered unobſtructed and unreguarded to run its malicious courſe, it will quickly vent its blunted arrows, and will die of diſappointment; whilſt all endeavours to appeaſe, all complaints of unkindneſs will but ſharpen againſt yourſelf the weapon's edge, and, by proving your ſenſibility of the wound, will give the wiſhed-for ſatisfaction to him who inflicts it. Prudence, in this caſe, directs more than ordinary circumſpection, that every part of your behaviour may be as blameleſs as poſſible, even to the abſtaining from the leaſt appearance of evil; and after you have, to the utmoſt of your power, ſtrove to merit approbation, expect not to meet with it: by theſe means you will eſcape the mortification of being diſappointed, which, often repeated, is apt to give a gloomy ſourneſs to the temper, incompatible with any degree of contentment. You muſt, ſo ſituated, learn to be ſatisfied with the conſciouſneſs of acting right, according to your beſt abilities, and, if poſſible, you ſhould look with an unconcerned indifference on the reception of every ſucceſsful attempt to pleaſe.

This, it muſt be owned, is a hard leſſen of philoſophy; it requires no leſs than an abſolute command over the paſſions; but let it be remembered, that ſuch a command will itſelf moſt amply recompenſe every difficulty; it will compenſate every pain, which it may coſt you to obtain it: beſides, it is, I believe, the only way to preſerve any tranquillity of mind, under ſo diſagreeable a connection.

As the want of underſtanding is by no art to be concealed, by no addreſs to be diſguiſed, it might be ſuppoſed impoſſible for a woman of ſenſe to unite herſelf to a perſon whoſe defect, in this inſtance, muſt render that ſort of rational ſociety which conſtitutes the chief happineſs of ſuch an union, impoſſible; yet, here, how often has the weakneſs of female judgment been conſpicuous! The advantages of great ſuperiority in rank of fortune have frequently proved ſo irreſiſtible a temptation, as, in opinion, to outweigh not only the folly but even the vices of its poſſeſſor: a grand miſtake, ever tacitly acknowledged by a ſubſequent repentance, when the expected pleaſures of affluence, equipage, and all the glittering pomp of uſeleſs pageantry have been experimentally found inſufficient to make amends for the want of that conſtant ſatisfaction, which reſults from the ſocial joy of converſing with a reaſonable friend! But however weak this motive muſt be acknowledged, it is more excuſable than another, which, I fear, has ſometimes had an equal influence on the mind; I mean, ſo great a love of ſway, as to induce her to give the preference to a perſon of weak intellectuals, in hopes thereby of holding, uncontrouled, the reins of government. The expectation is, in fact, ill-grounded obstinacy; and pride being generally the companion of folly, the silliest people are usually the most tenacious of their opinions, and consequently, the hardest of all others to be managed: but admit the contrary, the principle is in itself bad; it tends to invert the order of nature, and to counteract the design of Providence.

A woman can never be seen in a more ridiculous light than when she appears to govern her husband. If, unfortunately, the superiority of understanding is on her side, the apparent consciousness of that superiority betrays a weakness that renders her contemptible in the sight of every considerate person, and it may, very probably, fix in his mind a dislike never to be eradicated. In such a case, if it should ever be your own, remember that some degree of dissimulation is commendable, so far as to let your husband's defect appear unobserved. When he judges wrong, never flatly contradict, but lead him insensibly into another opinion, in so discreet a manner that it may seem entirely his own; and let the whole credit of every prudent determination rest on him without indulging the foolish vanity of claiming any merit to yourself. Thus a person of but an indifferent capacity may be so assisted as, in many instances, to shine with a borrowed lustre, scarce distinguishable from the native, and, by degrees, he may be brought into a kind of mechanical method of acting properly, in all the common occurrences of life. Odd as this position may seem, it is founded in fact; and I have seen the method successfully practised by more than one person, where a weak mind, on the governed side, has been so prudently set off as to appear the sole director; like the statue of the Delphic god, which was thought to give forth its own oracles, whilst the humble priest, who lent his voice, was by the shrine concealed, nor sought a higher glory than a supposed obedience to the power he would be thought to serve.

From hence it may be inferred, that by a perfect propriety of behaviour, ease, and contentment, at least, are attainable with a companion who has not the most exalted understanding; but then, virtue and good-nature are presupposed, or there will be nothing to work upon.

A vicious ill-natured fool being so untractable and tormenting an associate, there needs only to add jealousy to the composition, to make the curse compleat. This passion, once suffered to get footing in the heart, is hardly ever to be extirpated: it is a constant source of torment to the breast that gives it reception, and is an inexhaustible fund of vexation to the object of it. With a person of this unfortunate disposition, it is prudent to avoid the least appearance of concealment. A whisper in a mixed company, a message given in a low voice to a ſervant, have, by the power of a diſturbed imagination, being magnified into a material injury. Whatever has the air of ſecrecy raiſes terror in a mind naturally diſtruſtful. A perfect unreſerved openneſs, both in converſation and behaviour, ſtarves the anxious expectation of diſcovery, and may very probably lead into an habitual confidence, the only antidote againſt the poiſon of ſuſpicion. It is eaſier to prevent than remove a received ill impreſſion; and, conſequently, it is much wiſer to be ſometimes deficient in little points of civility, which, however indifferent in themſelves, may happen unaccountably to claſh with the eaſe of a perſon, whoſe repoſe it is both your duty and intereſt to promote. It is much more commendable, contentedly to incur the cenſure of a trifling diſpoſition, by a circumſtantial unaſked relation of inſignificant incidents, than to give any room for apprehending the leaſt degree of reſerve. Such a conſtant method of proceeding, together with a reaſonable compliance, is the moſt likely to cure this painful turn of mind; for, by with-holding every ſupport that could give ſtrength to it, the want of matter to feed on may probably in time cauſe its extinction. If, unhappily, it is ſo conſtitutional, ſo interwoven with the ſoul as to become, in a manner, inſeparably united with it, nothing remains but to ſubmit patiently to the Will of Heaven, under the preſſure of an unalterable evil; to guard carefully againſt the natural conſequence of repeated undeſerved ſuſpicions, namely, a growing indifference, which too frequently terminates in averſion; and, by conſidering ſuch a ſituation as a trial of obedience and reſignation, to receive the comfort that muſt ariſe from properly exerciſing one of the moſt exalted of the chriſtian virtues. I cannot diſmiſs this ſubject without adding a particular caution *to yourſelf* concerning it.

Jealouſy, is, on ſeveral accounts, ſtill more inexcuſable in a woman. There is not any thing that ſo much expoſes her to ridicule, or ſo much ſubjects her to the inſult of affrontive addreſſes: it is an inlet to almoſt every poſſible evil, the fatal ſource of innumerable indiſcretions, the ſure deſtruction of her own peace, and is frequently the bane of her huſband's affection. Give not a momentary harbour to its ſhadow in your heart; fly from it, as from the face of a fiend, that would lead your unwary ſteps into a gulph of unalterable miſery. When once embarked in the matrimonial voyage, the fewer faults you diſcover in your partner, the better. Never ſearch after what it will give you no pleaſure to find; never deſire to hear what you will not like to be told; therefore avoid that tribe of impertinents, who, either from a malicious love of diſcord, or from the meaner, tho' leſs criminal motive of ingratiating themſelves by gratifying the blameable curioſity of others, ſow diſſention wherever they gain admittance; and by telling unwelcome truths, or, more frequently, by inſinuating invented falſhoods, injure innocent people, diſturb domeſtic union, and deſtroy the peace of families. Treat theſe emiſſaries of Satan with the contempt they deſerve; hear not what they offer to communicate, but give them at once to underſtand, that you can never look on thoſe as your friends who ſpeak in a diſadvantageous manner of that perſon whom you would always chuſe to ſee in the moſt favourable light. If they are not effectually ſilenced by ſuch rebukes, be inacceſſible to their viſits, and break off all acquaintance with ſuch incorrigible peſts of ſociety, who will be ever upon the watch to ſeize an unguarded opportunity of diſturbing your repoſe.

Should the companion of your life be guilty of ſome ſecret indiſcretions, run not the hazard of being told by theſe malicious meddlers, what, in fact, it is better for you never to know; but if ſome unavoidable accident betrays an imprudent correſpondence, take it for a mark of eſteem, that he endeavours to conceal from you what he knows you muſt, upon a principle of reaſon and religion, diſapprove; and do not, by diſcovering your acquaintance with it, take off the reſtraint which your ſuppoſed ignorance lays him under, and thereby, perhaps, give a latitude to undiſguiſed irregularities. Be aſſured, whatever accidental ſallies the gaiety of inconſiderate youth may lead him into, you can never be indifferent to him, whilſt he is careful to preſerve your peace, by concealing what he imagines might be an infringement of it. Reſt then ſatisſied, that time and reaſon will moſt certainly get the better of all faults which proceed not from a bad heart; and that, by maintaining the firſt place in his eſteem, your happineſs will be built on too firm a foundation to be eaſily ſhaken.

I have been thus particular on the choice of a huſband, and on the material parts of conduct in a married life, becauſe thereon depends not only the temporal, but often the eternal felicity of thoſe who enter into that ſtate; a conſtant ſcene of diſagreement, of ill-nature and quarrels, neceſſarily unfitting the mind for every religious and ſocial duty, by keeping it in a diſpoſition directly oppoſite to that chriſtian piety, to that practical benevolence and rational compoſure, which alone can prepare it for everlaſting happineſs.

Inſtructions on this head, conſidering your tender age, may ſeem premature, and ſhould have been deferred 'till occaſion called for them, had our ſituation allowed me frequent opportunities of communicating my ſentiments to you; but that not being the caſe, I chuſe, in this epiſtle, at once to offer you my beſt advice in every circumſtance of great moment to your well being, both here and hereafter, leſt at a more proper ſeaſon it may not happen to be in my power. You may defer the particular conſideration of this part, 'till the deſign of entering into a new ſcene of life may make it uſeful to you; which, I hope, will not be for ſome years; an unhappy marriage being more generally the conſequence of a too early engagement, before reaſon has gained ſufficient ſtrength to form a ſolid judgment, on which only a proper choice can be determined. Great is the hazard of a miſtake, and irretrievable the effects of it! Many are the degrees between happineſs and miſery! Abſolute miſery, I will venture to affirm, is to be avoided by a proper behaviour, even under all the complicated ills of human life; but to arrive at that proper behaviour, requires the higheſt degree of chriſtian philoſophy. And who would voluntarily put themſelves upon a ſtate of trial ſo ſevere, in which not one of a thouſand has been found able to come off victorious? Betwixt this and poſitive happineſs there are innumerable ſteps of comparative evil; each has its ſeparate conflict, variouſly difficult, differently painful, under all which a patient ſubmiſſion and a conſcious propriety of behaviour is the only attainable good. Far ſhort indeed of poſſible temporal felicity is the eaſe ariſing from hence! Reſt not content with the proſpect of ſuch eaſe, but fix on a more eligible point of view, by aiming at true happineſs; and, take my word, *that* can never be found in a married ſtate, without the three eſſential qualifications already mentioned, Virtue, Good-Nature, and Good-Senſe, in a huſband.

Remember, therefore, my dear girl, this repeated caution, if you ever resolve on marriage, never to give your hand to a man who wants either of them, whatever other advantages he may be possessed of; so shall you not only escape all those vexations which thousands of unthinking mortals hourly repent of having brought upon themselves; but, most assuredly, if it is not your own fault, you will enjoy that uninterrupted domestic harmony, in the affectionate society of a virtuous companion, which constitutes the highest satisfaction of human life. Such an union, founded on reason and religion, cemented by mutual esteem and tenderness, is a kind of faint emblem, if the comparison may be allowed, of the promised reward of virtue in a future state; and most certainly, it is an excellent preparative for it, by preserving a perfect equanimity, by keeping a constant composure of mind, which naturally lead to the proper discharge of all the religious and social duties of life, the unerring road to everlasting peace—The first have been already spoken to; it remains only to mention some few of the latter.

Amongst these Œconomy may, perhaps, be thought improperly placed; yet many of the duties we owe to society being often rendered impracticable by the want of it, there is not so much impropriety in ranking it under this head, as may at first be imagined. For instance, a man who lives at an expence beyond what his income will ſupport, lays himſelf under a neceſſity of being unjuſt, by with-holding from his creditors what they have a right to demand from him as their due, according to all laws both human and divine; and thereby he often entails ruin on an innocent family, who, but for the loſs ſuſtained by his extravagance, might have comfortably ſubſiſted on the profits of their induſtry. He likewiſe puts it out of his own power to give that relief to the indigent, which, by the laws of humanity, they have a right to expect; the goods of fortune being given, as a great Divine excellently obſerves, for the uſe and ſupport of others, as well as for the perſon on whom they are beſtowed. Theſe are ſurely great breaches of that duty we owe to our fellow-creatures, and are effects very frequently and naturally produced by the want of œconomy.

You will find it a very good method, ſo to regulate your ſtated expences as to bring them always one-fourth part within your certain annual income: by theſe means you will avoid being at any time diſtreſſed by unforeſeen accidents, and you will have it more eaſily in your power materially to relieve thoſe who deſerve aſſiſtance. But the giving trifling ſums, *indiſcriminately*, to ſuch as appear neceſſitous, is far from being commendable; it is an injury to ſociety; it is an encouragement to idleneſs, and helps to fill the ſtreets with lazy beggars, who live upon miſapplied bounty, to the prejudice of the induſtrious poor. Theſe are uſeful members of the commonwealth; and on them ſuch benefactions might be ſerviceably beſtowed. Be ſparing therefore in this kind of indiſcriminate donations; they are too conſtantly an inſignificant relief to the receivers, ſuppoſing them really in want; and frequently repeated, they amount to a conſiderable ſum in the year's account. The proper objects of charity are thoſe, who, by unavoidable misfortunes, have fallen from affluent circumſtances into a ſtate of poverty and diſtreſs; thoſe alſo, who, by unexpected diſappointments in trade, are on the point of being reduced to an impoſſibility of carrying on that buſineſs, on which their preſent ſubſiſtence and their future proſpect in life depend, from the incapacity of raiſing an immediate ſum to ſurmount the difficulty; and thoſe who, by their utmoſt induſtry, can hardly ſupport their families above the miſeries of want; or who, by age or by illneſs, are rendered incapable of labour. Appropriate a certain part of your income to the relief of theſe real diſtreſſes. To the firſt, give as largely as your circumſtances will allow; to the ſecond, after the example of an excellent Prelate of our own church, lend, if it is in your power, a ſufficient ſum to prevent the threatened ruin, on condition of being repaid the loan, without intereſt, if Providence enables them, by future ſucceſs, to do it with convenience. The ſame method may be uſed where indigence renders induſtry unavailable, by depriving it of the means to lay in a ſmall original ſtock to be improved. Never take a note of hand or any acknowledgement of ſuch loan, leſt what you intended for a benefit ſhould be afterwards made the inſtrument of ruin to the receiver, by a different diſpoſition in your ſucceſſor. But ſuch aſſiſtance ought not to be given to any, without a thorough knowledge of their character, and from having good reaſon to believe them not only induſtrious but ſtrictly honeſt, which will be a ſufficient obligation on them for the repayment; and the ſums ſo repaid ought to be laid by, 'till an opportunity again offers of making them in like manner ſerviceable to others. The latter ſort, who are able to work, may, by a ſmall addition to the profits of their own labour, be reſcued from miſery, and may be put into a comfortable way of ſubſiſtence. Thoſe who, by age or by infirmity, are rendered utterly incapable of ſupporting themſelves, have an undoubted right, not only to the neceſſaries, but even to ſome of the conveniencies of life from all whom Providence has placed in the more happy ſtate of affluence and independence.

As your fortune and ſituation are yet undetermined, I have purpoſely laid down ſuch rules as may be adapted to every ſtation. A large fortune gives greater opportunity of doing good, and of communicating happineſs in a more extenſive degree; but a ſmall one is no excuſe for with-holding a proportionate relief from real and deſerving objects of compaſſion. To aſſiſt them is an indiſpenſible duty of chriſtianity. The firſt and great commandment is, To love God with all your heart; the ſecond, To love your neighbour as yourſelf: *Whoſo ſeeth his brother in need, and ſhutteth up his bowels of compaſſion, how dwelleth the love of God in him?* or how the love of his neighbour? If deficient in theſe primary duties, vain are the hopes of acceptance built on a partial obedience to the leſſer branches of the law!—Inability is often pleaded as an excuſe for the want of charity, by perſons who make no ſcruple of daily laviſhing on their pleaſures, what, if better applied, might have made an indigent family happy through life. Theſe perſons loſe ſight of real felicity, by the miſtaken purſuit of its ſhadow: the pleaſures which engroſs their attention die in the enjoyment, are often ſucceeded by remorſe, and always by ſatiety; whereas the true joy, the ſweet complacency reſulting from benevolent actions, encreaſes by reflection, and muſt be immortal as the ſoul. So exactly, ſo kindly is our duty made to coincide with our preſent as well as future intereſt, that incomparably more ſatisfaction will accrue to a conſiderate mind from denying itſelf even ſome of the agreeables of life, in order the more effectually to relieve the unfortunate, than could ariſe from a full indulgence of every temporal gratification.

However ſmall your income may be, remember that a part of it is due to merit in diſtreſs. Set by an annual ſum for this purpoſe, even though it ſhould oblige you to abate ſome unneceſſary expence to raiſe the fund: By this method perſons of ſlender fortune have been enabled to do much good, and to give happineſs to many. If your ſtock will not admit of frequent draughts upon it, be the more circumſpect with regard to the merit of thoſe you relieve, that bounties not in your power to repeat often, may not be miſapplied. But if Providence, by a more ample fortune, ſhould bleſs you with a larger ability of being ſerviceable to your fellow-creatures, prove yourſelf worthy of the truſt repoſed in you by making a proper uſe of it. Wide as your influence can extend, turn the cry of diſtreſs and danger into the ſong of joy and ſafety; feed the hungry, clothe the naked, comfort the afflicted, give medicine to the ſick, and, with either, beſtow all the alleviation their unfortunate circumſtances can admit of. Thus may you truly make a friend of the unrighteous Mammon. Thus you may turn the periſhable goods of fortune into everlaſting bleſſings. Upon earth you will partake that happineſs you impart to others, and you will lay up for yourſelf *Treaſures in Heaven, where neither moth nor ruſt can corrupt, and where thieves do not break through nor ſteal.*

A perſon who has once experienced the advantages of a right action, will be led by the motive of preſent ſelf-intereſt, as well as by future expectation, to the continuance of it. There is no injunction of chriſtianity that a ſincere chriſtian, by obedience, will not find ſo calculated as to be directly, in ſome meaſure, its own reward.

The forgiveneſs of injuries, to which is annexed the promiſe of pardon for our own offences, and which is required by the goſpel, not only ſo far as to forbear all kinds of retaliation, but alſo to render us equally diſpoſed to ſerve with our utmoſt power thoſe perſons who have wilfully injured us, as if no ſuch injury had been received from them, has by ſome been accounted a hard precept; yet the difficulty of it ariſes merely from, and is proportionable to, the badneſs of the heart by which it is ſo eſteemed. A good diſpoſition finds a ſuperlative pleaſure in returning good for evil; and, by an inexpreſſible ſatisfaction of mind in ſo doing, feels the preſent reward of obedience: whereas a ſpirit of revenge is incompatible with happineſs, an implacable temper being a conſtant torment to its poſſeſſor; and the man who returns an injury, feels more real miſery from the rancour of his own heart, than it is in his power to inflict upon another.

Should a friend wound you in the moſt tender part, by betraying a confidence repoſed, prudence forbids the expoſing yourſelf to a ſecond deception, by placing any future truſt in ſuch a perſon. But though here all obligations of intimacy ceaſe, thoſe of benevolence and humanity remain ſtill in full force, and are equally binding, alſo every act of ſervice and aſſiſtance, even to the ſuffering a leſſer evil yourſelf, in order to ſecure a much greater good to the perſon by whom you have been thus ill-uſed. This is in general allowed to be the duty of every individual to all, as a member of ſociety; but it is particularly inſtanced in the preſent caſe to ſhew, that not even a breach of friendſhip, the higheſt of all provocations, will cancel the duty, at all times equally and unalterably binding—the duty of promoting both the temporal and eternal happineſs of all your fellow-creatures by every method in your power.

It has been by many thought impertinent at any time to offer unaſked advice; the reaſon of which may be chiefly owing to its being too frequently tendered with a ſupercilious air that implies a conceited conſciouſneſs of ſuperior wiſdom: it is the manner, therefore, more than the thing itſelf which gives diſguſt.

If thoſe with whom you have any degree of intimacy are guilty of what to you appears either wrong or indiſcreet, ſpeak your opinion to them with freedom, though you ſhould even loſe a nominal friend by ſo doing. Silence makes you, in ſome meaſure, an acceſſary to the fault; but having thus once diſcharged your duty, reſt there—they are to judge for themſelves: to repeat ſuch admonitions is both uſeleſs and impertinent, and they will then be thought to proceed rather from pride than from good nature. To the perſons concerned only are you to ſpeak your diſapprobation of their conduct: when they are cenſured by others, ſay all that truth or probability will permit in their juſtification.

It often happens, that upon an accidental quarrel between friends, they ſeparately appeal to a third perſon. In ſuch caſe, alternately take the oppoſite ſide, alledging every argument in favour of the abſent party, and placing the miſtakes of the complainer in the ſtrongeſt light. This method may probably at firſt diſpleaſe, but is always right, as it is the moſt likely to procure a reconciliation. If that takes place, each, equally obliged, will thankfully approve your conduct: if not, you will have the ſatisfaction of, at leaſt, endeavouring to have been the reſtorer of peace. A contrary behaviour, which generally proceeds from the mean deſire of pleaſing by flattery at the expence of truth, often widens a trifling breach into open and irreconcileable enmity. People of this diſpoſition are the worſt ſort of incendiaries, the greateſt plague of human ſociety, becauſe the moſt difficult to be guarded againſt, from their always wearing the ſpecious diſguiſe of pretended approbation and friendſhip to the preſent, and equally deceitful reſentment againſt the abſent perſon or company.

To enumerate all the ſocial duties would lead me too far; ſuffice it, therefore, my dear, in few words to ſum up what remains.

Let truth ever dwell upon your tongue.

Scorn to flatter any, and deſpiſe the perſon who would practiſe ſo baſe an art upon yourſelf.

Be honeſtly open in every part of your behaviour and converſation.

All, with whom you have any intercourſe, even down to the meaneſt ſtation, have a right to civility and good-humour from you. A ſuperiority of rank or fortune is no licence for a proud ſupercilious behaviour: the diſadvantages of a dependent ſtate are alone ſufficient to labour under; 'tis both unjuſt and cruel to encreaſe them, either by a haughty deportment, or by the unwarrantable exerciſe of a capricious temper.

Examine every part of your conduct towards others by the unerring rule of ſuppoſing a change of places. This will certainly lead to an impartial judgment. Do then what appears to you right, or in other words, *what you would they ſhould do unto you;* which comprehends every duty relative to ſociety.

Aim at perfection, or you will never reach to an attainable height of virtue.

Be religious without hypocrisy, pious without enthusiasm.

Endeavour to merit the favour of God by a sincere and uniform obedience to whatever you know, or believe, to be his will; and should afflictive evils be permitted to cloud the sun-shine of your brightest days, receive them with submission; satisfied that a Being equally wise, omniscient, and beneficient, at once sees and intends the good of his whole creation; and that every general or particular dispensation of His providence towards the rational part of it, is so calculated as to be productive of ultimate happiness, which nothing but the misbehaviour of individuals can prevent to themselves.

This truth is surely an unanswerable argument for absolute resignation to the Will of God; and such a resignation, founded upon reason and choice, not enforced by necessity, is unalterable peace of mind, fixed on too firm a basis to be shaken by adversity. Pain, poverty, ingratitude, calumny, and even the loss of those we hold most dear, may each transiently affect, but united cannot mortally wound it. Upon this principle, you will find it possible not only to be content, but cheerful, under all the disagreeable circumstances this state of probation is liable to; and, by making a proper use of them, you may effectually remove the garb of terror from the laſt of all temporal evils. Learn then, with grateful pleaſure, to meet approaching death as the kind remover of every painful ſenſation, the friendly guide to perfect and to everlaſting happineſs.

Believe me this is not mere theory. My own experience every moment proves the fact undeniably true. My conduct in all thoſe relations which ſtill ſubſiſt with me, nearly as human imperfection will allow, is governed by the rules here laid down for you; and it produces the conſtant rational compoſure which conſtitutes the moſt perfect felicity of human life: for with truth I can aver, that I daily feel incomparably more real ſatisfaction, more true contentment in my preſent retirement, than the gayeſt ſcenes of feſtive mirth ever afforded me. I am pleaſed with this life, without an anxious thought for the continuance of it, and am happy in the hope of hereafter exchanging it for a life infinitely better. My ſoul, unſtained by the crimes unjuſtly imputed to me, moſt ſincerely forgives the malicious authors of theſe imputations; it anticipates the future pleaſure of an open acquittal, and in that expectation loſes the pain of preſent undeſerved cenſure. By this is meant the inſtance that was made the ſuppoſed foundation for the laſt of innumerable injuries which I have received through him from whom I am conſcious of having deſerved the kindeſt treatment. Other faults, no doubt, I might have many; to him I had very few: nay, for ſeveral years, I cannot, upon reflection, accuſe myſelf of any thing but of a too abſolute, too unreſerved obedience to every injunction, even where plainly contrary to the dictates of my own reaſon. How wrong ſuch a compliance was, has been clearly proved by many inſtances, in which it has been ſince moſt ungenerouſly and moſt ungratefully urged as a circumſtantial argument againſt me.

It muſt indeed be owned, that for the two or three laſt years, tired with a long ſeries of repeated inſults, of a nature almoſt beyond the power of imagination to conceive, my temper became ſoured: a conſtant fruitleſs endeavour to oblige was changed into an abſolute indifference about it; and ill humour, occaſioned by frequent diſappointment—a conſequence I have experimentally warned you againſt—was perhaps ſometimes too much indulged. How far the unequalled provocations may be allowed as an excuſe for this, Heaven only muſt determine, whoſe goodneſs has thought fit to releaſe me from the painful ſituation; though by a method, at preſent, not the moſt eligible, as it is the cauſe of a ſeparation *from my children alſo*, and thereby has put it out of my power to attend in the manner I could have wiſhed to their education; a duty that inclination would have led me with equal care and pleaſure more amply to fulfill, had they continued under my direction. But as Providence has thought fit otherwise to determine, contented I submit to every dispensation, convinced that all things are ordered for the best, and that they will in the end work together for good to them that fear God, and who sincerely endeavour to keep his commandments. If in these I err, I am certain it is owing to a mistake in the judgement, not to a defect of the will.

Thus have I endeavoured, my dear girl, in some measure, to compensate both to you and to your sisters the deprivation of a constant maternal care, by advising you, according to my best ability, in the most material parts of your conduct through life, as particularly as the compass of a letter would allow me. May these few instructions be as serviceable to you as my wishes would make them! and may that Almighty Being, to whom my daily prayers ascend for your preservation, grant you His heavenly benediction! May he keep you from all moral evil, lead you into the paths of righteousness and peace, and may He give us all a happy meeting in that future state of unalterable felicity, which is *prepared for those who, by patient continuance in well-doing, seek after glory and immortality!*

ADVICE

OF A

MOTHER

TO

HER DAUGHTER.

BY THE

MARCHIONESS DE LAMBERT.

"——The dearest task a parent knows."

CARTWRIGHT.

——DUBLIN;——

PRINTED BY GRAISBERRY AND CAMPBELL,

FOR JOHN ARCHER, NO. 80, DAME-STREET.

1790.

ADVICE

OF A

MOTHER

TO

HER DAUGHTER.

BY THE

MARCHIONESS DE LAMBERT.

ADVICE

OF A

MOTHER

TO

HER DAUGHTER.

THE world has in all ages been very negligent in the education of daughters; all their care is laid out entirely upon the men; and as if the women were a distinct species, they leave them to themselves without any helps, without thinking that they compose one half of the world; that the two sexes are necessarily united together by alliances; that the women make either the happiness or misery of the men, who always feel the want of having them reasonable; that they are a great means of the rise and ruin of families;

that they are entrusted with the education of the children in their early youth, a season of life in which they receive the liveliest and deepest impressions. What would they have them inspire into their children, when from their very infancy they are left themselves in the hands of governantes, who, as they are generally taken out of the low world, inspire them with low sentiments, encourage all the timorous passions, and form them to superstition instead of religion. 'Twould be a subject worthier of their thoughts to contrive how to make certain vices hereditary to their families, by conveying them down from the mother to the children, than how to secure their estates by entails. Nothing therefore is so much mistaken as the education which they give to young women: they design them to please; they give them no instructions but for the ornament and graces of the body; they flatter their self-love; they give them up to effeminacy, to the world, and to false opinions; they give them no lectures of virtue and fortitude: surely it is unreasonable or rather downright madness to imagine that such an education should not turn to their prejudice.

It may be necessary, my Daughter, to observe all the outward rules of *Decorum;* but this is not enough to gain you the esteem of the world; 'tis the sentiments of the mind that form the character of a person; that lead the understanding; that govern the will; that ſecure the reality and duration of all our virtues: but religion ſhould be the principle and foundation of theſe ſentiments. When religion is once engraven on our heart, all the virtues will naturally flow from that ſource; all the duties of life will be regularly practiſed in their reſpective order. 'Tis not enough for the conduct of young perſons to oblige them to do their duty; they muſt be brought to love it. Authority is a tyrant only over the outward behaviour, it has no ſway over the inward ſentiments. When one preſcribes a conduct, we ſhould repreſent the reaſons and the motives of it, and give them a reliſh for what we adviſe them.

'Tis ſo much for our intereſt to practiſe virtue, that we ſhould never conſider it as our enemy, but rather as the ſource of happineſs, of glory, and of peace.

You are juſt coming into the world; enter it, my daughter, with ſome principles; you cannot fortify yourſelf too much againſt what you will meet with there: bring along with you all your religion: nouriſh it in your heart by your ſentiments; confirm it in your mind by proper reflections, and by reading adapted to encourage it.

There is nothing more neceſſary, and indeed more happy for us than to keep up a ſentiment that makes us love and hope; that gives us a proſpect of an agreeable futurity; that reconciles all times; that insures all the duties of life; that answers for us to ourselves, and is our guarantee with regard to others. What a support will you find from religion under the misfortunes that threaten you! for a certain number of misfortunes must fall to your share. 'Twas a saying of one of the Antients, "That he wrapped himself up in the mantle of his Virtue:" Wrap yourself up in that of your Religion; it will be a great help to you against the weakness of youth, and a sure refuge in your riper years.

Women that have cultivated all their understanding with nothing but the maxims of the world, are presented at last with an universal blank, and find themselves in a terrible want of thought and employment, the most irksome situation in life. As they advance in age the world quits them, and reason tells them they should quit the world; but where must they go for relief? The time past furnishes us with regrets, the present with inquietudes, and the time to come with fears. Religion alone calms all our uneasiness, and comforts us under all misfortunes; by uniting you to God, it reconciles you with the world, and yourself too.

A young person when she comes into the world frames to herself an high notion of the happiness reserved for her. She sets herself to obtain it; 'tis the source of all her cares. She is always on the hunt after her notion, and in hopes of finding a perfect happineſs: this is the occaſion of lightneſs and inconſtancy.

The pleaſures of the world are deceitful; they promiſe more than they perform; the queſt of them is full of anxiety: their enjoyment is far from yielding any true ſatisfaction, and their loſs is attended with vexation.

To fix your deſires, think that no ſolid or laſting happineſs is to be found any where but in your own breaſt. Honours and riches have no charms that are laſting for any length of time; their poſſeſſion extends our view, and gives us new deſires. Pleaſures when they grow familiar, loſe their reliſh. Before you have taſted them, you may do without them; whereas enjoyment makes that neceſſary to you, which was once ſuperfluous, and you are worſe at your eaſe than you were before; by enjoying them you grow uſed to them, and when you loſe them, they leave you nothing but emptineſs and want. What affects us ſenſibly is the paſſage from one circumſtance of life to another; the interval between a miſerable ſeaſon and a happy one. The ſenſe of pleaſure wears off as ſoon as we grow habituated to it. 'Twould be a great advantage if reaſon could at once lay before us all that is neceſſary for our happineſs. Experience brings us back to ourſelves; ſpare yourſelf that expence, and lay it early down for a maxim, with a firmneſs and reſolution to determine your conduct, that "true felicity conſiſts in peace of mind, in reaſon, and in the diſcharge of our duty." Let us not fancy ourſelves happy, my Daughter, till we feel our pleaſures of this ſort flow from the bottom of our ſoul.

Theſe reflections ſeem too ſtrong for a young perſon, and are proper for a riper age: however, I believe you capable of them; and beſides, I am inſtructing myſelf. We cannot engrave the precepts of wiſdom too deeply in our hearts; the impreſſions that they make are always too light; but it can't be denied that ſuch as uſe themſelves to make reflections, and fortify their hearts with principles, are in a fairer way to virtue than ſuch as neglect them. If we are unhappy enough to be defective in the practice of our duty, let us at leaſt not be wanting in our affections to it: let us then, my Daughter, make uſe of theſe precepts for a continual help to our virtue.

'Tis commonly ſaid there are two prejudices with which every body muſt comply: Religion and Honour. 'Tis a wrong expreſſion to call Religion a prejudice. A prejudice is an opinion that may be ſubſervient to error as well as truth; the term ought never to be applied but to things that are uncertain; and Religion is not ſo.

Honour is indeed an invention merely human; yet nothing is more real than the evils that people ſuffer who would get rid of it; 'twould be dangerous to ſhake it off; we ſhould rather do all we can to fortify a ſentiment that ought to be a rule to our conduct, ſince nothing is more deſtructive of our quiet, or makes our life more unequal, than to think one way and act another. Poſſeſs your heart as much as is poſſible with ſentiments for the conduct that you ought to obſerve; fortify this prejudice of Honour in your mind; you cannot be too ſcrupulouſly nice on this ſubject.

Never warp in the leaſt from theſe principles; never entertain a notion, as if the virtue of women was a virtue only enjoined by cuſtom; nor allow yourſelf to think you have ſufficiently diſcharged your obligations, if you can but eſcape the eyes of the world. There are two courts before which you muſt inevitably appear in judgment, your Conſcienee and the World; you may poſſibly get clear of the World, but you can never get clear of Conſcience. Secure her teſtimony in favour of your honeſty; 'tis what you owe to yourſelf; but withal do not neglect the approbation of the public, for a contempt of reputation naturally leads to a contempt of virtue.

When you are a little acquainted with the world, you will find that there is no need of the ſanctions and terror of laws to keep you within the bounds of your duty; the example of ſuch as have deviated from it, and the calamities that have ever attended them, is enough to ſtop any inclination in the midſt of its career; for there is no coquet but muſt own, if ſhe would be ſincere, that is is the greateſt misfortune in the world to be forgot and neglected.

Shame is a paſſion that might be of excellent advantage to us, if we managed it well: I do not mean that falſe ſhame which only ſerves to diſturb our quiet, without being of any ſervice to our behaviour; I ſpeak of that which keeps us from evil out of fear of diſhonour: we muſt confeſs this ſhame is ſometimes the ſureſt guard of the women's virtue; there are very few virtuous for virtue itſelf.

There are ſome great virtues, which, when they are carried to a certain degree, make a great many defects be over-looked; ſuch as extraordinary valour in the men, and extreme modeſty in the women. Agrippina, the wife of Germanicus, was excuſed of all her faults on account of her chaſtity. This Princeſs was ambitious and haughty; but, ſays Tacitus, "all her paſſions were conſecrated by her chaſtity."

If you are ſenſible and nice in the point of reputation, if you are apprehenſive of being attacked as to eſſential virtues, there is one ſure means to calm your fears and ſatisfy your nicety; 'tis to be virtuous. Be ſure always to keep well with yourſelf; 'tis a ſure income of pleaſures; and will gain you praiſe, and a good reputation to boot; in a word, be but truly virtuous, and you'll find admirers enough.

The virtues that make a figure in the world do not fall to the women's ſhare; there virtues are of a ſimple and peaceable nature: Fame will have nothing to do with us. 'Twas a ſaying of one of the Antients, that "the great virtues are for the men!" he allows the women nothing but the ſingle merit of being unknown; and "ſuch as are moſt praiſed, "(ſays he) are not always the perſons that deſerve "it beſt; but rather ſuch as are not talked of at all." The notion ſeems to me to be wrong; but to reduce this maxim into practice, I think it beſt to avoid the world, and making a figure, which always ſtrike at modeſty, and be contented with being one's own ſpectator.

The virtues of the women are difficult, becauſe they have no help from glory to practiſe them. To live at home; to meddle with nothing but one's ſelf and family; to be ſimple, juſt, and modeſt, are painful virtues, becauſe they are obſcure. One muſt have a great deal of merit to ſhun making a figure, and a great deal of courage to bring one's ſelf to be virtuous only to one's own eyes. Grandeur and reputation ſerve for ſupports to our weakneſs, for ſuch in reality is our deſire to diſtinguiſh and raiſe ourſelves. The mind reſts in the public approbation, but true glory conſiſts in being ſatisfied without it. Let it not enter then into the motives of your actions; 'tis enough that it is the recompence of them.

Be assured, my Daughter, that perfection and happiness cling together; that you can never be happy but by virtue, and scarce ever unhappy but by ill conduct. Whoever examines themselves strictly, will find that they never had any grievous affliction, but they occasioned it themselves by some fault, or by being wanting in some duty. Anxiety always follows the loss of innocence; but virtue is ever attended with an inward satisfaction, that is a constant spring of felicity to all its votaries.

Do not however imagine that your only virtue is modesty; there are abundance of women that have no notion of any other, and fancy, that by practising it they discharge all the duties of society: they think they have a right to neglect all the rest, and to be as proud and censorious as they please. Anne of Bretagne, a proud and imperious Princess, made Lewis XII suffer exceedingly; and the good Prince was used to say, when he submitted to her humour, "we must pay dear for the women's chastity." Make nobody pay for yours; think rather that it is a virtue which regards only yourself, and loses its greatest lustre, if it be not attended with the other virtues.

We should be very tender in our modesty; inward corruption passes from the heart to the mouth, and occaſions looſe diſcourſe. The moſt violent paſſions have need of modeſty to ſhew themſelves in a ſeducing form; it ſhould diſtinguiſh itſelf in all your actions; it ſhould ſet off and embelliſh all your perſon.

They ſay that when Jove formed the paſſions, he aſſigned every one of them its diſtinct abode. Modeſty was forgot; and when ſhe was introduced to him, he could not tell where to place her: ſhe was therefore allowed to conſort with all the reſt. Ever ſince that time ſhe is inſeparable from them; ſhe is the friend of Truth, and betrays the lie that dares attack it; ſhe is in a ſtrict and intimate union with Love; ſhe always attends, and frequently diſcovers and proclaims it: Love, in a word, loſes his charms, whenever he appears without her; there is not a more glorious ornament for a young lady than modeſty.

Let the chief part of your finery then be modeſty it has great advantages; it ſets off beauty, and ſerves for a veil to uglineſs: modeſty is the ſupplement of beauty. The great misfortune of uglineſs is, that it ſmothers and buries the merit of women. People do not go to look in a forbidding figure for the engaging qualities of the mind and heart; 'tis a very difficult affair when merit muſt make its way, and ſhine through a diſagreeable outſide.

You do not want Graces to make you agreeable, but you are no Beauty: this obliges you to lay up a ſtock of merit: the world will compliment you with nothing. Beauty has great advantages. One of the Antients ſaid of it, that it was "a ſhort tyranny, "and the greateſt privilege in Nature; that hand-"ſome perſons carry letters of recommendation in "their looks."

Beauty inſpires a pleaſing ſentiment which prepoſſeſſes people in its favour. If you have made no ſuch impreſſions, you muſt expect to be taken to pieces. Take care that there be nothing in your air or manners to make any body think that you do not know yourſelf: an air of confidence in an ordinary figure is ſhocking enough. Let nothing in your diſcourſe or dreſs look like art, at leaſt let it not be eaſy to find it out; the moſt refined art never lets itſelf be ſeen.

You are not to neglect the accompliſhments and ornaments proper to make you agreeable, for women are deſigned to pleaſe; but you ſhould rather think of acquiring a ſolid merit, than of employing yourſelf in trifling things. Nothing is ſhorter than the reign of beauty; nothing is more melancholy than the latter part of the lives of women who never knew any thing but that they were handſome. If any body makes their court to you for the ſake of your agreeable accompliſhments, make their regards center in friendſhip, and ſecure the continuance of that friendſhip by your merits.

'Tis a difficult matter to lay down any ſure rules to pleaſe. The Graces without merit cannot pleaſe long; and merit without the Graces may command the eſteem of men, but can never move them. Women therefore muſt have an amiable merit, and join the Graces to the Virtues. I do not confine the merit of women merely to modeſty; I give it much a larger extent. A valuable woman exerts the manly virtues of friendſhip, probity, and honour, in the punctual diſcharge of all her obligations. An amiable woman ſhould not only have the exterior graces, but all the graces of the heart and fine ſentiments of the mind. There is nothing ſo hard as to pleaſe without being ſo intent upon it, that it ſhall look a little like coquetry. Women generally pleaſe the men of the world more by their faults than their good qualities. The men are for making their advantages of the weakneſſes of amiable women: they would have nothing to do with their virtues; they do not care to eſteem them; they had much rather be amuſed by perſons of little or no merit, than be forced to admire ſuch as are virtuous.

One muſt know human nature if one deſigns to pleaſe. The men are much more affected with what is new, than with what is excellent: but the flower of novelty ſoon fades; what pleaſed when it was new, ſoon diſpleaſes when it grows common. To keep up this taſte of novelty, we muſt have a great many resources and various kinds of merit within ourselves; we must not stick only at the agreeable accomplishments: we must strike their fancy with a variety of graces and merits to keep up their inclinations, and make the same object afford them all the pleasures of inconstancy.

Women are born with a violent desire to please; as they find themselves barred from all the ways that lead to glory and authority, they take another road to árrive at them, and make themselves amends by their agreeableness. Beauty imposes on the person that has it, and infatuates the soul; yet remember that there is but a very small number of years difference between a fine woman and one that is no longer so. Get over this excessive desire to please; at least keep from shewing it. We must not be extravagant in our dress, or let it take up all our time; the real Graces do not depend on a studied finery; we must submit to the mode as a troublesome sort of slavery, but comply with it no more than we are obliged in decency. The mode would be reasonable if it could be fixed to a point of perfection, convenience, and gracefulness; but to be always changing is inconstancy, rather than politeness and a good taste.

A good taste avoids all excessive niceness; it treats little things as little ones, and gives itself very little trouble about them. Neatness is indeed agreeable, and deserves to be ranked among things that are graceful, but it commences littleneſs, when it is carried to an exceſs; it is a much better temper to be careleſs in things of little conſequence than to be too nice about them.

Young perſons are very ſubject to the ſpleen; as they are quite deſtitute of knowledge, they run with eagerneſs towards ſenſible objects; the ſpleen, however, is the leaſt evil they have to dread: exceſſive joys are no part of the train of virtue. All violent and moving pleaſures are dangerous. Though one is diſcreet enough not to break through the rules of decency, and to keep within the bounds of modeſty; yet when the heart is once moved with the pleaſure it feels, a ſort of ſoftneſs diffuſes itſelf over the ſoul, and takes away its reliſh for every thing that is called virtue: it ſtops and makes you cool in the practice of your duty. A young perſon does not ſee the conſequences of this flattering poiſon, the leaſt miſchief of which is to diſturb the quiet of life, to deprave the taſte, and render all ſimple pleaſure inſipid. When one ſees a young perſon happy enough not to have had her heart touched (as there is a natural diſpoſition in us to a union, and this diſpoſition has not been exerciſed), ſhe eaſily complies, and gives herſelf naturally to the perſon deſigned for her.

Be very cautious on the article of plays, and the like public diverſions. There is no dignity in ſhewing one's ſelf continually, nor is it an eaſy matter to preſerve a ſtrict modeſty in a conſtant hurry of diverſions. It is miſtaking one's intereſt to frequent them: if you have beauty, you muſt not wear out the taſte of the world by ſhewing yourſelf continually: you muſt be ſtill more reſerved if you want graces to ſet you off; beſides, the conſtant uſe of diverſions leſſens the reliſh of them.

When all your life has been ſpent in pleaſures, and they come to leave you, either becauſe your taſte for them is over, or becauſe your reaſon forbids you the enjoyment of them, your mind finds itſelf in a moſt uneaſy ſituation for want of employment. If you would therefore have your pleaſures and amuſements laſt, uſe them only as diverſions to relieve you after more ſerious occupations. Entertain yourſelf with your own reaſon; keep up that correſpondence, and the abſence of pleaſures will not leave you any time upon your hands, nor any hankering after them.

It behoves us therefore to huſband our taſtes; there is no reliſhing life without them, but innocence only can preſerve them in their integrity; irregularity is ſure to deprave them.

When we have found a heart, we make an advantage of every thing, and turn it into a ſource of pleaſure. We come frequently to pleaſures with a ſick's man's palate: we fancy ourſelves nice, when we are only ſurfeited and out of taſte. When we have not ſpoiled our mind and heart by ſentiments that ſeduce the fancy, or by any flaming paſſion, it is eaſy to find delight: health and innocence are the true fountains of joy. But when we have had the misfortune to habituate ourſelves to vehement pleaſures, we become inſenſible to moderate ones. We ſpoil our taſte by diverſions, and uſe ourſelves ſo much to violent pleaſures, that we cannot take up with ſuch as are ſimple and regular.

We ſhould always dread ſuch great emotions of the ſoul as leave us flat and out of ſorts. Young perſons have the greater reaſon to fear them, in that they are leſs capable of reſiſting what flatters their ſenſe. "Temperance," ſaid one of the Antients, "is the beſt caterer for luxury." With this temperance, which makes the health both of mind and body, one has always a pleaſing and an equal joy; one has no need of diverſions and expence; reading, work, and converſation, afford a purer joy than all the train of the greateſt pleaſures. In a word, innocent delights are of moſt advantage; they are always ready at hand; they are beneficent, and are never purchaſed at too dear a rate. Other pleaſures flatter, but they do miſchief: they alter the conſtitution of the mind, and ſpoil it like that of the body.

Be regular in all your views and in all your actions; it would be happy if our fortune was ſuch as to make computations of our income unneceſſary; but as yours is narrow, it obliges us to be regular. Be diſcreet in the article of your expences; if you do not obſerve a moderation in them, you will ſoon ſee your affairs in diſorder; as ſoon as you lay aſide œconomy, you can anſwer for nothing.

Pompous living is the high road to ruin, and the ruin of people's fortune is almoſt always followed with corruption of manners: but in order to be regular, it is no way neceſſary to be covetous. Remember that avarice is of little ſervice, and diſhonours a perſon infinitely. All that one ſhould aim at in a regular management, is to avoid the ſhame and injuſtice that always attend an irregular conduct. We muſt retrench ſuperfluous expences only to be in a better condition to afford ſuch as decency, friendſhip and charity engage us to make.

It is good order, and not the looking into little matters, that turns to any great account. Pliny, when he ſent his friend back a bond for a conſiderable ſum which his father owed him, with a general acquittance, told him, "I have but a ſmall eſtate, "and am obliged to be at great expences; but my "frugality ſerves for a fund to ſupply me wherewith "to do the ſervice that I render to my friends." Borrow from your fancies and diverſions, that you may have ſomething to gratify the ſentiments of generofity, which every perfon of a genteel fpirit ought to have.

Never mind the wants that vanity creates. "We "muft be," they fay, "like others;" this *like* goes a vaft way. Have a nobler emulation, and allow nobody to have more honour, probity, and integrity than yourfelf. Be always fenfible of the neceffity of virtue: poornefs of foul is worfe than poverty of fortune.

Whilft you are young, form your reputation, raife your credit: put your affairs in order: you would have more trouble about it in another feafon of life. Charles the Fifth ufed to fay, that "Fortune loved "young folks." In the time of youth, all the world offer themfelves to you, and lend you a helping hand: young people govern without thinking of it. But in more advanced age, you have no helps from any quarter; you have no longer that bewitching charm which has an influence on every body: you have nothing for you but reafon and truth, which do not ordinarily govern the world.

"You are going," faid Montagne to fome young people, "towards reputation and credit; but I am "returning back." When you ceafe to be young, you have no acquifition left you to make, but in point of virtue. In all your undertakings and actions, always aim at the higheft perfection; form no project, and fet about nothing without faying to yourfelf,

"Could not I do better?" By this means you will insensibly contract a habit of justice and virtue, which will make the practice thereof easier to you. Do what Seneca advised his friend Lucilius: "Choose," said he to him, "among great men "some one that you think is most to be admired: "do nothing but in his presence; give him an account "of all your actions." Happy the man that is esteemed enough to be pitched on for this purpose! This is the more easy, because young folks have a natural disposition to imitation. They run less hazard when they choose their patterns from antiquity, where we generally meet with none but great examples. Among the moderns it may have its inconveniences; the copies of them very rarely succeed. It has been said long ago, that every copy ought to tremble before its original; they never follow it but at a distance; and yet it takes away your natural character, which is generally the truest and the most simple. You are apt to grow negligent as to yourself, when you fix yourself to a model; besides, a great part of our faults come from imitation. Learn then to reverence and stand in awe of yourself: let your scrupulousness be your own censor.

Use all your application to make yourself happy in your station of life; improve all the means you have; you lose a thousand advantages for want of it. It is our attention, and comparing of things, that makes us happy.

The more addreſs and capacity you have, the more will you make of your circumſtances, and the more will you extend your pleaſures. It is not poſſeſſion that makes us happy, it is enjoyment, and enjoyment lies in attention.

If people knew how to hug and enjoy themſelves in their condition, they would not be troubled either with ambition or envy, and would be bleſſed with a perfect tranquillity; but we do not live enough in the preſent moment, our deſires and hopes are always puſhing us on towards futurity.

There are two ſorts of madmen in the world; the one always live upon futurity, and feed themſelves with nothing but hopes; and as they are not wiſe enough to calculate them rightly, they paſs their lives in a continual miſtake. Reaſonable perſons are never taken up with any deſires but ſuch as are within their reach; they often gain their point, and though they ſhould be miſtaken, they would eaſily conſole themſelves under the diſappointment, they know likewiſe that our fondneſs for things wears off upon the poſſeſſion of them, or ceaſes upon ſeeing the impoſſibility of obtaining what we deſire: wiſe men always make themſelves eaſy with ſuch reflections. There is another ſort of madmen that make too much of the preſent, and take no manner of care for futurity;

they ruin their fortune. their reputation, and their taſte of life, by not managing them diſcrectly. Men of ſenſe join theſe two times together; they enjoy the preſent, and yet do not neglect the future.

It is a duty, my Daughter, to employ our time, but what uſe do we make of it? Few people know how to value it as it deſerves. "Account to your-"ſelf," ſays one of the Antients, "for every mo-"ment of your time; that after making a juſt uſe of "the preſent, you may have leſs occaſion for the "future." Time flies with rapidity: learn to live, that is, to make a good uſe of your time; but life is ſpent too often in vain hopes, in queſt of fortune, or in waiting for it. All mankind feel the vanity of their condition, always taken up without being ever ſatisfied. Remember that life does not conſiſt in the ſpace of time that you live, but in the uſe you ſhould make of it: conſider that you have a mind to cultivate and feed with truth; a heart to purify and regulate; and a religious worſhip to pay to the Deity.

As the firſt years of life are precious, remember, Daughter, to make an advantageous uſe of them. Whilſt the mind eaſily receives impreſſions, embelliſh your memory with valuable things, and conſider that you are laying in a proviſion for your whole life. The memory is formed and improved by exerciſing it.

Curioſity is a ſentiment that you ſhould not ſtifle, it wants only to be managed, and placed on a right object. Curioſity is a knowledge begun, which makes you advance farther and quicker in the road of truth; it is a natural diſpoſition that meets inſtruction half-way; it ſhould not be ſtopped by lazineſs and love of eaſe.

It is very uſeful for young perſons to employ their time in ſolid ſciences; the Greek and Roman Hiſtory elevate the mind, and raiſes the courage by the great actions that we ſee there related. We ought to know the Hiſtory of France; nobody ſhould be ignorant of the hiſtory of their own country. I ſhould not even blame a little philoſophy, eſpecially the new, if one has a capacity for it: it helps to give you a clear judgment, to diſtinguiſh your ideas, and teach you to think juſtly. I would likewiſe have a little morality: by the bare reading of Cicero, Pliny, and others, one gets a taſte for virtue: it makes an inſenſible impreſſion on us, that is of great advantage to our morals. The inclination to vice is corrected by the example of ſo many virtues, and you will rarely find an evil diſpoſition have any reliſh for this ſort of reading. We do not love to ſee what is always upbraiding and condemning us.

As for languages, though a woman ought to be ſatisfied with ſpeaking that of her own country, I ſhould not thwart the inclination one might have for Latin. It is the language of the Church: it opens you a gate to all the ſciences: it lets you into converſation with the beſt part of the world in all ages. Women are ready enough to learn Italian; but I think it dangerous; it is the language of love: the Italian writers are not very correct; you ſee in all their works a gingle of words, and a looſe imagination inconſiſtent with a juſt way of thinking.

Poetry may produce ſome inconveniences; I ſhould however be loth to forbid the reading of the fine tragedies of Corneille: but the beſt of them often give you lectures of virtue, and leave you an impreſſion of vice.

The reading of romances is ſtill more dangerous: I would not have them much uſed; they inure the mind to falſhoods. Romances having no foundation of truth to ſupport them, warm the imagination, impair modeſty, put the heart in diſorder, and let a young perſon have but the leaſt diſpoſition to tenderneſs, they hurry on and fire her inclination. One ſhould not increaſe the charms and deluſions of love; the more it is ſoftened, and the more modeſt it appears, the more dangerous it is. I would not forbid them; all prohibitions intrench upon liberty, and raiſe the deſire: but we ſhould, as much as we are able, uſe ourſelves to ſolid readings, which improve the underſtanding and fortify the heart: we cannot too carefully avoid ſuch as leave impreſſions hard to be effaced.

Moderate your fondneſs for extraordinary ſciences; they are dangerous, and generally teach one nothing but a vaſt deal of vanity: they depreſs the activity of the ſoul. If you have a very warm and active imagination, and a curioſity which nothing can ſtop, it is much better to employ theſe diſpoſitions in the ſciences, than to run the hazard of their being turned to ſerve your paſſions: but remember, that a young lady ſhould have almoſt as nice a modeſty in the article of ſciences, as ſhe has with regard to vice.

Guard yourſelf therefore againſt the inclination of ſetting up for a virtuoſo; do not amuſe yourſelf in running after vain ſciences, and ſuch as are above your reach. Our ſoul is much better qualified for enjoyment than it is for knowledge; we have all the knowledge that is proper and neceſſary for our well being; but we will not ſtick there, we are ſtill running after truths that were not deſigned for us.

Before we engage in enquiries that are above our capacities, we ſhould know the juſt extent of our underſtanding, and what rule we ſhould have for determining our perſuaſion: we ſhould learn to diſtinguiſh between opinion and knowledge, and ſhould have reſolution enough to doubt, when we have no clear notion of things, as well as courage to be ignorant of what ſurpaſſes us.

The better to prevent a vain opinion of our capacity, and abate a confidence in our underſtanding, let us conſider that the two principles of all our knowledge, reaſon and the ſenſes, want ſincerity, and often deceive us. The ſenſes impoſe on reaſon, and reaſon miſleads them in its turn. Theſe are our two guides, and both of them lead us out of the way. Such reflections ſhould naturally put us out of conceit with abſtracted ſciences; it is much better for us to employ our time in uſeful points of knowledge.

Docility is a quality very neceſſary for a young perſon, who ſhould never have much confidence in herſelf: but this docility muſt not be carried too far. In point of religion, indeed, it muſt ſubmit to authority; but on any other ſubject it muſt receive nothing but from reaſon and evidence. By carrying docility too far, you do an injury to your reaſon; you make no uſe of your own judgment and underſtanding, which are impaired for want of exerciſe. You ſet too narrow bounds to your ideas, when you confine them to to thoſe of other people. The teſtimony of men only deſerves credit in proportion to the degree of certainty which they have acquired by examining into facts. There lies no preſcription againſt truth: it is for all perſons and of all times. In a word, as a great man ſays, "To be a Chriſtian, one muſt be-"lieve implicitly: but to be a wiſe man, one muſt "ſee clearly."

Accuſtom yourſelf to exerciſe your underſtanding, and make more uſe of it than of your memory. We fill our heads with the notions of other people, and take no care to form any of our own. We fancy that we have made a great progreſs, when we load our memory with hiſtories and facts; but this is of very little ſervice to perfect our underſtanding. We muſt uſe ourſelves to thinking. The underſtanding extends and improves itſelf by exerciſe; yet few perſons take care to exert it.

Among our ſex the art of thinking is a ſort of dormant talent. Hiſtorical facts, and the opinions of philoſophers, will not defend you againſt a calamity that preſſes you: you will not find yourſelf much the ſtronger for them. When an affliction comes upon you, you have recourſe to Seneca and Epictetus: Is it for their reaſon to give you conſolation? Is it not rather the buſineſs of your own? Make uſe of your own ſtock; in the calm of life make a proper proviſion againſt the time of affliction, which you are ſure to meet with: you will find yourſelf much better ſupported by your own reaſon than by that of other people.

If you can govern your imagination, and make it ſubmit to reaſon and truth, it will be a great ſtep towards your perfection and happineſs. Women are generally governed by their imagination; as they are not employed in any thing ſolid, and are not in the courſe of their lives troubled either with the care of their fortune, or the management of their affairs, they give themſelves up entirely to their pleaſures. Plays, dreſs, romances, and inclinations, all depend upon imagination. I know well enough that if you keep it within due bounds, you take ſo much off from your pleaſures; for Imagination is the ſource of them; and the things that pleaſe us moſt, derive from her the charm and illuſion in which all their agreeableneſs conſiſts: but for one pleaſure of her creating, what evils doth ſhe not make us ſuffer? She ſtands continually between Truth and us: Reaſon dares not ſhew herſelf where Imagination bears the ſway. We ſee only as ſhe pleaſes, and thoſe that are led by her know what they ſuffer from her by woeful experience. It would be a very happy compoſition to make with her, to give her back all her pleaſures, on condition that ſhe made you feel none of her pains: in a word, there is nothing ſo inconſiſtent with happineſs, as a fine lively and too heated imagination.

Poſſeſs yourſelf with a true notion of things, and take not up with the ſentiments of the people: form your own judgment without giving into received opinions, and get over the prejudices of your infancy. When you feel yourſelf under any uneaſineſs, take the following method: I have found the uſe of it: Examine into the occaſion of your trouble; ſtrip it of all the diſguiſe that is about it, and of all the embroidery of imagination, and you will find that it is generally nothing at all, or at leaſt great allowances are to be made. Value things only according to their real worth. We have a great deal more reaſon to complain of our falſe notions than of our fortune; it is very frequently not ſo much things that hurt us, as the opinion that we have of them.

In order to be happy, we muſt think rightly: we owe a great reſpect to the common opinions, when they concern religion; but we ought to think very differently from the vulgar in what regards morality and the happineſs of life. By the vulgar, I mean every body that has a low and vulgar way of thinking; the court is filled with ſuch ſort of creatures; and the world talks of nothing but fortune and credit: all the cry there is, "Go on, make haſte "forwards;" whereas Wiſdom ſays, "Take up "with ſimple things; chooſe an obſcure but quiet "life; get out of the hurry of the world; avoid a "croud." Fame is not all the recompence of virtue; the main part of it lies in the teſtimony of your own conſcience. A great virtue is ſurely enough to comfort you for the loſs of a little glory.

Be aſſured, that the greateſt ſcience is to know how to be independent. "I have learnt," ſaid one of the Antients, "to be my own friend, ſo I ſhall "never be alone." You muſt provide yourſelf ſome reſources againſt the inquietudes of life, and ſome equivalent for the goods you had depended on.

Secure yourſelf a retreat and place of refuge in your own breaſt; you can always return thither, and be ſure to find yourſelf again. When the world is leſs neceſſary to you, it will have leſs power over you: when you do not, by ſome ſolid inclinations, place your dependance on yourſelf, you depend upon every thing elſe.

Uſe yourſelf to ſolitude: there is nothing more uſeful and neceſſary to weaken the impreſſion that ſenſible objects make upon us. You ſhould therefore from time to time retire from the world to be alone. Aſſign ſome hours in the day for reading, and for making your own reflections. "Reflection," ſays a Father of the Church, "is the eye of the ſoul; it "lets light and trnth into it."—"I will lead him "into ſolitude," ſays Wiſdom, "and there I will "ſpeak to his heart." It is there indeed where Truth gives her inſtructions; where prejudices vaniſh, where prepoſſeſſion wears off, and where opinion, that governs all, begins to loſe its influence. When one conſiders the uſeleſſneſs and inſignificancy of life, one is forced to ſay with Pliny, "It is much better "to paſs one's life in doing nothing at all, than in "doing trifles of nothing."

I have told you already, Daughter, that happineſs conſiſts in peace of mind: you cannot enjoy the pleaſures of the mind without health of mind: every thing almoſt is a pleaſure to a ſound mind. If you would live with tranquillity, theſe are the rules you are to obſerve. The firſt is, not to give yourſelf up to things that pleaſe; to uſe them only occaſionally; not to expect too much from the men, for fear of being diſappointed; to be your own principal friend. Solitude too will enſure you tranquillty, and is a friend to wiſdom: it is within you that Peace and Truth take up their abode. Avoid the great world, there is no ſecurity in it; it always awakens ſome ſentiment or other that we had almoſt cruſhed; there are but too many people in it that encourage looſeneſs; the more one converſes with it, the more authority do one's paſſions gain; it is hard to reſiſt the attack of vice when it comes ſo well attended: in a word, one comes back from it much weaker, leſs modeſt, and more unjuſt, for having been among the men. The world eaſily inſtills its poiſon into tender ſouls. We ſhould likewiſe ſhut up all the avenues to the Paſſions; it is much eaſier to keep them off, than vanquiſh them; and though one ſhould be happy enough to baniſh them, yet from the time that they made their impreſſion, they make us pay dear for their abode. The firſt motions of them is what cannot be refuſed to Nature, but ſhe often carries her influence too far; and when you come to yourſelf again, you find abundant reaſon to repent.

One ſhould always have ſome reſources and laſt ſhifts: calculate your ſtrength and your courage; and for this end, in all cafes where you have any apprehenfions, confider every thing at the worft. Wait for the misfortune that may happen to you with firmnefs: look it bravely in the face; view it in all its moft terrible circumftances, and do not let yourfelf fink under it.

A favourite raifed to the height of grandeur was fhewing his riches to a friend. As he took out a box, he faid to him, "Here it is that my treafure "lies." His friend preffed him to fhew it him, and he allowed him to open the box: there was nothing in it but an old ragged coat. His friend feemed furprized at it: the favourite faid to him, "When for-"tune fhall fend me back to my original condition, "I am ready for it." What a noble refource is it to confider every thing at the worft, and feel fortitude enough in one's felf to ftand the fhock.

How ftrongly foever you wifh for any thing, begin with examining the thing you wifh: fet before your eyes the good which it promifes you, and the evils that follow it: remember the paffage of Horace, "Pleafure goes before you, but keeps her retinue "out of fight." You will ceafe to fear, as foon as ever you ceafe to defire. Depend upon it, a wife man does not run after felicity, but makes his own happinefs; it muft be your own doing, and it is in your own power. Remember that a very fmall matter will ferve for all the real needs of life, but there muſt be an infinite deal to ſatisfy the imaginary needs of opinion; and that you will much ſooner reduce your deſires to the level of your fortune, than raiſe your fortune to the level of your deſires. If honours and riches could ſatiate us, we might heap them up; but the thirſt of them increaſes by acquiring them: he that deſires moſt, is certainly the moſt indigent.

Young perſons live upon hope, M. de la Rochefoucault ſays, "that it carries one an agreeable road "to the end of life." It would be indeed ſhort enough, if hope did not lengthen it; it is a very comfortable ſentiment, but may prove dangerous, by occaſioning you often a great many diſappointments. The leaſt evil that happens from it is, that we often loſe what we poſſeſs, by waiting for what we deſire.

Our ſelf-love makes us blind to ourſelves, and diminiſhes all our defects. We live with them as we do with the perfumes that we wear, we do not ſmell them; they only incommode others: to ſee them in their right light, we muſt ſee them in other people. View your own imperfections with the ſame eyes with which you view thoſe of others: be always exact in keeping to this rule, it will accuſtom you to equity. Examine your own nature, and make the beſt of your defects: there is none of them but may be tacked to ſome virtues, and be made to favour them. Morality does not propoſe to deſtroy nature, but to perfect it. Are you vain-glorious? Make uſe of that ſentiment to raiſe yourſelf above the weakneſſes of your ſex, and to avoid the faults that abaſe it. Every unruly paſſion has a pain and ſhame annexed to it, which ſolicit you to quit it. Are you timorous? Turn that weakneſs into prudence; let it keep you from expoſing yourſelf. Are you laviſh? Do you love to give? It is eaſy to turn prodigality into generoſity. Give with choice and judgment; but do not neglect indifferent people: lend when it is neceſſary; but give to ſuch as cannot return your kindneſs; by ſo doing you ſtrike in with your inclination, and do good actions: there is no weakneſs, but, if you pleaſe, virtue can make a good uſe of it.

In the afflictions which befal you, and which make you ſenſible of your little ſtock of merit, inſtead of fretting and oppoſing the opinion that you have of yourſelf to the injuſtice which you pretend has been done you, conſider that the perſons who are the authors of it are better able to judge of you than you are yourſelf; that you ſhould ſooner believe them than ſelf-love, which always flatters; and that with regard to what concerns yourſelf, your enemy is nearer truth than you are; that you ſhould have no merit in your own eyes, but what you have in other people's. One has too great a diſpoſition to flatter one's ſelf, and men are too near themſelves to judge impartially in the caſe.

These are general precepts for oppofing the vices of the mind; but your firft care fhould be to perfect your heart and your fentiments: it depends on your heart to make your virtue fure and lafting; it is properly that which forms your character; and to make yourfelf miftrefs of it, obferve this method. When you feel yourfelf agitated with a ftrong and violent paffion, defire it to allow you a little time, and compound with your weaknefs; if without hearing it a moment, you are for facrificing every thing to your reafon and your duty, there is room to fear that your paffion may rebel, and grow ftronger than ever. You are under its command, and muft manage it with addrefs: you will receive more help than you think of from fuch a conduct: you will find fome fure remedies even in your paffion. If it be that of hatred, you will fee that you have not altogether fo much reafon to hate and revenge yourfelf, as you at firft imagined. If by misfortune it be the contrary fentiment that has feized you, there is no paffion which furnifhes you furer remedies againft itfelf.

If your heart has the misfortune to be attacked by love, thefe are the remedies to ftop its progrefs: Think that its pleafures are neither folid nor conftant; they quit you; and if this was all the harm they would do you, 'tis enough. In paffions the foul propofes itfelf an object, and is more intimately united to it either by defire or enjoyment, than it is to its own being; it places all its felicity in its poſſeſſion, and all its miſery in the loſs of the object. Yet this felicity of the imagination, this good of the ſoul's choice, is neither ſolid nor laſting: it depends upon others; it depends upon yourſelf; and you cannot anſwer either for others or for yourſelf.

Love in the beginning offers you nothing but flowers, and hides all the danger from you; it impoſes on you; it always takes ſome form which is not its own: the heart being in ſecret intelligence with it conceals its inclination from you, for fear of alarming your reaſon and modeſty. You fancy it a mere amuſement; it is only the perſon's wit or good ſenſe that pleaſes us. In a word, Love is almoſt always unknown till he has got the maſtery. As ſoon as he comes to be felt, fly that inſtant, and hearken not to the complaints of your heart: Love is not rooted out of the ſoul with ordinary efforts, it has too many partizans within us: as ſoon as it has ſurprized you, every thing is on its ſide againſt you, and nothing will ſerve you againſt Love. It is the moſt cruel ſituation a rational perſon can be in; where there is nothing to ſupport you; where you have no ſpectator but yourſelf. You muſt ſummon up your courage immediately, and remember that you muſt make a much more ſorrowful uſe of it, if you yield to your paſſion in the leaſt.

Reflect upon the fatal consequences of passions, and you will find but too many examples to instruct you; but we are often convinced of our mistake, without being cured of our passion. Reckon up, if possible, the evils that flow from Love: it imposes on the reason; it fills the soul and the senses with trouble; it takes away the flower of innocence; it stuns virtue; it blasts the reputation, shame being almost always the consequence of Love. Nothing debases you to such a degree, and sinks you so much below yourself, as the Passions: they degrade you: there is nothing but reason that can maintain your dignity. It is far more unhappy to stand in need of one's courage to bear a misfortune, than to avoid it; the pleasure of doing one's duty is a comfort to you; but never applaud yourself, for fear of being humbled. Remember that you carry your enemy about with you; stick strictly to a conduct that may answer for you to yourself. Avoid plays and passionate representations; you must not see what you would not feel; music, poetry, all this is of the retinue of sensual pleasure. Use yourself to reading on solid subjects, to fortify your reason.

Do not converse with your Imagination; it will paint Love to you with all its charms; it is all seduction and illusion, when she makes the representation: there is always a great drawback when you quit her to come to the reality. St. Augustine has given us a deſcription of his condition, when he was minded to quit love and pleaſures. He ſays, that what he loved preſented itſelf to him under a charming figure; he repreſents what paſſed in his heart in ſuch moving terms, that there is no reading it without danger. One muſt paſs ſlightly over the pictures of Pleaſure; ſhe is always to be feared, even at the very time we are taking meaſures againſt her; and when we are fulleſt of the diſaſters ſhe has occaſioned, we are ſtill to miſtruſt ourſelves. The paſſion is apt to get ground by the examining of one's ſelf; forgetfulneſs is the only ſecurity to be taken againſt Love: you muſt call yourſelf ſeriouſly to account, and ſay, "What do I "mean to do with the inclination that is ſeizing me? "Are not ſuch and ſuch misfortunes ſure to attend "me, if I have the weakneſs to yield to it."

Borrow forces and ſuccour from your enemy and the very nature of Love; if you would not flatter him, he will ſupply you with them. Strip him of all the charms that your fancy gives him; lend him nothing, give him no favour, and you will ſee he will have but little left. After this, think no more of him; take a firm reſolution to fly from him; and depend upon it, we are as ſtrong as we reſolve to be. Diverſion and ſimple amuſements are neceſſary; but we muſt ſhun all pleaſures that affect the heart.

It is not always our faults that ruin us, but the manner of our conduct after we have committed them.

An humble acknowledgment of our faults diſarms reſentment, and ſtops the violence of anger. Women that have had the misfortune to deviate from their duty, to break through decorum, to part with their virtue and modeſty, owe ſo much regard to cuſtom, and ought to have ſuch a ſenſe of their breach of chaſtity, as to appear with a mortified air; it is a ſort of ſatisfaction that the public expects from them; it is ſure to remember your faults whenever you appear to forget them. Repentance inſures a change of your conduct; prevent the malignity which is natural to mankind; put yourſelf in the place that their pride allots you, they would have you humbled; and when you have made yourſelf ſo to their hands, they will have no more to ſay to you: but ſhe that is proud after commiting faults, calls them to mind, and makes them immortal.

Let us now paſs, my Daughter, to the Social Duties. I thought I was in the firſt place to draw you out of the common education and the prejudices of childhood, and that it was neceſſary to fortify your reaſon, and give you ſome ſolid principles to ſupport you. I thought moſt of the diſorders of life were owing to falſe opinions; that falſe opinions produced looſe ſentiments; and that when the underſtanding is not enlightened, the heart is expoſed to paſſions: that there muſt be ſome truths fixed in the mind to preſerve us from error, and that one muſt have ſome ſentiments in the heart to keep out the paſſions. When you have once a knowledge of truth, and a love for juſtice, there is no danger of all the other virtues.

The firſt duty of civil life is to take care of others; ſuch as live only for themſelves fall into contempt, and are neglected by every body. If you are for requiring too much from others, they will refuſe you every thing, their friendſhip, their affections, and their ſervices. Civil life is a mutual intercourſe of good offices: the moſt valuable part of mankind go ſtill further: by promoting the hapineſs of others, you inſure your own; 'tis the trueſt politics to think in this manner.

Nothing can be more odious than people that make every body ſee that they live only for themſelves. An extravagant ſelf-love is the ſource of great crimes; ſome degrees lower it occaſions vices; but let there be never ſo little a ſpice of it in a perſon, it impairs all the virtues and charms of ſociety.

'Tis impoſſible to make a friendſhip with perſons who have a predominant ſelf-love, and take care to ſhew it; and yet we can never ſtrip ourſelves of it entirely; as long as we are attached to life, we ſhall be attached to ourſelves.

But there is a qualified ſelf-love, that is not exerciſed at the expence of others.

We fancy we exalt ourſelves by depreſſing our equals: this makes us cenſorious and envious. Good-nature turns to more account than malignity. Do good when it is in your power; ſpeak well of all the world, and never judge with rigour. Such acts of goodneſs and generoſity frequently repeated will gain you at laſt a great and excellent reputation, All the world is engaged to commend you, to extenuate your defects, and enhance your good qualities. You ſhould found your reputation upon your own virtues, and not upon the demerit of others: conſider that their good qualities take nothing at all from you, and that the diminution of your reputation can be imputed to no body but yourſelf.

One of the things that contributes moſt to make us unhappy is, that we depend too much upon the men; 'tis the ſource too of our injuſtice. We pick quarrels with them, not on account of what they owe us, or of what they have promiſed us, but on account of what we have hoped from them. We depend abſolutely upon our hopes, which occaſion us abundance of diſappointments.

Be not raſh in your judgments, and give no ear to calumnies: never give in to the firſt appearance of things, nor be in haſte to condemn any body. Remember that there are things probable which are not true, as there are things true which are not probable.

We ſhould, in our private judgments, imitate the equity of ſolemn judgments. Judges never decide without having examined, heard and confronted the witneſſes with the parties concerned; but we, without any commiſſion, ſet up for umpires of reputation; and every proof is ſufficient, every authority appears good, when the buſineſs is to condemn. Prompted by our natural malignity, we fancy that we give ourſelves what we take away from others: hence ariſes animoſities and enmities; for every thing is ſure to be known.

Be equitable therefore in your judgments; the ſame juſtice that you do to others, they will return to you. Would you have them think and ſpeak well of you, never ſpeak ill of any body.

Civility, which is an imitation of charity, is another of the ſocial virtues: it puts you above others when you have it in a more eminent degree; but it is practiſed and maintained at the expence of ſelf-love. Civility is always borrowing ſomething from yourſelf, and turning it to the advantage of others. 'Tis one of the great bonds of ſociety, and the only quality that makes one ſafe and eaſy in the intercourſe of life.

We naturally love to govern; 'tis an unjuſt inclination. Whence have we our right to pretend to exalt ourſelves above others? There is but one juſt and allowable ſuperiority, 'tis that which virtue gives you; have more goodneſs and generoſity than others: be beforehand with them more in ſervices than benefits; 'tis the way to raiſe yourſelf. A great diſintereſtedneſs makes you as independent, and raiſes you higher than the ampleſt fortune: nothing ſinks us ſo much as a fondneſs for our own intereſt.

The qualities of the heart have the greateſt concern in the commerce of life: the underſtanding does not endear us to others, and you frequently ſee men very odious with great parts; they are for giving you a good opinion of themſelves; they are for getting an aſcendant over and depreſſing others.

Though humility has only been conſidered as a chriſtian virtue, it muſt be owned to be a ſocial virtue; and ſo neceſſary a one, that without it 'tis a very ticklish matter to have to do with you. 'Tis the conceit that you have of yourſelf which makes you maintain your rights with ſo much arrogance, and intrench on thoſe of other people.

We muſt never be ſtrict in calling any body to account. Exact civility does not inſiſt on all that is due to you. Do not be afraid of being before-hand with your friends: if you have a mind to be a true friend, never inſiſt on any thing too ſtiffly; but that your behaviour may not be inconſiſtent, as it expreſſes your inward diſpoſition, make often ſerious reflections on your weakneſſes, and take yourſelf to pieces. This examination will make you entertain ſentiments of humility for yourſelf, and of indulgence with regard to others.

Be humble without being baſhful. Shame is a ſecret pride ; and pride is an error with regard to one's own worth, and an injuſtice with regard to what one has a mind to appear to others.

Reputation is an advantage very deſirable ; but it is a weakneſs to court it with too much ardor, and do nothing but with a view to it ; we ought to content ourſelves with deſerving it. We ſhould not diſcourage ſenſibility for glory ; 'tis the ſureſt help we have to virtue ; but the buſineſs is to make choice of true glory.

Accuſtom yourſelf to ſee what is above you without either admiration or envy ; and what is below you without contempt. Do not let the pomp of greatneſs impoſe on you ; none but little ſouls fall down and worſhip grandeur ; admiration is only due to virtue.

To uſe yourſelf to value men by their proper qualities, conſider the condition of a perſon loaded with honours, dignities and riches, who ſeems to want nothing at all, but really wants every thing, by being deſtitute of true goods, of thoſe internal qualities that are neceſſary to the enjoyment and uſe of them : he ſuffers as much as if his poverty was real, ſo long as he has the ſenſe of poverty, and is wiſhing for more. " There is nothing worſe," ſays one of the Antients, " than poverty in the midſt of riches, becauſe the " evil lies in the mind." The man that is in this ſituation feels all the evils of opinion, without enjoying the goods of fortune; he is blinded by error, and tormented by his paſſions: whilſt a reaſonable perſon who has nothing at all, but ſubſtitutes wiſe and ſolid reflections to ſupply the place of riches and honours, enjoys a tranquillity which nothing can equal: the happineſs of the one, and the miſery of the other, come only from their different manner of thinking.

If you find yourſelf diſpoſed to reſentment and revenge, ſtrive to keep down that ſentiment; there is nothing ſo mean as to revenge one's ſelf. If you meet with ill-treatment from any body, you owe them only contempt; 'tis a debt eaſy to be paid. If they have offended you only in ſlight matters, you owe them indulgence; but there are certain ſeaſons in life when you muſt meet with injuries; ſeaſons when the friends for whom you have done moſt, fall foul upon and condemn you: in ſuch a caſe, after having done all you can to undeceive them, do not be obſtinate in diſputing with them. One ought to court the eſteem of one's friends; but when you find people that will only view you through their prejudices, when you have diſputes with ſuch hot and fiery imaginations as will admit of nothing but what favours their injuſtice, you have nothing to do but retire and ſet your heart at reſt. Do what you will, you'll get nothing from them but diſcontent. When you thus ſuffer from their ill-uſage and ſhame of recanting, comfort yourſelf in your innocence, and the aſſurance that you have not offended. Think that if your worth was not greater at the time they raiſed you, it is not at all leſs now they are for cruſhing you: you ſhould, without being more mortified at it, pity them, and not be exaſperated if poſſible, but ſay, "They ſee "in a wrong light." Conſider that with good qualities one may at laſt get over reſentment and envy. Let the hopes you draw from virtue keep up your courage, and be your conſolatic...

Do not think of revenging yourſelf any way but by uſing more moderation in your conduct, than thoſe that attack you have malice. None but ſublime ſouls are touched with the glory of pardoning injuries.

Set yourſelf to deſerve your own eſteem, the better to conſole yourſelf for the eſteem which others deny you. You can allow yourſelf but one ſort of vengeance; 'tis that of doing good to ſuch as have offended you: 'tis the moſt exquiſite revenge, and the only one that is allowable: you gratify your paſſion, and you intrench upon no virtue. Cæſar has ſet us an example of it; his lieutenant Labienus deſerted from him at a time that he ſtood in moſt need of him, and went over to Pompey, leaving great riches in Cæſar's camp. Cæſar ſent them after him, with a meſſage to tell him, "that was the manner of Cæſar's re-"venge."

'Tis prudent to make a good uſe of other people's faults, even when they do us miſchief; but very often they only begin the wrongs, and we finiſh them; they give us indeed a right againſt themſelves, but we make an ill uſe of it: we are for taking too much advantage of their faults. This is an injuſtice and a violence that makes the ſtanders-by againſt us. If we ſuffered with moderation all the world would be for us, and the faults of thoſe that attack us would be doubled by our patience.

When you know that your friends have not treated you as they ought, take no notice of it; as ſoon as ever you ſhew that you perceive it, their malignity increaſes, and you give a looſe to their hatred: whereas by diſſembling it, you flatter their ſelf-love; they enjoy the pleaſure of impoſing on you; they fancy themſelves your ſuperiors, as long as they are not diſcovered; they triumph in your miſtake, and feel another pleaſure in not ruining you quite. By not letting them ſee that you know them, you give them time to repent and come to themſelves; and there needs nothing but a ſeaſonable piece of ſervice, and a different manner of taking things, to make them more attached to you than ever.

Be inviolable in your word; but to gain it an entire confidence, remember that you muſt be extremely ſcrupulous in keeping it. Shew your regard to truth even in things indifferent; and conſider that there is nothing ſo deſpicable as to deviate from it. 'Tis a common ſaying, that lying ſhews that people deſpiſe God, and ſtand in fear of man; and that the man who ſpeaks truth and does good reſembles the Deity. We ſhould likewiſe avoid ſwearing; the bare word of an honeſt perſon ſhould have all the credit and authority of an oath.

Politeneſs is a deſire of pleaſing: nature gives it, education and the world improve it. Politeneſs is a ſupplement to Virtue. They ſay it came into the world when that daughter of Heaven abandoned it. In ruder times, when Virtue bore a greater ſway, they knew leſs of Politeneſs; it came in with Voluptuouſneſs; it is the daughter of Luxury and Delicacy. It has been diſputed, whether it approaches neareſt to vice or virtue. Without pretending to decide the queſtion, or define politeneſs, may I be allowed to ſpeak my ſentiments of it? I take it to be one of the greateſt bonds of ſociety, as it contributes moſt to the peace of it; 'tis a preparation to charity, and an imitation too of humility. True politeneſs is modeſt; and as it aims to pleaſe, it knows that the way to carry its point, is to ſhew that we do not prefer ourſelves to others, but give them the firſt rank in our eſteem.

Pride keeps us off from ſociety: our ſelf-love gives us a peculiar rank, which is always diſpoſed with us. Such a high eſteem of ourſelves as makes others feel it, is almoſt always puniſhed with an univerſal contempt. Politeneſs is the art of reconciling agreeably what we owe to others, and what one owes to one's ſelf; for theſe duties have their bounds, which when they exceed, 'tis flattery with regard to others, and pride with regard to yourſelf; 'tis the moſt ſeducing quality in nature.

The moſt polite perſons have generally a good deal of ſweetneſs in their converſation, and engaging qualities: 'tis the girdle of Venus; it ſets off, and gives graces and charms to all that wear it; and with it you cannot fail to pleaſe.

There are ſeveral degrees of politeneſs. You carry it to a higher point in proportion to the delicacy of your way of thinking: it diſtinguiſhes itſelf in all your behaviour, in your converſation, and even in your ſilence.

Perfect politeneſs forbids us to diſplay our parts and talents with aſſurance; it even borders upon cruelty, to ſhew one's ſelf happy when we have certain misfortunes before our eyes. Converſation in the world is enough to poliſh our outward behaviour; but there muſt be a good deal of delicacy to form a politeneſs of mind. A nice politeneſs formed with art and taſte, will make the world excuſe you a great many failings, and improve your good qualities. Such as are defective in point of behaviour have the greater need of ſolid qualities, and make ſlow advances in gaining a reputation. In a word, politeneſs coſts but little, and is of vaſt advantage.

Silence always becomes a young perſon; there is a modeſty and dignity in keeping it; you ſit in judgment upon others, and run no hazard yourſelf: but guard yourſelf againſt a proud and inſulting ſilence; it ſhould be the reſult of your prudence, and not the conſequence of your pride. But as there is no holding our peace always, it is fit for us to know that the principal rule for ſpeaking well is to think well.

When your notions are clear and diſtinct, your diſcourſe will be ſo too; let a proper decorum and modeſty run through them. In all your diſcourſes pay a regard to received cuſtoms and prejudices; expreſſions declare the ſentiments of the heart, and the ſentiments form the behaviour.

Be particularly careful not to ſet up for a joker; 'tis an ill part to act, and by making others laugh, we ſeldom make ourſelves eſteemed. Pay a great deal more attention to others than to yourſelf, and think how to ſet them out rather than to ſhine yourſelf: we ſhould learn how to liſten to other people's diſcourſe, and not betray an abſence of mind either by our eyes or our manner. Never dwell upon ſtories: if you chance to tell any, do it in a genteel and cloſe manner; let what you ſay be new, or at leaſt give a new turn. The world is full of people, that are dinning things into your ears, without ſaying any thing to entertain the mind. Whenever we ſpeak, we ſhould take care either to pleaſe or inſtruct; when you call for the attention of the company, you ſhould make them amends by the agreeableneſs of what you ſay: an indifferent diſcourſe cannot be too ſhort.

You may approve what you hear, but ſhould very ſeldom admire it: admiration is proper to blockheads. Never let your diſcourſe have an air of art and cunning; the greateſt prudence lies in ſpeaking little, and ſhewing more diffidence of one's ſelf than of other people. An upright conduct, and a reputation for probity, gains more confidence and eſteem, and at the long-run more advantages too in point of fortune, than any by-ways. Nothing makes you ſo worthy of the greateſt matters, and raiſes you ſo much above others, as an exact probity.

Uſe yourſelf to treat your ſervants with kindneſs and humanity. 'Tis a ſaying of one of the Antients, " that we ought to conſider them as unhappy friends." Remember that the vaſt difference between you and them is owing merely to chance; never make them uneaſy in their ſtate of life, or add weight to the trouble of it. There is nothing ſo poor and mean as to be haughty to any body that is in your ſervice.

Never uſe any harſh language; it ſhould never come out of the mouth of a delicate and polite perſon.

Servitude being ſettled in oppoſition to the natural equality of mankind, it behoves us to ſoften it. What right have we to expect our ſervants ſhould be without faults, when we are giving them inſtances every day of our own? Let us rather bear with them. When you ſhew yourſelf in all your humours and fits of paſſion, (for we often lay ourſelves open before our ſervants) how do you expoſe yourſelf to them? Can you have any right afterwards to reprimand them? A mean familiarity with them is indeed ever to be avoided; but you owe them aſſiſtance, advice, and bounties ſuitable to their condition and wants.

One ſhould keep up authority in one's family, but it ſhould be a mild authority. We ſhould not indeed always threaten without puniſhing, for fear of bringing our threats into contempt; but we ſhould not call in authority till perſuaſion has failed. Remember that humanity and chriſtianity put all the world on the ſame foot. The impatience and heat of youth, joined to the falſe notion they give you of yourſelf, make you look upon your ſervants as creatures of a different ſpecies; but how contrary are ſuch ſentiments to the modeſty that you owe to yourſelf, and the humanity you owe to others.

Never reliſh or encourage the flattery of ſervants; and to prevent the impreſſion which their fawning ſpeeches frequently repeated may make upon you, conſider that they are hirelings paid to ſerve your weakneſſes and pride.

If by misfortune, Daughter, you ſhould not think fit to follow my Advice and Precepts, though they be loſt upon you, they will ſtill be uſeful to myſelf, as laying me under new obligations. Theſe reflections are freſh engagements to me to exert myſelf in the way of virtue. I fortify my reaſon even againſt myſelf; for I am now under a neceſſity of following it, or elſe I expoſe myſelf to the ſhame of having known it, and yet been falſe to it.

There is nothing, my Daughter, more mortifying than to write upon ſubjects that put me in mind of all my faults: by laying them open to you, I give up my right to reprimand you; I furniſh you with arms againſt myſelf. And I allow you freely to uſe them, if you ſee any vices in me inconſiſtent with the virtues that I recommend to you; for all Advice and Precepts want authority, when they are not ſupported by example.

F A B L E S

FOR THE

FEMALE SEX.

FABLES

FOR THE

FEMALE SEX.

BY EDWARD MOORE.

TENTH EDITION.

" Truth under fiction I impart,
" To weed out folly from the heart,
" And shew the paths, that lead astray
" The wand'ring nymph from wisdom's way."

—D U B L I N;—

PRINTED BY GRAISBERRY AND CAMPBELL,
FOR JOHN ARCHER, NO. 80, DAME-STREET.

1790.

TABLE

OF

CONTENTS.

TABLE OF CONTENTS.

TABLE OF CONTENTS.

FABLE I.

THE EAGLE, AND THE ASSEMBLY OF BIRDS.

TO HER

ROYAL HIGHNESS

THE

PRINCESS OF WALES.

THE moral lay, to beauty due,
I write, *fair Excellence*, to you;
Well pleas'd to hope my vacant hours
Have been employ'd to ſweeten yours.
Truth under fiction I impart,
To weed out folly from the heart,
And ſhew the paths, that lead aſtray
The wandring nymph from wiſdom's way.

M

I flatter none. The great and good
Are by their actions underſtood;
Your monument if actions raiſe,
Shall I deface by idle praiſe?
I echo not the voice of fame,
That dwells delighted on your name;
Her friendly tale, however true,
Were flatt'ry, if I told it you.

The proud, the envious, and the vain,
The jilt, the prude, demand my ſtrain;
To theſe, deteſting praiſe, I write,
And vent, in charity, my ſpite,
With friendly hand I hold the glaſs
To all, promiſcuous as they paſs;
Should folly there her likeneſs view,
I fret not that the mirror's true;
If the fantaſtic form offend,
I made it not, but would amend.

Virtue, in every clime and age,
Spurns at the folly-ſoothing page,
While ſatire, that offends the ear
Of vice and paſſion, pleaſes her.

Premiſing this, your anger ſpare,
And claim the fable, you, who dare.

The birds in place, by factions preſs'd,
To Jupiter their pray'rs addreſs'd;
By ſpecious lies the ſtate was vex'd,
Their counſels libellers perplexed;
They begg'd (to ſtop ſeditious tongues)
A gracious hearing of their wrongs.
Jove grants their ſuit. The Eagle ſate,
Decider of the grand debate.

The Pye, to truſt and pow'r preferr'd,
Demands permiſſion to be heard.
Says he, prolixity of phraſe
You know I hate. This libel ſays,
" Some birds there are, who prone to noiſe,
" Are hir'd to ſilence wiſdom's voice,
" And ſkill'd to chatter out the hour,
" Riſe by their emptineſs to pow'r."
That this is aim'd direct at me,
No doubt, you'll readily agree;
Yet well this ſage aſſembly knows,
By parts to government I roſe;

My prudent counſels prop the ſtate;
Magpies were never known to prate.

The Kite roſe up. His honeſt heart
In virtue's ſuff'rings bore a part.
That there were birds of prey he knew;
So far the libeller ſaid true.
" Voracious, bold, to rapine prone,
" Who knew no int'reſt but their own;
" Who hov'ring o'er the farmer's yard,
" Nor pigeon, chick, nor duckling ſpar'd."
This might be true, but if apply'd
To him, in troth, the ſland'rer ly'd.
Since ign'rance then might be miſled,
Such things, he thought, were beſt unſaid.

The Crow was vex'd. As yeſter-morn
He flew acroſs the new ſown corn,
A ſcreaming boy was ſet for pay,
He knew, to drive the crows away:
Scandal had found him out in turn,
And buzz'd abroad, that crows love corn.

The Owl aroſe, with ſolemn face,
And thus harangu'd upon the caſe.

That Magpies prate, it may be true,
A Kite may be voracious too,
Crows ſometimes deal in new ſown peaſe;
He libels not, who ſtrikes at theſe;
The ſlander's here—" But there are birds,
" Whoſe wiſdom lies in looks, not words;
" Blund'rers, who level in the dark,
" And always ſhoot beſide the mark."
He names not me; but, theſe are hints,
Which manifeſt at whom he ſquints;
I were indeed that blund'ring fowl,
To queſtion if he meant an owl.

Ye wretches, hence! the Eagle cries;
'Tis conſcience, conſcience, that applies;
The virtuous mind takes no alarm,
Secur'd by innocence from harm,
While guilt, and his aſſociate fear,
Are ſtartled at the paſſing air.

FABLE II.

THE PANTHER, THE HORSE, AND OTHER BEASTS.

THE man, who ſeeks to win the fair,
(So cuſtom ſays) muſt truth forbear;
Muſt fawn and flatter, cringe and lie,
And raiſe the goddeſs to the ſky;
For truth is hateful to her ear,
A rudeneſs which ſhe cannot bear——
A rudeneſs?—Yes,—I ſpeak my thoughts;
For truth upbraids her with her faults.

How wretched, Cloe, then am I
Who love you, and yet cannot lie,
And ſtill to make you leſs my friend,
I ſtrive your errors to amend?
But ſhall the ſenſeleſs fop impart
The ſofteſt paſſion to your heart,
While he, who tells you honeſt truth,
And points to happineſs your youth,

Determines, by his care, his lot,
And lives neglected, and forgot?

Trust me, my dear, with greater ease,
Your taste for flatt'ry I could please.
And similies in each dull line,
Like glow-worms in the dark, should shine.
What if I say your lips disclose
The freshness of the op'ning rose?
Or that your cheeks are beds of flow'rs,
Enripen'd by refreshing show'rs?
Yet certain as these flow'rs shall fade,
Time ev'ry beauty will invade.
The butterfly of various hue,
More than the flow'r resembles you;
Fair, flutt'ring, fickle, busy thing,
To pleasure ever on the wing,
Gayly coquetting for an hour,
To die, and ne'er be thought of more.
Would you the bloom of youth should last?
'Tis virtue that must bind it fast,
An easy carriage, wholly free
From sour reserve, or levity;

Good-natur'd mirth, an open heart,
And looks unſkill'd in any art;
Humility, enough to own
The frailties, which a friend makes known,
And decent pride, enough to know
The worth that virtue can beſtow.

These are the charms which ne'er decay,
Tho' youth, and beauty fade away,
And time, which all things elſe removes,
Still heightens virtue, and improves.

You'll frown, and aſk to what intent,
This blunt addreſs to you is ſent?
I'll ſpare the queſtion, and confeſs
I'd praiſe you, if I lov'd you leſs;
But rail, be angry, or complain,
I will be rude, while you are vain.

Beneath a Lion's peaceful reign,
When beaſts met friendly on the plain,
A Panther, of majeſtic port,
(The vaineſt female of the court)
With ſpotted ſkin, and eyes of fire,
Fill'd ev'ry boſom with deſire;

Where'er ſhe mov'd, a ſervile croud
Of fawning creatures cring'd and bow'd;
Aſſemblies ev'ry week ſhe held,
(Like modern belles) with coxcombs fill'd,
Where noiſe, and nonſenſe, and grimace,
And lies and ſcandal, fill'd the place.

Behold the gay, fantaſtic thing,
Encircled by the ſpacious ring;
Low-bowing, with important look,
As firſt in rank, the monkey ſpoke.
"Gad take me, madam, but I ſwear,
"No angel ever look'd ſo fair——
"Forgive my rudeneſs, but I vow,
"You were not quite divine till now,
"Thoſe limbs! that ſhape! and then thoſe eyes
"O cloſe them, or the gazer dies!"

Nay, gentle Pug, for goodneſs huſh,
I vow, and ſwear, you make me bluſh;
I ſhall be angry at this rate——
'Tis ſo like flatt'ry which I hate.

The Fox, in deeper cunning vers'd,
The beauties of her mind rehears'd,

And talk'd of knowledge, taſte, and ſenſe,
To which the fair have moſt pretence;
Yet well he knew them always vain
Of what they ſtrive not to attain,
And play'd ſo cunningly his part,
That Pug was rivall'd in his art.

The Goat avow'd his am'rous flame,
And burnt—for what he durſt not name;
Yet hop'd a meeting in the wood
Might make his meaning underſtood.
Half angry at the bold addreſs,
She frown'd; but yet ſhe muſt confeſs,
Such beauties might inflame his blood,
But ſtill his phraſe was ſomewhat rude.
The Hog her neatneſs much admir'd;
The formal Aſs her ſwiftneſs fir'd;
While all to feed her folly ſtrove,
And by their praiſes ſhar'd her love.

The Horſe, whoſe gen'rous heart diſdain'd
Applauſe, by ſervile flatt'ry gain'd,
With graceful courage, ſilence broke,
And thus with indignation ſpoke.

When flatt'ring monkeys fawn and prate,
They justly raise contempt, or hate;
For merit's turn'd to ridicule,
Applauded by the grinning fool.
The artful fox your wit commends,
To lure you to his selfish ends;
From the vile flatt'rer turn away,
For knaves make friendships to betray.
Dismiss the train of fops, and fools,
And learn to live by wisdom's rules.
Such beauties might the lion warm,
Did not your folly break the charm;
For who would court that lovely shape,
To be the rival of an ape?

He said; and snorting in disdain,
Spurn'd at the croud, and sought the plain.

FABLE III.

THE NIGHTINGALE, AND GLOW-WORM.

THE prudent nymph, whofe cheeks difclofe
The lilly, and the blufhing rofe,
From public view her charms will fkreen,
And rarely in the croud be feen;
This fimple truth fhall keep her wife,
" The faireft fruits attract the flies."

One night, a Glow-worm, proud and vain,
Contemplating her glitt'ring train,
Cry'd, fure there never was in nature
So elegant, fo fine a creature,
All other infects that I fee,
The frugal ant, induftrious bee,
Or filk-worm, with contempt I view;
With all that low, mechanic crew,

Who ſervilely their lives employ
In buſineſs, enemy to joy.
Mean, vulgar herd! ye are my ſcorn,
For grandeur only I was born,
Or ſure am ſprung from race divine,
And plac'd on earth to live, and ſhine.
Thoſe lights, that ſparkle ſo on high,
Are but the glow-worms of the ſky,
And kings on earth their gems admire,
Becauſe they imitate my fire.

She ſpoke. Attentive on a ſpray,
A nightingale forbore his lay;
He ſaw the ſhining morſel near
And flew, directed by the glare;
A while he gaz'd with ſober look,
And thus the trembling pray beſpoke.

Deluded fool, with pride elate,
Know, 'tis thy beauty brings thy fate;
Leſs dazling, long thou might'ſt have lain
Unheeded on the velvet plain;
Pride, ſoon or late, degraded mourns,
And beauty wrecks, whom ſhe adorns.

FABLE IV.

HYMEN AND DEATH.

SIXTEEN, d'ye ſay? Nay, then 'tis time
Another year deſtroys your prime.
But ſtay—The ſettlement! "That's made."
Why then's my ſimple girl afraid?
Yet hold a moment, if you can,
And heedfully the fable ſcan.

The ſhades were fled, the morning bluſh'd,
The winds were in their caverns huſh'd,
When Hymen, penſive and ſedate,
Held o'er the fields his muſing gait.
Behind him, through the green-wood ſhade,
Death's meagre form the God ſurvey'd,
Who quickly with gigantic ſtride,
Out-went his pace, and join'd his ſide.
The chat on various ſubjects ran,
Till angry Hymen thus began.

Relentleſs Death, whoſe iron ſway,
Mortals reluctant muſt obey,
Still of thy pow'r ſhall I complain,
And thy too partial hand arraign?
When Cupid brings a pair of hearts,
All over ſtuck with equal darts,
Thy cruel ſhafts my hopes deride,
And cut the knot, that Hymen ty'd.

Shall not the bloody, and the bold,
The miſer, hoarding up his gold,
The harlot, reeking from the ſtew,
Alone thy fell revenge purſue?
But muſt the gentle, and the kind
Thy fury, undiſtinguiſh'd, find?

The monarch calmly thus reply'd;
Weigh well the cauſe, and then decide.
That friend of yours, you lately nam'd,
Cupid, alone is to be blam'd;
Then let the charge be juſtly laid;
That idle boy neglects his trade,
And hardly once in twenty years,
A couple to your temple bears.

The wretches, whom your office blends,
Silenus now, or Plutus ſends;
Hence care, and bitterneſs, and ſtrife
Are common to the nuptial life.

Believe me; more than all mankind,
Your vot'ries my compaſſion find;
Yet cruel am I call'd, and baſe,
Who ſeek the wretched to releaſe,
The captive from his bonds to free,
Indiſſoluble, but for me.

'Tis I entice him to the yoke;
By me, your crouded altars ſmoke;
For mortals boldly dare the nooſe,
Secure that Death will ſet them looſe.

FABLE V.

THE POET, AND HIS PATRON.

WHY, Celia, is your ſpreading waiſt
So looſe, ſo negligently lac'd?
Why muſt the wrapping bed-gown hide
Your ſnowy boſom's ſwelling pride?
How ill that dreſs adorns your head,
Diſtain'd, and rumpled from the bed!
Thoſe clouds, that ſhade your blooming face,
A little water might diſplace.
As nature ev'ry morn beſtows
The cryſtal dew to cleanſe the roſe.
Thoſe treſſes, as the raven black,
That wav'd in ringlets down your back,
Uncomb'd, and injur'd by neglect,
Deſtroy the face, which once they deck'd.

Whence this forgetfulneſs of dreſs?
Pray, madam, are you marry'd? Yes.

Nay, then indeed the wonder ceafes,
No matter now how loofe your drefs is ;
The end is won, your fortune's made,
Your fifter now may take the trade.

Alas ! what pity 'tis to find
This fault in half the female kind !
From hence proceed averfion, ftrife,
And all that fours the wedded life.
Beauty can only point the dart,
'Tis neatnefs guides it to the heart ;
Let neatnefs then, and beauty ftrive
To keep a wav'ring flame alive.

'Tis harder far (you'll find it true)
To keep the conqueft, than fubdue ;
Admit us once behind the fcreen,
What is there farther to be feen ?
A newer face may raife the flame,
But ev'ry woman is the fame.

Then ftudy chiefly to improve
The charm, that fix'd your hufband's love ;
Weigh well his humour. Was it drefs,
That gave your beauty pow'r to blefs ?

Purſue it ſtill; be neater ſeen,
'Tis always frugal to be clean;
So ſhall you keep alive deſire,
And time's ſwift wing ſhall fan the fire.

In garret high (as ſtories ſay)
A Poet ſung his tuneful lay;
So ſoft, ſo ſmooth his verſe, you'd ſwear,
Appollo, and the Muſes there;
Thro' all the town his praiſes rung,
His ſonnets at the play-houſe ſung;
High waveing o'er his lab'ring head,
The goddeſs Want her pinions ſpread,
And with poetic fury fir'd,
What Phœbus faintly had inſpir'd.

A noble youth, of taſte and wit,
Approv'd the ſprightly things he writ,
And ſought him in his cobweb dome,
Diſcharg'd his rent, and brought him home.

Behold him at the ſtately board,
Who, but the Poet, and my Lord!

Each day, delicioufly he dines,
And greedy quaffs the gen'rous wines;
His fides were plump, his fkin was fleek,
And plenty wanton'd on his cheek;
Aftonifh'd at the change fo new,
Away th' infpiring goddefs flew.

Now, dropt for politics, and news,
Neglected lay the drooping mufe,
Unmindful whence his fortune came,
He ftifled the poetic flame;
Nor tale, nor fonnet, for my lady,
Lampoon, nor epigram was ready.

With juft contempt his patron faw,
(Refolv'd his bounty to withdraw)
And thus, with anger in his look,
The late-repenting fool befpoke.

Blind to the good that courts thee grown,
Whence has the fun of favour fhone?
Delighted with thy tuneful art,
Efteem was growing in my heart,

But idly thou reject'st the charm,
That gave it birth, and kept it warm.

Unthinking fools alone despise
The arts, that taught them first to rise.

FABLE VI.

THE WOLF, THE SHEEP, AND THE LAMB.

DUTY demands, the parent's voice
Should ſanctify the daughter's choice;
In that is due obedience ſhewn;
To chooſe belongs to her alone.

May horror ſeize his midnight hour,
Who builds upon a parent's pow'r,
And claims by purchaſe vile and baſe,
The loathing maid for his embrace;
Hence virtue ſickens; and the breaſt,
Where peace had built her downy neſt,
Becomes the troubled ſeat of care,
And pines with anguiſh and deſpair.

A Wolf, rapacious, rough, and bold,
Whoſe nightly plunders thin'd the fold,
Contemplating his ill-ſpent life,
And cloy'd with thefts, would take a wife.
His purpoſe known, the ſavage race,
In num'rous crowds, attend the place;
For why, a mighty Wolf he was,
And held dominion in his jaws.
Her fav'rite whelp each mother brought,
And humbly his alliance ſought;
But cold by age, or elſe too nice,
None found acceptance in his eyes.

It happen'd, as at early dawn,
He ſolitary croſs'd the lawn,
Stray'd from the fold, a ſportive Lamb
Skip'd wanton by her fleecy Dam;
When Cupid, foe to man and beaſt,
Diſcharg'd an arrow at his breaſt.
The tim'rous breed the robber knew,
And trembling o'er the meadow flew;
Their nimbleſt ſpeed the Wolf o'ertook,
And courteous, thus the Dam beſpoke.

Stay, fairest, and suspend your fear,
Trust me, no enemy is near;
These jaws, in slaughter oft imbru'd,
At length have known enough of blood,
And kinder business brings me now,
Vanquish'd at beauty's feet to bow.
You have a daughter——Sweet forgive
A Wolf's address——In her I live;
Love from her eye like lightning came,
And set my marrow all on flame;
Let your consent confirm my choice,
And ratify our nuptial joys.
Me ample wealth, and pow'r attend,
Wide o'er the plains my realms extend;
What midnight robber dare invade
The fold, if I the guard am made?
At home the shepherd's cur may sleep,
While I secure his master's sheep.
Discourse like this, attention claim'd;
Grandeur the mother's breast inflam'd;
Now fearless by his side she walk'd
Of settlements, and jointures talk'd,

Propos'd, and doubled her demands
Of flow'ry fields, and turnip-lands.
The Wolf agrees. Her bosom swells;
To miss her happy fate she tells.
And of the grand alliance vain,
Contemns her kindred of the plain.

The loathing Lamb with horror hears,
And wearies out her Dam with pray'rs;
But all in vain; mamma best knew
What unexperienc'd girls should do;
So, to the neighb'ring meadow carry'd,
A formal ass the couple marry'd,

Torn from the tyrant-mother's side,
The trembler goes, a victim-bride,
Reluctant meets the rude embrace,
And bleats among the howling race.
With horror oft her eyes behold
Her murder'd kindred of the fold;
Each day a sister-lamb is serv'd,
And at the glutton's table carv'd;
The crashing bones he grinds for food,
And slakes his thirst with streaming blood.

Love, who the cruel mind deteſts,
And lodges but in gentle breaſts,
Was now no more. Enjoyment paſt,
The ſavage hunger'd for the feaſt;
But (as we find in human race,
A maſk conceals the villain's face)
Juſtice muſt authorize the treat;
Till then he long'd, but durſt not eat.

As forth he walk'd, in queſt of prey,
The hunters met him on the way;
Fear wings his flight; the marſh he ſought,
The ſnuffing dogs are ſet at fault.
His ſtomach baulk'd, now hunger gnaws,
Howling he grinds his empty jaws;
Food muſt be had——and lamb is nigh;
His maw invokes the fraudful lye.
Is this (diſſembling rage, he cry'd)
The gentle virtue of a bride?
That, league'd with man's deſtroying race,
She ſets her huſband for the chace?
By treach'ry prompts the noiſy hound
To ſcent his footſteps on the ground?

Thou trait'ress vile! for this thy blood
Shall glut my rage, and dye the wood!

So saying, on the lamb he flies,
Beneath his jaws the victim dies.

FABLE VII.

THE GOOSE, AND THE SWANS.

I HATE the face, however fair,
That carries an affected air;
The lisping tone, the shape constrain'd,
The study'd look, the passion feign'd,
Are fopperies, which only tend
To injure what they strive to mend.
With what superior grace enchants
The face which nature's pencil paints!
Where eyes, unexercis'd in art,
Glow with the meaning of the heart!
Where freedom, and good-humour sit,
And easy gaiety, and wit!
Tho' perfect beauty be not there,
The master lines, the finish'd air,
We catch from ev'ry look delight,
And grow enamour'd at the sight;

For beauty, tho' we all approve,
Excites our wonder, more than love,
While the agreeable ſtrikes ſure,
And gives the wounds, we cannot cure.

Why then, my Amoret, this care,
That forms you, in effect, leſs fair?
If nature on your cheek beſtows
A bloom, that emulates the roſe,
Or from ſome heav'nly image drew
A form, Appelles never knew,
Your ill-judg'd aid will you impart,
And ſpoil by meretricious art?
Or had you, nature's error, come
Abortive from the mother's womb,
Your forming care ſhe ſtill rejects,
Which only heightens her defects.
When ſuch of glitt'ring jewels proud,
Still preſs the foremoſt in the croud,
At ev'ry public ſhew are ſeen,
With look aw'ry, and aukward mien,
The gaudy dreſs attracts the eye,
And magnifies deformity.

Nature may under-do her part,
But ſeldom wants the help of art;
Truſt her, ſhe is your ſureſt friend,
Nor made your form for you to mend.

A Gooſe, affected, empty, vain,
The ſhrilleſt of the cackling train.
With proud, and elevated creſt,
Precedence claim'd above the reſt.

Says ſhe, I laugh at human race,
Who ſay, geeſe hobble in their pace;
Look here!——the ſland'rous lie detect;
Not haughty man is ſo erect.
That peacock yonder! lord how vain
The creature's of his gaudy train!
If both were ſtript, I'd pawn my word,
A gooſe would be the finer bird.
Nature, to hide her own defects,
Her bungled work with fin'ry decks;
Were geeſe ſet off with half that ſhow,
Would men admire the peacock? no.

Thus vaunting, croſs the mead ſhe ſtalks,
The cackling breed attend her walks,
The ſun ſhot down his noon-tide beams,
The Swans were ſporting in the ſtreams;
Their ſnowy plumes, and ſtately pride
Provok'd her ſpleen. Why there ſhe cry'd
Again, what arrogance we ſee!—
Thoſe creatures! how they mimic me!
Shall ev'ry fowl the waters ſkim,
Becauſe we geeſe are known to ſwim?
Humility, they ſoon ſhall learn,
And their own emptineſs diſcern.

So ſaying, with extended wings,
Lightly upon the waves ſhe ſprings,
Her boſom ſwells, ſhe ſpreads her plumes,
And the ſwan's ſtately creſt aſſumes.
Contempt and mockery enſu'd,
And burſts of laughter ſhook the flood.

A ſwan, ſuperior to the reſt,
Sprung forth, and thus the fool addreſs'd.
Conceited thing! elate with pride,
Thy affectation all deride;

Theſe airs thy aukwardneſs impart,
And ſhew thee plainly as thou art.
Among thy equals of the flock,
Thou had'ſt eſcap'd the public mock,
And as thy parts to good conduce
Been deem'd an honeſt hobbling gooſe.

Learn hence, to ſtudy wiſdom's rules;
Know, foppery's the pride of fools,
And ſtriving nature to conceal,
You only her defects reveal.

FABLE VIII.

THE LAWYER, AND JUSTICE.

LOVE! thou divineſt good below,
Thy pure delights few mortals know.
Our rebel hearts thy ſway diſown,
While tyrant luſt uſurps thy throne!
The bounteous god of nature made,
The ſexes for each other's aid,
Their mutual talents to employ,
To leſſen ills, and heighten joy.
To weaker woman he aſſign'd
That ſoft'ning gentleneſs of mind,
That can with ſympathy impart
Its likeneſs, to the rougheſt heart.
Her eyes with magic pow'r endu'd
To fire the dull, and awe the rude.
His roſy fingers on her face
She'd laviſh ev'ry blooming grace.

And ſtamp'd (perfection to diſplay)
His mildeſt image on her clay.

Man, active, reſolute, and bold,
He faſhion'd in a diff'rent mould.
With uſeful arts his mind inform'd,
His breaſt with nobler paſſions warm'd;
He gave him knowledge, taſte, and ſenſe,
And courage for the fair's defence.
Her frame, reſiſtleſs to each wrong,
Demands pretection from the ſtrong;
To man ſhe flies when fear alarms,
And claims the temple of his arms.
By nature's author thus declar'd
The woman's ſov'reign and her guard,
Shall man, by treach'rous wile invade
The weakneſs, he was meant to aid?
While beauty, given to inſpire
Protecting love, and ſoft deſire,
Lights up a wild-fire in the heart,
And to its own breaſt points the dart,
Becomes the ſpoiler's baſe pretence
To triumph over innocence?

The wolf, that tears the tim'rous ſheep,
Was never ſet the fold to keep;
Nor was the tyger, or the pard
Meant the benighte.. trav'lers guard;
But man, the wildeſt beaſt of prey,
Wears friendſhips ſemblance to betray;
His ſtrength againſt the weak employs,
And where he ſhould protect, deſtroys.

Paſt twelve o'clock, the watchman cry'd,
His brief the ſtudious Lawyer ply'd;
The all-prevailing fee lay nigh,
The earneſt of to-morrow's lie;
Sudden the furious winds ariſe,
The jarring caſement ſhatter'd flies,
The doors admit a hollow ſound,
And rattling from their hinges bound;
When Juſtice in a blaze of light
Reveal'd her radiant form to ſight.

The wretch with thrilling horror ſhook,
Looſe ev'ry joint, and pale his look,
Not having ſeen her in the courts,
Or found her mentioned in reports,

He aſk'd, with fault'ring tongue, her name,
Her errand there, and whence ſhe came?

Sternly the white-rob'd ſhade reply'd,
(A crimſon glow her viſage dy'd)
Can'ſt thou be doubtful who I am?
Is Juſtice grown ſo ſtrange a name?
Were not your courts for Juſtice rais'd
'Twas there of old my altars blaz'd.
My guardian thee did I elect,
My ſacred temple to protect,
That thou and all thy venal tribe
Should ſpurn the goddeſs for a bribe?
Aloud the ruin'd client cries,
Juſtice has neither ears, nor eyes!
In foul alliance with the bar,
'Gainſt me the judge denounces war,
And rarely iſſues his decree,
But with intent to baffle me.

She paus'd. Her breaſt with fury burn'd,
The trembling Lawyer thus return'd.
I own the charge is juſtly laid,
And weak th' excuſe that can be made;

Yet ſearch the ſpacious globe, and ſee
If all mankind are not like me.
The gown-man ſkill'd in Romiſh lies,
By faith's falſe glaſs deludes our eyes,
O'er conſcience rides without controul,
And robs the man, to ſave his ſoul.

The doctor, with important face,
By ſly deſign, miſtakes the caſe,
Preſcribes, and ſpins out the diſeaſe,
To trick the patient of his fees.
The ſoldier, rough with many a ſcar
And red with ſlaughter, leads the war;
If he a nation's truſt betray,
The foe has offer'd double pay.

When vice o'er all mankind prevails,
And weighty int'reſt turns the ſcales.
Muſt I be better than the reſt,
And harbour Juſtice in my breaſt?
On one ſide only take the fee,
Content with poverty and thee?

Thou blind to ſenſe, and vile of mind,
Th' exaſperated ſhade rejoin'd,

If virtue from the world is flown,
Will others' faults excuſe thy own?
For ſickly ſouls the prieſt was made,
Phyſicians, for the body's aid,
The ſoldier guarded liberty,
Man woman, and the lawyer me,
If all are faithleſs to their truſt,
They leave not thee the leſs unjuſt.
Henceforth your pleadings I diſclaim,
And bar the ſanction of my name;
Within your courts it ſhall be read,
That Juſtice from the law is fled.

She ſpoke; and hid in ſhades her face,
'Till HARDWICK ſooth'd her into grace.

FABLE IX.

THE FARMER, THE SPANIEL, AND THE CAT.

WHY knits my dear her angry brow?
What rude offence alarms you now?
I ſaid, that Delia's fair, 'tis true,
But did I ſay, ſhe equall'd you?
Can't I another's face commend,
Or to her virtues be a friend,
But inſtantly your forehead lours,
As if her merit leſſen'd yours?
From female envy never free,
All muſt be blind, becauſe you ſee.
Survey the gardens, fields, and bow'rs,
The buds, the bloſſoms, and the flow'rs,
Then tell me where the wood-bine grows,
That vies in ſweetneſs with the roſe?

Or where the lilly's ſnowy white,
That throws ſuch beauties on the ſight?
Yet folly is it to declare,
That theſe are neither ſweet, nor fair.
The chryſtal ſhines with fainter rays,
Before the di'amond's brighter blaze;
And fops will ſay the di'mond dies
Before the luſtre of your eyes;
But I, who deal in truth, deny
That neither ſhine when you are by.

When zephirs o'er the bloſſoms ſtray,
And ſweets along the air convey,
Shan't I the fragrant breeze inhale,
Becauſe you breathe a ſweeter gale?

Sweet are the flow'rs that deck the field,
Sweet is the ſmell the bloſſoms yield,
Sweet is the ſummer gale that blows,
And ſweet, tho' ſweeter you, the roſe.

Shall envy then torment your breaſt,
If you are lovelier than the reſt?
For while I give to each her due,
By praiſing them, I flatter you,

And praiſing moſt, I ſtill declare
You faireſt, where the reſt are fair.

As at his board a Farmer ſate,
Repleniſh'd by his homely treat,
His fav'rite Spaniel near him ſtood,
And with his maſter ſhar'd the food;
The crackling bones his jaws devour'd,
His lapping tongue the trenchers ſcour'd;
Till ſated now, ſupine he lay,
And ſnor'd the riſing fumes away.

The hungry Cat, in turn, drew near,
And humbly crav'd a ſervant's ſhare;
Her modeſt worth the maſter knew,
And ſtrait the fat'ning morſel threw;
Enrag'd, the ſnarling cur awoke,
And thus, with ſpiteful envy, ſpoke.

They only claim a right to eat,
Who earn by ſervices their meat;
Me, zeal and induſtry inflame
To ſcour the fields and ſpring the game,

Or, plunged in the wintry wave,
For man the wounded bird to ſave,
With watchful diligence I keep,
From prowling wolves, his fleecy ſheep;
At home, his midnight hours ſecure,
And drive the robber from the door.
For this, his breaſt with kindneſs glows;
For this, his hand the food beſtows;
And ſhall, thy Indolence impart,
A warmer friendſhip to his heart,
That thus he robs me of my due,
To pamper ſuch vile things as you?
I own (with meekneſs puſs reply'd)
Superior merit on your ſide;
Nor does my breaſt with envy ſwell,
To find it recompenc'd ſo well;
Yet I, in what my nature can,
Contribute to the good of man.
Whoſe claws deſtroy the pilf'ring mouſe?
Who drives the vermin from the houſe?
Or, watchful for the lab'ring ſwain,
From lurking rats ſecure the grain?

From hence if he rewards beſtow,
Why ſhould your heart with gall o'erflow?
Why pine my happineſs to ſee,
Since there's enough for you and me?

Thy words are juſt, the Farmer cry'd,
And ſpurn'd the ſnarler from his ſide.

FABLE X.

THE SPIDER, AND THE BEE.

THE nymph, who walks the public ſtreets,
And ſets her cap at all ſhe meets,
May catch the fool, who turns to ſtare
But men of ſenſe avoid the ſnare.

As on the margin of the flood,
With ſilken line, my Lydia ſtood,
I ſmil'd to ſee the pains you took,
To cover o'er the fraudful hook.
Along the foreſt as we ſtray'd,
You ſaw the boy his lime-twigs ſpread;
Gueſs'd you the reaſon of his fear,
Leſt, heedleſs, we approach'd too near?
For as behind the buſh we lay,
The linnet flutter'd on the ſpray.

Needs there ſuch caution to delude
The ſcaly fry, and feather'd brood?
And think you, with inferior art,
To captivate the human heart?
The maid, who modeſtly conceals
Her beauties, while ſhe hides, reveals,
Give but a glimpſe, and fancy draws,
Whate'er the Grecian Venus was.
From Eve's firſt fig-leaf to brocade,
All dreſs was meant for fancy's aid,
Which evermore delighted dwells
On what the baſhful nymph conceals.

When Celia ſtruts in man's attire,
She ſhews too much to raiſe deſire,
But from the hoop's bewitching round
Her very ſhoe has power to wound.
The roving eye, the boſom bare,
The forward laugh, the wanton air
May catch the fop; for gudgeons ſtrike
At the bare hook, and bait, alike,
While ſalmon play regardleſs by,
'Till art, like nature, forms the fly.

Beneath a peaſant's homely thatch,
A Spider long had held her watch;
From morn to night with reſtleſs care,
She ſpun her web, and wove her ſnare.
Within the limits of her reign,
Lay many a heedleſs captive ſlain,
Or flutt'ring ſtruggled in the toils,
To burſt the chains, and ſhun her wiles.
A ſtraying Bee, that perch'd hard by,
Beheld her with diſdainful eye.
And thus began. Mean thing give o'er,
And lay thy ſlender threads no more;
A thoughtleſs fly, or two at moſt,
Is all the conqueſt thou can'ſt boaſt,
For bees of ſenſe, thy arts evade,
We ſee ſo plain the nets are laid.

The gaudy tulip, that diſplays
Her ſpreading foliage to the gaze,
That points her charms at all ſhe ſees,
And yields to ev'ry wanton breeze,
Attracts not me. Where bluſhing grows,
Guarded with thorns, the modeſt roſe,

Enamour'd, round and round I fly,
Or on her fragrant bofom lie;
Reluctant, fhe my ardor meets,
And bafhful renders up her fweets.

To wifer heads attention lend,
And learn this leffon from a friend.
She, who with modefty retires,
Adds fewel to her lover's fires,
While fuch incautious jilts as you,
By folly your own fchemes undo.

FABLE XI.

THE YOUNG LION, AND THE APE.

'TIS true, I blame your lover's choice,
Tho' flatter'd by the public voice,
And peevifh grow, and fick to hear
His exclamations, O how fair!
I liften not to wild delights,
And tranfports of expected nights;
What is to me your hoard of charms,
The whitenefs of your neck and arms?
Needs there no acquifition more,
To keep contention from the door?
Yes; pafs a fortnight, and you'll find,
All beauty cloys, but of the mind.

Senfe, and good-humour ever prove
The fureft cords to faften love.

Yet, Phillis (ſimpleſt of your ſex)
You never think, but to perplex.
Coquetting it with ev'ry ape,
That ſtruts abroad in human ſhape;
Not that the coxcomb is your taſte,
But that it ſtings your lover's breaſt;
To-morrow you reſign the ſway,
Prepar'd to honour, and obey,
The tyrant-miſtreſs change for life,
To the ſubmiſſion of a wife.
Your follies, if you can, ſuſpend,
And learn inſtruction from a friend.
Reluctant hear the firſt addreſs,
Think often, 'ere you anſwer, yes;
But once reſolv'd, throw off diſguiſe,
And wear your wiſhes in your eyes.
With caution ev'ry look forbear,
That might create one jealous fear.
A lover's rip'ning hopes confound,
Or give the gen'rous breaſt a wound.
Contemn the girliſh arts to teaze,
Nor uſe your pow'r, unleſs to pleaſe;

For fools alone with rigour ſway,
When, ſoon or late, they muſt obey,

The king of brutes, in life's decline,
Reſolv'd dominion to reſign;
The beaſts were ſummon'd to appear,
And bend before the royal heir.
They came; a day was fix'd; the croud
Before their future monarch bow'd.

A dapper Monkey, proud and vain,
Step'd forth, and thus addreſs'd the train.

Why cringe my friends with ſlaviſh awe,
Before this pageant king of ſtraw?
Shall we anticipate the hour,
And 'ere we feel it, own his pow'r?
The counſels of experience prize,
I know the maxims of the wiſe;
Subjection let us caſt away,
And live the monarchs of to-day;
'Tis ours the vacant hand to ſpurn,
And play the tyrant each in turn,

So ſhall he right from wrong diſcern,
And mercy, from oppreſſion learn,
At others woes be taught to melt,
And loath the ills himſelf has felt.

He ſpoke; his boſom ſwell'd with pride,
The youthful Lion thus reply'd.

What madneſs prompts thee to provoke
My wrath, and dare th' impending ſtroke?
Thou wretched fool! can wrongs impart
Compaſſion to the feeling heart?
Or teach the grateful breaſt to glow,
The hand to give, or eye to flow?
Learn'd in the practice of their ſchools,
From women thou haſt drawn thy rules;
To them return, in ſuch a cauſe,
From only ſuch expect applauſe;
The partial ſex I don't condemn,
For liking thoſe, who copy them.

Would'ſt thou the gen'rous lion bind,
By kindneſs bribe him to be kind;
Good offices their likeneſs get,
And payment leſſens not the debt;

With multiplying hand he gives
The good from others he receives;
Or for the bad makes fair return,
And pays with int'reſt, ſcorn for ſcorn.

FABLE XII.

THE COLT, AND THE FARMER.

TELL me, Corinna, if you can,
Why ſo averſe, ſo coy to man?
Did nature, laviſh of her care,
From her beſt pattern form you fair,
That you ungrateful to her cauſe,
Should mock her gifts and ſpurn her laws?
And miſer-like, with-hold that ſtore,
Which, by imparting, bleſſes more?
Beauty's a gift, by heaven aſſign'd,
The portion of the female kind;
For this the yielding maid demands
Protection at her lover's hands;
And tho' by waſting years it fade,
Remembrance tells him, once 'twas paid.

And will you then this wealth conceal,
For age to ruſt, or time to ſteal?
The ſummer of your youth to rove,
A ſtranger to the joys of love?
Then, when life's winter haſtens on,
And youth's fair heritage is gone,
Dow'rleſs to court ſome peaſant's arms,
To guard your wither'd age from harms?
No gratitude to warm his breaſt,
For blooming beauty, once poſſeſs'd;
How will you curſe that ſtubborn pride,
Which drove your bark acroſs the tide,
And ſailing before folly's wind,
Left ſenſe and happineſs behind?

Corinna, leſt theſe whims prevail,
To ſuch as you, I write my tale.

A Colt, for blood and mettled ſpeed,
The choiceſt of the running breed,
Of youthful ſtrength, and beauty vain,
Refus'd ſubjection to the rein;
In vain the groom's officious ſkill
Oppos'd his pride, and check'd his will;

In vain the maſter's forming care
Reſtrain'd with threats, or ſooth'd with pray'r;
Of freedom proud, and ſcorning man,
Wild o'er the ſpacious plains he ran.
Where e'er luxuriant nature ſpread
Her flow'ry carpet o'er the mead,
Or bubbling ſtreams, ſoft-gliding paſs,
To cool and freſhen up the graſs,
Diſdaining bounds, he crop'd the blade,
And wanton'd in the ſpoil he made.

In plenty thus the ſummer paſs'd,
Revolving winter came at laſt;
The trees no more a ſhelter yield,
The verdure withers from the field,
Perpetual ſnows inveſt the ground,
In icy chains the ſtreams are bound,
Cold, nipping winds, and rattling hail
His lank, unſhelter'd ſides aſſail.

As round he caſt his rueful eyes,
He ſaw the thatch-roof'd cottage riſe;
The proſpect touch'd his heart with cheer,
And promis'd kind deliv'rance near.

A ſtable, erſt his ſcorn, and hate,
Was now become his wiſh'd retreat;
His paſſion cool, his pride forgot,
A Farmer's welcome yard he ſought.

The maſter ſaw his woeful plight,
His limbs, that totter'd with his weight,
And friendly to the ſtable led.
And ſaw him litter'd, dreſs'd, and fed.
In ſlothful eaſe, all night he lay;
The ſervants roſe at break of day;
The market calls. Along the road
His back muſt bear the pond'rous load;
In vain he ſtruggles, or complains,
Inceſſant blows reward his pains.
To-morrow varies but his toil;
Chain'd to the plough, he breaks the ſoil;
While ſcanty meals at night repay
The painful labours of the day.

Subdu'd by toil, with anguiſh rent,
His ſelf-upbraidings found a vent.
Wretch that I am! he ſighing ſaid
By arrogance, and folly led;

Had but my reſtive youth been brought
To learn the leſſon nature taught,
Then had I, like my ſires of yore,
The prize from ev'ry courſer bore;
While man, beſtow'd rewards, and praiſe,
And females crown'd my latter days.
Now laſting ſervitude's my lot,
My birth contemn'd, my ſpeed forgot,
Doom'd am I, for my pride to bear
A living death, from year to year.

FABLE XIII.

THE OWL, AND THE NIGHTINGALE.

TO know the miſtreſs' humour right,
See if her maids are clean and tight,
If Betty waits without her ſtays,
She copies but her ladies ways.
When miſs comes in with boiſt'rous ſhout,
And drops no court'ſey, going out,
Depend upon't, mamma is one,
Who reads, or drinks too much alone.

If bottled beer her thirſt aſſwage,
She feels enthuſiaſtic rage,
And burns with ardor to inherit
The gifts and workings of the ſpirit.
If learning crack her giddy brains,
No remedy, but death remains.

Sum up the various ills of life,
And all are ſweet to ſuch a wife.
At home, ſuperior wit ſhe vaunts,
And twits her huſband with his wants;
Her ragged offspring all around,
Like pigs, are wallowing on the ground.
Impatient ever of controul,
And knows no order but of ſoul;
With books her litter'd floor is ſpread
Of nameleſs authors, never read;
Foul linen, petticoats, and lace
Fill up the intermediate ſpace.
Abroad, at viſitings, her tongue
Is never ſtill, and always wrong,
All meanings ſhe defines away,
And ſtands, with truth and ſenſe, at bay.

If e'er ſhe meets a gentle heart,
Skill'd in the houſewife's uſeful art,
Who makes her family her care,
And builds contentment's temple there,
She ſtarts at ſuch miſtakes in nature,
And cries, lord help us!—what a creature!

Melissa, if the moral strike,
You'll find the fable not unlike.

An Owl, puff'd up with self-conceit,
Lov'd learning better than his meat;
Old manuscripts he treasur'd up,
And rummag'd ev'ry grocer's shop;
At pastry-cooks was known to ply,
And strip, for science, every pye.
For modern poetry and wit,
He had read all that Blackmore writ.
So intimate with Curl was grown,
His learned treasures were his own,
To all his authors had access,
And sometimes would correct the press.
In logic he acquir'd such knowledge,
You'd swear him fellow of a college.
Alike to ev'ry art and science,
His daring genius bid defiance.
And swallow'd wisdom, with that haste,
That cits do custard at a feast.

Within the shelter of a wood,
One ev'ning, as he musing stood,

Hard by, upon a leafy ſpray,
A Nightingale began his lay.
Sudden he ſtarts, with anger ſtung,
And ſcreeching interrupts the ſong.

Pert, buſy thing, thy airs give o'er,
And let my contemplations ſoar.
What is the muſic of thy voice,
But jarring diſſonance and noiſe?
Be wiſe. True harmony thou'lt find,
Not in the throat, but in the mind;
By empty chirping not attain'd,
But by laborious ſtudy gain'd.
Go read the authors, Pope explodes,
Fathom the depth of Cibber's odes.
With modern plays improve thy wit,
Read all the learning, Henley writ,
And if thou needs muſt ſing, ſing then,
And emulate the ways of men:
So ſhalt thou grow, like me, refin'd,
And bring improvement to thy kind.

Thou wretch, the little warbler cry'd,
Made up of ignorance and pride,

Aſk all the birds, and they'll declare,
A greater blockhead wings not air.
Read o'er thyſelf, thy talents ſcan,
Science was only meant for man.
No ſenſeleſs authors me moleſt,
I mind the duties of my neſt,
With careful wing protect my young,
And chear their ev'nings with a ſong.
Make ſhort the weary trav'ler's way,
And warble in the poet's lay.

Thus, following nature, and her laws,
From men and birds I claim applauſe,
While nurs'd in pedantry and ſloth,
An Owl is ſcorn'd alike by both.

FABLE XIV.

THE SPARROW, AND THE DOVE.

IT was, as learn'd traditions ſay,
Upon an April's blithſome day,
When pleaſure, ever on the wing,
Return'd, companion of the ſpring,
And chear'd the birds with am'rous heat,
Inſtructing little hearts to beat;
A ſparrow, frolick, gay, and young,
Of bold addreſs, and flippant tongue,
Juſt left his lady of a night,
Like him, to follow new delight.

The youth, of many a conqueſt vain,
Flew off to ſeek the chirping train;
The chirping train he quickly found,
And with a ſaucy eaſe, bow'd round.

For every ſhe his boſom burns,
And this, and that he woes by turns;
And here a ſigh, and there a bill,
And here——thoſe eyes! ſo form'd to kill!
And now with ready tongue, he ſtrings
Unmeaning, ſoft, reſiſtleſs things;
With vows, and dem—me's ſkill'd to woo,
As other pretty fellows do.
Not that he thought this ſhort eſſay
A prologue needful to his play;
No, truſt me, ſays our learned letter,
He knew the virtuous ſex much better;
But theſe he held as ſpecious arts,
To ſhew his own ſuperior parts,
The form of decency to ſhield,
And give a juſt pretence to yield.

Thus finiſhing his courtly play,
He mark'd the fav'rite of a day;
With careleſs impudence drew near,
And whiſper'd Hebrew in her ear;
A hint, which like the maſon's ſign,
The conſcious can alone divine.

The fluttering nymph, expert at feigning,
Cry'd, Sir!—pray Sir, explain your meaning—
Go prate to those that may endure ye——
To me this rudeness!——I'll assure ye!——
Then off she glided, like a swallow,
As saying——you guess where to follow.

To such as know the party set,
'Tis needless to declare they met;
The parson's barn, as authors mention,
Confess'd the fair had apprehension.
Her honour there secure from stain,
She held all farther trifling vain,
No more affected to be coy,
But rush'd, licentious, on the joy.

Hist, love! the male companion cry'd,
Retire a while, I fear we're spy'd;
Nor was the caution vain; he saw
A Turtle, rustling in the straw,
While o'er her callow brood she hung,
And fondly thus address'd her young.

Ye tender objects of my care!
Peace, peace, ye little helpless pair;

Anon he comes, your gentle ſire,
And brings you all your hearts require.
For us, his infants and his bride,
For us, with only love to guide,
Our lord aſſumes an eagle's ſpeed,
And like a lion, dares to bleed.
Nor yet by wint'ry ſkies confin'd,
He mounts upon the rudeſt wind,
From danger tears the vital ſpoil,
And with affection ſweetens toil.
Ah ceaſe, too vent'rous! ceaſe to dare,
In thine, our dearer ſafety ſpare,
From him, ye cruel falcons ſtray,
And turn, ye fowlers, far away!

Should I ſurvive to ſee the day,
That tears me from myſelf away,
That cancels all that heav'n could give,
The life, by which alone, I live,
Alas, how more than loſt were I,
Who, in the thought, already die!

Ye pow'rs, whom men and birds obey,
Great rulers of your creatures, ſay,

Why mourning comes, by bliſs convey'd,
And ev'n the ſweets of love allay'd?
Where grows enjoyment, tall, and fair,
Around it twines entangling care;
While fear, for what our ſouls poſſeſs,
Enervates ev'ry pow'r to bleſs;
Yet friendſhip forms the bliſs above,
And, life! what art thou, without love?
Our hero, who had heard apart,
Felt ſomething moving in his heart,
But quickly, with diſdain, ſuppreſs'd
The virtue, riſing in his breaſt;
And firſt he feign'd to laugh aloud,
And next, approaching, ſmil'd and bow'd.

Madam, you muſt not think me rude;
Good manners never can intrude;
I vow I came thro' pure good nature!
(Upon my ſoul a charming creature)
Are theſe the comforts of a wife?
This careful, cloiſter'd, moaping life?
No doubt, that odious thing, call'd duty
Is a ſweet province for a beauty.

Thou pretty ignorance! thy will
Is meaſur'd to thy want of ſkill;
That good old-faſhion'd dame, thy mother,
Has taught thy infant years no other—
The greateſt ill in the creation
Is ſure the want of education.

But think ye?—tell me without feigning,
Have all theſe charms no farther meaning?
Dame nature, if you don't forget her,
Might teach your ladyſhip much better.
For ſhame, reject this mean employment,
Enter the world, and taſte enjoyment;
Where time, by circling bliſs, we meaſure;
Beauty was form'd alone for pleaſure;
Come, prove the bleſſing, follow me,
Be wiſe, be happy, and be free.

Kind Sir, reply'd our matron chaſte,
Your zeal ſeems pretty much in haſte;
I own, the fondneſs to be bleſs'd,
Is a deep thirſt in ev'ry breaſt;
Of bleſſings too I have my ſtore,
Yet quarrel not, ſhould heav'n give more;

Then prove the change to be expedient,
And think me, Sir, your moſt obedient.
Here turning, as to one inferior,
Our gallant ſpoke, and ſmil'd ſuperior.
Methinks, to quit your boaſted ſtation
Requires a world of heſitation,
Where brats, and bonds are held a bleſſing,
The caſe, I doubt, is paſt redreſſing,
Why, child, ſuppoſe the joys I mention,
Were the mere fruits of my invention,
You've cauſe ſufficient for your carriage,
In flying from the curſe of marriage;
That ſly decoy, with vary'd ſnares.
That takes your widgeons in by pairs;
Alike to huſband, and to wife,
The cure of love, and bane of life;
The only method of forecaſting,
To make misfortune firm, and laſting;
The ſin, by heav'n's peculiar ſentence,
Unpardon'd, thro' a life's repentance.
It is the double ſnake, that weds
A common tail to diff'rent heads,

That leads the carcaſs ſtill aſtray,
By dragging each a diff'rent way.
Of all the ills, that may attend me,
From marriage, mighty gods, defend me!

Give me frank nature's wild demeſne,
And boundleſs tract of air ſerene,
Where fancy, ever wing'd for change,
Delights to ſport, delights to range;
There, Liberty! to thee is owing
Whate'er of bliſs is worth beſtowing,
Delights, ſtill vary'd, and divine,
Sweet goddeſs of the hills are thine.

What ſay you now, you pretty pink you?
Have I, for once, ſpoke reaſon, think you?
You take me now for no romancer——
Come, never ſtudy for an anſwer;
Away, caſt ev'ry care behind ye,
And fly where joy alone ſhall find you.

Soft yet, return'd our female fencer,
A queſtion more, or ſo——and then Sir.

You've rally'd me with ſenſe exceeding,
With much fine wit, and better breeding;
But pray Sir, how do you contrive it?
Do thoſe of your world never wive it?
" No, no,"—How then?—" Why dare I tell
" What does the buſineſs full as well."
Do you ne'er love?—" An hour at leiſure."
Have you no friendſhips?——" Yes, for pleaſure."
No care for little ones?—" We get 'em,
" The reſt the mothers mind—and let 'em."

Thou wretch, rejoin'd the kindling dove,
Quite loſt to life, as loſt to love!
Whene'er misfortune comes, how juſt!
And come misfortune ſurely muſt;
In the dread ſeaſon of diſmay,
In that your hour of trial, ſay,
Who then ſhall prop your ſinking heart,
Who bear affliction's weightier part.

Say, when the black-brow'd welkin bends.
And winter's gloomy ſtorm impends,
To mourning turns all tranſient cheer,
And blaſts the melancholy year;

For times at no perſuaſion, ſtay,
Nor vice can find perpetual May;
Then where's that tongue, by folly led,
That ſoul of pertneſs, whither fled?
All ſhrunk within thy lonely neſt,
Forlorn, abandon'd, and unbleſs'd;
No friends, by cordial bonds ally'd,
Shall ſeek thy cold, unſocial ſide,
No chirping pratlers to delight,
Shall turn the long-enduring night,
No bride her words of balm impart,
And warm thee at her conſtant heart.

Freedom, reſtrain'd by reaſon's force,
Is as the ſun' unvarying courſe,
Benignly active, ſweetly bright,
Affording warmth, affording light;
But torn from virtue's ſacred rules,
Becomes a comet, gaz'd by fools.
Foreboding cares, and ſtorms, and ſtrife,
And fraught with all the plagues of life.

Thou fool! by union ev'ry creature
Subſiſts, thro' univerſal nature;

And this, to beings void of mind,
Is wedlock, of a meaner kind.

While womb'd in ſpace, primæval clay
A yet unfaſhion'd embryo lay,
The ſource of endleſs good above
Shot down his ſpark of kindling love;
Touch'd by the all-enliv'ning flame,
Then motion firſt exulting came,
Each atom ſought its ſep'rate claſs,
Thro' many a fair enamour'd maſs,
Love caſt the central charm around,
And with eternal nuptials bound.
Then form, and order o'er the ſky,
Firſt train'd their bridal pomp on high,
The ſun diſplay'd his orb to ſight,
And burn'd with hymeneal light.

Hence nature's virgin womb conceiv'd,
And with the genial burthen heav'd;
Forth came the oak, her firſt-born heir,
And ſcal'd the breathing ſteep of air;
Then infant ſtems, of various uſe,
Imbib'd her ſoft, maternal juice,

The flow'rs, in early bloom diſclos'd,
Upon her fragrant breaſt repos'd;
Within her warm embraces grew
A race of endleſs form, and hue;
Then pour'd her leſſer offspring round,
And fondly cloth'd their parent ground.

Nor here alone the virtue reign'd,
By matter's cumb'ring form detain'd,
But thence, ſubliming, and refin'd,
Aſpir'd, and reach'd its kindred mind.
Caught in the fond celeſtial fire,
The mind perceiv'd unknown deſire,
And now with kind effuſion flow'd,
And now with cordial ardours glow'd,
Beheld the ſympathetic fair,
And lov'd its own reſemblance there;
On all with circling radiance ſhone,
But cent'ring, fix'd on one alone;
There claſp'd the heav'n appointed wife,
And doubled every joy of life.

Here ever bleſſing, ever bleſs'd,
Reſides this beauty of the breaſt.

As from his palace, here the god
Still beams effulgent bliſs abroad,
Here gems his own eternal round,
The ring, by which the world is bound,
Here bids his ſeat of empire grow,
And builds his little heav'n below.

The bridal partners thus ally'd,
And thus in ſweet accordance ty'd,
One body, heart and ſpirit live,
Enrich'd by ev'ry joy they give;
Like echo, from her vocal hold,
Return'd in muſic twenty fold.
Their union firm, and undecay'd,
Nor time can ſhake, nor pow'r invade,
But as the ſtem, and ſcion ſtand,
Ingrafted by a ſkilful hand,
They check the tempeſt's wint'ry rage,
And bloom and ſtrengthen into age.
A thouſand amities unknown,
And pow'rs, perceiv'd by love alone,
Endearing looks, and chaſte deſire,
Fan and ſupport the mutual fire,

Whoſe flame, perpetual, as refin'd,
Is fed by an immortal mind.

Nor yet the nuptial ſanction ends,
Like Nile it opens and deſcends,
Which, by apparent windings led,
We trace to its celeſtial head.
The ſire, firſt ſpringing from above,
Becomes the ſource of life and love,
And gives his filial heir to flow,
In fondneſs down on ſons below;
Thus roll'd in one continu'd tide,
To time's extremeſt verge they glide,
While kindred ſtreams, on either hand,
Branch forth in bleſſings o'er the land.

Thee, wretch! no liſping babe ſhall name,
No late-returning brother claim,
No kinſman on thy road rejoice,
No ſiſter greet thy ent'ring voice,
With partial eyes no parents ſee,
And bleſs their years, reſtor'd in thee.

In age rejected, or declin'd,
An alien, even among thy kind,

The partner of thy ſcorn'd embrace,
Shall play the wanton in thy face,
Each ſpark unplume thy little pride,
All friendſhip fly thy faithleſs ſide,
Thy name ſhall like thy carcaſs rot,
In ſickneſs ſpurn'd, in death forgot.

All giving pow'r! great ſource of life!
O hear the parent! hear the wife!
That life, thou lendeſt from above,
Tho' little, makes it large in love;
O bid my feeling heart expand
To ev'ry claim, on ev'ry hand,
To thoſe, from whom my days I drew,
To theſe, in whom thoſe days renew,
To all my kin, however wide,
In cordial warmth, as blood ally'd,
To friends with ſteely fetters twin'd,
And to the cruel, not unkind.
But chief, the lord of my deſire,
My life, my ſelf, my ſoul, my fire,
Friends, children, all that wiſh can claim,
Chaſte paſſion claſp, and rapture name;

O ſpare him, ſpare him, gracious pow'r!
O give him to my lateſt hour!
Let me my length of life employ,
To give my ſole enjoyment joy,
His love, let mutual love excite,
Turn all my cares to his delight,
And ev'ry needleſs bleſſing ſpare,
Wherein my darling wants a ſhare.

When he with graceful action wooes,
And ſweetly bills, and fondly cooes,
Ah! deck me to his eyes alone,
With charms attractive as his own.
And in my circling wings careſs'd,
Give all the lover to my breaſt.
Then in our chaſte, connubial bed,
My boſom pillow'd for his head,
His eyes, with bliſsful ſlumbers cloſe,
And watch, with me, my lord's repoſe,
Your peace around his temples twine,
And love him with a love like mine.

And, for I know his gen'rous flame,
Beyond whate'er my ſex can claim,

Me too to your protection take,
And ſpare me for my huſband's ſake;
Let one unruffled calm delight
The loving, and belov'd unite,
One pure deſire our boſoms warm,
One will direct, one wiſh inform;
Thro' life, one mutual aid ſuſtain,
In death, one peaceful grave contain.

While, ſwelling with the darling theme,
Her accents pour'd an endleſs ſtream,
The well-known wings a ſound impart,
That reach'd her ear, and touch'd her heart:
Quick dropp'd the muſic of her tongue,
And forth with eager joy ſhe ſprung.
As ſwift her ent'ring conſort flew,
And plum'd and kindled at the view;

Their wings, their ſouls embracing meet,
Their hearts with anſw'ring meaſure beat;
Half loſt in ſacred ſweets, and bleſs'd
With raptures felt, but ne'er expreſs'd.

Strait to her humble roof ſhe led
The partner of her ſpotleſs bed;

Her young, a flutt'ring pair, arise,
Their welcome sparkling in their eyes,
Transported, to their sire they bound,
And hang with speechless action round.
In pleasure wrapt, the parents stand,
And see their little wings expand;
The sire, his life sustaining prize
To each expecting bill applies,
There fondly pours the wheaten spoil,
With transport giv'n, tho' won with toil;
While all collected at the sight
And silent thro' supreme delight,
The fair high heav'n of bliss beguiles,
And on her lord, and infants smiles.

The Sparrow, whose attention hung
Upon the Dov's enchanting tongue,
Of all his little slights disarm'd,
And from himself, by virtue, charm'd,
When now he saw, what only seem'd,
A fact, so late a fable deem'd,
His soul to envy he resign'd,
His hours of folly to the wind,

In ſecret wiſh'd a turtle too,
And ſighing to himſelf, withdrew.

FABLE XV.

THE FEMADE SEDUCERS.

'TIS ſaid of widow, maid, and wife,
That honour is a woman's life;
Unhappy ſex! who only claim
A being in the breath of fame,
Which tainted, not the quick'ning gales,
That ſweep Sabæa's ſpicy vales,
Nor all the healing ſweets reſtore,
That breathe along Arabia's ſhore.

The trav'ler, if he chance to ſtray,
May turn uncenſur'd to his way;
Polluted ſtreams again are pure,
And deepeſt wounds admit a cure;
But woman! no redemption knows,
The wounds of honour never cloſe.

Tho' diſtant ev'ry hand to guide,
Nor ſkill'd on life's tempeſtuous tide,
If once her feeble bark recede,
Or deviate from the courſe decreed,
In vain ſhe ſeeks the friendly ſhore,
Her ſwifter folly flies before;
The circling ports againſt her clóſe,
And ſhut the wand'rer from repoſe,
'Till by conflicting waves oppreſt,
Her found'ring pinnace ſinks to reſt.

Are there no off'rings to atone
For but a ſingle error?——None.
Tho' woman is avow'd of old,
No daughter of celeſtial mould,
Her temp'ring not without allay,
And form'd but of the finer clay,
We challenge from the mortal dame,
The ſtrength angelic natures claim;
Nay more; for ſacred ſtories tell,
That ev'n immortal angels fell.

Whatever fills the teeming ſphere
Of humid earth, and ambient air,

With varying elements endu'd,
Was form'd to fall. aad riſe renew'd.

The ſtars no fix'd duration know,
Wide oceans ebb, again to flow,
The moon repletes her waining face,
All-beauteous, from her late diſgrace,
And ſuns, that mourn approaching night,
Refulgent riſe, with new-born light.

In vain may death, and time ſubdue,
While nature mints her race anew,
And holds ſome vital ſpark apart,
Like virtue, hid in ev'ry heart;
'Tis hence, reviving warmth is ſeen,
To cloath a naked world in green.
No longer barr'd by winter's cold,
Again the gates of life unfold:
Again each inſect tries his wing,
And lifts freſh pinions on the ſpring;
Again from ev'ry latent root
The bladed ſtem, and tendril ſhoot,
Exhaling incenſe to the ſkies,
Again to periſh, and to riſe.

And muſt weak woman then diſown
The change to which a world is prone?
In one meridian brightneſs ſhine
And ne'er like ev'ning ſuns decline?
Reſolv'd and firm alone?——————Is this
What we demand of woman!—Yes.

But ſhould the ſpark of veſtal fire,
In ſome unguarded hour expire,
Or ſhould the nightly thief invade
Heſperia's chaſte, and ſacred ſhade,
Of all the blooming ſpoils poſſeſs'd,
The dragon honour charm'd to reſt,
Shall virtue's flame no more return?
No more with virgin ſplendor burn?
No more the ravag'd garden blow
With ſpring's ſucceeding bloſſom?—No.
Pity may mourn, but not reſtore,
And woman falls———to riſe no more.

Within this ſublunary ſphere,
A country lies———no matter where;

The clime may readily be found,
By all, who tread poetic ground.
A ſtream, call'd life, acroſs it glides,
And equally the land divides;
And here, of vice the province lies,
And there, the hills of virtue riſe.

Upon a mountain's airy ſtand,
Whoſe ſummit look'd to either land,
An antient pair their dwelling choſe,
As well for proſpect, as repoſe;
For mutual faith they long were fam'd,
And Temp'rance, and Religion, nam'd.

A num'rous progeny divine,
Confeſs'd the honours of their line;
But in a little daughter fair,
Was center'd more than half their care;
For heav'n to gratulate her birth,
Gave ſigns of future joy to earth;
White was the robe this infant wore,
And chaſtity the name ſhe bore.

As now the maid in ſtature grew,
(A flow'r juſt op'ning to the view)

Oft' thro' her native lawns ſhe ſtray'd,
And wreſtling with the lambkins play'd,
Her looks diffuſive ſweets bequeath'd,
The breeze grew purer as ſhe breath'd,
The morn her radiant bluſh aſſum'd,
The ſpring with earlier fragrance bloom'd,
And nature, yearly, took delight,
Like her, to dreſs the world in white.

But when her riſing form was ſeen,
To reach the criſis of fifteen,
Her parents up the mountain's head,
With anxious ſtep their darling led;
By turns they ſnatch'd her to their breaſt,
And thus the fears of age expreſs'd.

O joyful cauſe of many a care!
O daughter, too divinely fair!
Yon world, on this important day,
Demands thee to a dang'rous way;
A painful journey, all muſt go,
Whoſe doubted period none can know,
Whoſe due direction who can find,
Where reaſon's mute, and ſenſe is blind?

Ah, what unequal leaders these,
Thro' such a wide, perplexing maze!
Then mark the warnings of the wise,
And learn, what love and years advise.

Far to the right thy prospect bend,
Where yonder tow'ring hills ascend;
Lo, there the arduous path's in view,
Which virtue and her sons pursue;
With toil o'er less'ning earth they rise,
And gain, and gain upon the skies.
Narrow's the way her children tread,
No walk for pleasure smoothly spread,
But rough, and difficult, and steep,
Painful to climb, and hard to keep.

Fruits immature those lands dispense,
A food indelicate to sense,
Of taste unpleasant, yet from those
Pure health, with chearful vigour flows,
And strength, unfeeling of decay,
Throughout the long, laborious way.

Hence, as they scale that heav'nly road,
Each limb is lighten'd of its load;

From earth refining ſtill they go
And leave the mortal weight below.
Then ſpreads the ſtrait, the doubtful clears,
And ſmooth the rugged path appears,
For cuſtom turns fatigue to eaſe,
And, taught by virtue, pain can pleaſe.

At length, the toilſome journey o'er,
And near the bright, celeſtial ſhore,
A gulph, black, fearful, and profound,
Appears, of either world the bound.
Thro' darkneſs, leading up to light,
Senſe backward ſhrinks, and ſhuns the ſight,
For there the tranſitory train,
Of time, and form, and care, and pain,
And matter's groſs, incumb'ring maſs,
Man's late aſſociates, cannot paſs,
But ſinking, quit the immortal charge,
And leave the wond'ring ſoul at large;
Lightly ſhe wings her obvious way,
And mingles with eternal day.

Thither, O thither wing thy ſpeed,
Tho' pleaſure charm, or pain impede;

To ſuch th' all-bounteous pow'r has giv'n,
For preſent earth, a future heav'n;
For trivial loſs, unmeaſur'd gain,
And endleſs bliſs, for tranſient pain.
Then fear, ah! fear to turn thy ſight,
Where yonder flow'ry fields invite;
Wide on the left the path-way bends,
And with pernicious eaſe deſcends;
There ſweet to ſenſe, and fair to ſhow,
New-planted Edens ſeem to blow,
Trees, that delicious poiſon bear,
For death is vegetable there.

Hence is the frame of health unbrac'd,
Each ſinew ſlack'ning at the taſte,
The ſoul to paſſion yields her throne,
And ſees with organs not her own;
While, like the ſlumb'rer in the night,
Pleas'd with the ſhadowy dream of light,
Before her alienated eyes,
The ſcenes of fairy-land ariſe;
The puppet-world's amuſing ſhow,
Dipt in the gayly-colour'd bow,

Scepters, and wreaths, and glitt'ring things,
The toys of infants, and of kings,
That tempt along the baneful plain,
The idly wiſe, and lightly vain,
'Till verging on the gulphy ſhore,
Sudden they ſink, and riſe no more.

But liſt to what thy fates declare,
Tho' thou art woman, frail as fair,
If once thy ſliding foot ſhould ſtray,
Once quit yon heav'n appointed way,
For thee, loſt maid, for thee alone,
Nor pray'rs ſhall plead, nor tears attone;
Reproach, ſcorn, infamy, and hate,
On thy returning ſteps ſhall wait.
Thy form be loath'd by ev'ry eye,
And ev'ry foot thy preſence fly.

Thus arm'd with words of potent ſound,
Like guardian-angels plac'd around,
A charm, by truth divinely caſt,
Forward our young advent'rer paſs'd.
Forth from her ſacred Eye-lids ſent,
Like morn, fore-running radiance went,

While honour, hand-maid late aſſign'd,
Upheld her lucid train behind.

Awe-ſtruck the much admiring croud
Before the virgin viſion bow'd,
Gaz'd with an ever new delight,
And caught freſh virtue at the ſight;
For not of earth's unequal frame
They deem'd the heav'n-compounded dame,
If matter, ſure the moſt refin'd,
High-wrought, and temper'd into mind,
Some darling daughter of the day,
And body'd by her native ray.

Where-e'er ſhe paſſes, thouſands bend,
And thouſands, where ſhe moves, attend,
Her ways obſervant eyes confeſs,
Her ſteps purſuing praiſes bleſs;
While to the elevated maid
Oblations, as to heav'n, are paid.

'Twas on an ever-blithſome day,
The jovial birth of roſy May,
When genial warmth, no more ſuppreſs'd,
New melts the froſt in ev'ry breaſt,

The cheek with ſecret fluſhing dyes,
And looks kind things from chaſteſt eyes;
The ſun with healthier viſage glows,
Aſide his clouded kerchief throws,
And dances up th' etherial plain,
Where late he us'd to climb with pain,
While nature, as from bonds ſet free,
Springs out, and gives a looſe to glee.

And now for momentary reſt,
The nymph her travel'd ſtep repreſs'd,
Juſt turn'd to view the ſtage attain'd,
And glory'd in the height ſhe gain'd.

Out-ſtretch'd before her wide ſurvey,
The realms of ſweet perdition lay,
And pity touch'd her ſoul with woe,
To ſee a world ſo loſt below;
When ſtrait the breeze began to breathe
Airs, gently wafted from beneath,
That bore commiſſion'd witchcraft thence,
And reach'd her ſympathy of ſenſe;
No ſounds of diſcord, that diſcloſe
A people ſunk, and loſt in woes.

But as of preſent good poſſeſs'd,
The very triumph of the bleſs'd.
The Maid in wrapt attention hung,
While thus approaching Sirens ſung.

Hither, faireſt, hither haſte,
Brighteſt beauty, come and taſte
What the pow'rs of bliſs unfold,
Joys, too mighty to be told;
Taſte what extaſies they give,
Dying raptures taſte, and live.

In thy lap, diſdaining meaſure,
Nature empties all her treaſure,
Soft deſires, that ſweetly languiſh,
Fierce delights, that riſe to anguiſh;
Faireſt, doſt thou yet delay?
Brighteſt beauty come away.

Liſt not, when the froward chide,
Sons of pedantry, and pride,
Snarlers, to whoſe feeble ſenſe,
April ſunſhine is offence;
Age and envy will adviſe
Ev'n againſt the joys they prize.

Come, in pleaſure's balmy bowl,
Slake the thirſtings of thy ſoul,
'Till thy raptur'd pow'rs are fainting
With enjoyment, paſt the painting;
Faireſt, doſt thou yet delay?
Brighteſt beauty, come away.

So ſung the Sirens, as of yore,
Upon the falſe Auſonian ſhore;
And, O! for that preventing chain,
That bound Ulyſſes on the main,
That ſo our Fair One might withſtand
The covert ruin now at hand.

The ſong her charm'd attention drew,
When now the tempters ſtood in view;
Curioſity with prying eyes,
And hands of buſy, bold emprize;
Like Hermes, feather'd were her feet,
And, like fore-running fancy fleet,
By ſearch untaught, by toil untir'd,
To novelty ſhe ſtill aſpir'd,
Taſteleſs of ev'ry good poſſeſs'd,
And but in expectation bleſs'd,

With her, aſſociate, Pleaſure came,
Gay Pleaſure, frolic-loving dame,
Her mien, all ſwimming in delight,
Her beauties, half reveal'd to ſight;
Looſe flow'd her garments from the ground,
And caught the kiſſing winds around.
As erſt Meduſa's looks were known
To turn beholders into ſtone,
A dire reverſion here they felt,
And in the eye of pleaſure melt.
Her glance with ſweet perſuaſion charm'd,
Unnerv'd the ſtrong, the ſteel'd diſarm'd;
No ſafety ev'n the flying find,
Who vent'rous, look but once behind.

Thus was the much admiring Maid,
While diſtant, more than half betray'd.
With ſmiles, and adulation bland,
They join'd her ſide, and ſeiz'd her hand;
Their touch envenom'd ſweets inſtill'd,
Her frame with new pulſations thrill'd,
While half conſenting, half denying,
Reluctant now, and now complying,

Amidſt a war of hopes, and fears,
Of trembling wiſhes, ſmiling tears,
Still down, and down, the winning Pair
Compell'd the ſtruggling, yielding Fair.

As when ſome ſtately veſſel bound,
To bleſt Arabia's diſtant ground,
Borne from her courſes, haply lights
Where Barca's flow'ry clime invites,
Conceal'd around whoſe treach'rous land,
Lurks the dire rock, and dang'rous ſand;
The pilot warns with ſail and oar,
To ſhun the much ſuſpected ſhore,
In vain; the tide too ſubtly ſtrong,
Still bears the wreſtling bark along,
Till found'ring, ſhe reſigns to fate,
And ſinks, o'erwhelm'd, with all her freight.

So, baffling ev'ry bar to ſin,
And heav'n's own pilot, plac'd within,
Along the devious ſmooth deſcent,
With pow'rs increaſing as they went,
The Dames accuſtom'd to ſubdue,
As with a rapid current drew,

And o'er the fatal bounds convey'd
The loſt, the long reluctant Maid.

Here ſtop, ye fair ones, and beware,
Nor ſend your fond affections there;
Yet, yet your darling, now deplor'd,
May turn, to you, and heav'n, reſtor'd;
Till then, with weeping honour wait,
The ſervant of her better fate,
With honour, left upon the ſhore,
Her friend, and handmaid now no more;
Nor, with the guilty world, upbraid
The fortunes of a wretch, betray'd,
But o'er her failing caſt a veil,
Rememb'ring, you yourſelves are frail.
And now from all-enquiring light,
Faſt fled the conſcious ſhades of night,
The Damſel, from a ſhort repoſe,
Confounded at her plight, aroſe.

As when, with ſlumb'rous weight oppreſs'd,
Some wealthy miſer ſinks to reſt,
Where felons eye the glitt'ring prey,
And ſteal his hoard of joys away;

He, borne where golden Indus ſtreams,
Of pearl, and quarry'd di'mond dreams,
Like Midas, turns the glebe to ore,
And ſtands all wrapt amidſt his ſtore,
But wakens, naked, and deſpoil'd
Of that, for which his years had toil'd.

So far'd the Nymph, her treaſure flown,
And turn'd, like Niobe, to ſtone,
Within, without, obſcure, and void,
She felt all ravag'd, all deſtroy'd.
And, O thou curs'd, inſidious coaſt!
Are theſe the bleſſings thou canſt boaſt?
Theſe, virtue! theſe the joys they find,
Who leave thy heav'n-topt hills behind?
Shade me ye pines, ye caverns hide,
Ye mountains cover me, ſhe cry'd!

Her trumpet Slander rais'd on high,
And told the tidings to the ſky;
Contempt, diſcharg'd a living dart,
A ſide-long viper to her heart;
Reproach breath'd poiſons o'er her face,
And ſoil'd, and blaſted ev'ry grace;

Officious Shame, her handmaid new,
Still turn'd the mirror to her view,
While thoſe in crimes the deepeſt dy'd,
Approach'd to whiten at her ſide,
And ev'ry lewd, inſulting dame
Upon her folly roſe to fame.

What ſhould ſhe do? Attempt once more
To gain the late-deſerted ſhore?
So truſting, back the Mourner flew,
As faſt the train of fiends purſue.

Again, the farther ſhore's attain'd,
Again the land of virtue gain'd;
But echo, gathers in the wind;
And ſhows her inſtant foes behind.
Amaz'd, with headlong ſpeed ſhe tends,
Where late ſhe left an hoſt of friends;
Alas! thoſe ſhrinking friends decline,
Nor longer own that form divine,
With fear they mark the following cry,
And from the lonely Trembler fly,
Or backward drive her on the coaſt,
Where peace was wreck'd and honour loſt.

From earth, thus hoping aid in vain.
To heav'n, not daring to complain,
No truce, by hoftile clamour giv'n,
And from the face of friendfhip driv'n,
The Nymph funk proftrate on the ground,
With all her weight of woes around.

Enthron'd within a circling fky,
Upon a mount o'er mountains high,
All radiant fate, as in a fhrine,
Virtue, firft effluence divine;
Far, far above the fcenes of woe,
That fhut this cloud-rapt world below;
Superior goddefs, effence bright,
Beauty of uncreated light,
Whom fhould mortality furvey,
As doom'd upon a certain day,
The breath of frailty muft expire,
The world diffolve in living fire,
The gems of heav'n, and folar flame
Be quench'd by her eternal beam,
And nature, quick'ning in her eye,
To rife a new-born phœnix, die.

Hence, unreveal'd to mortal view,
A veil around her form ſhe threw,
Which three ſad ſiſters of the ſhade,
Pain, care, and melancholy made.

Thro' this her all-enquring eye,
Attentive ſtom her ſtation high,
Beheld, abandon'd to deſpair,
The ruins of her fav'rite Fair;
And with a voice, whoſe awful ſound,
Appall'd the guilty world around,
Bid the tumultuous winds be ſtill,
To numbers bow'd each liſt'ning hill,
Uncurl'd the ſurging of the main,
And ſmooth'd the thorny bed of pain,
The golden harp of heav'n ſhe ſtrung,
And thus the tuneful goddeſs ſung.

Lovely Penitent, ariſe,
Come and claim thy kindred ſkies,
Come, thy ſiſter angels ſay,
Thou haſt wept thy ſtains away.

Let experience now decide,
'Twixt the good, and evil try'd,

In the ſmooth, enchanted ground,
Say, unfold the treaſures found.

Structures, rais'd by morning dreams,
Sands, that trip the flitting ſtreams,
Down, that anchors on the air,
Clouds, that paint their changes there.

Seas, that ſmoothly dimpling lie,
While the ſtorm impends on high,
Showing, in an obvious glaſs,
Joys, that in poſſeſſion paſs.

Tranſient, fickle, light, and gay,
Flatt'ring, only to betray·
What, alas, can life contain!
Life! like all its circles——vain.

Will the ſtork, intending reſt,
On the billow build her neſt?
Will the bee demand his ſtore
From the bleak and bladeleſs ſhore?

Man alone, intent to ſtray,
Ever turns from wiſdom's way,

Lays up wealth in foreign land,
Sows the ſea, and plows the ſand.

Soon this elemental maſs,
Soon th' encumbring world ſhall paſs,
Form be wrapt in waſting fire,
Time be ſpent, and life expire.

Then, ye boaſted works of men,
Where is your aſylum then?
Sons of pleaſure, ſons of care,
Tell me, mortals, tell me where?

Gone, like traces on the deep,
Like a ſcepter, graſp'd in ſleep,
Dews, exhal'd from morning glades,
Melting ſnows, and gliding ſhades.

Paſs the world, and what's behind?
Virtue's gold, by fire refin'd;
From an univerſe deprav'd,
From the wreck of nature ſav'd.

Like the life-ſupporting grain
Fruit of patience, and of pain,

On the ſwain's autumnal day,
Winnow'd from the chaff away.

Little trembler, fear no more,
Thou haſt plenteous crops in ſtore,
Seed, by genial ſorrows ſown,
More than all thy ſcorners own.

What tho' hoſtile earth deſpiſe,
Heav'n beholds with gentler eyes;
Heav'n thy friendleſs ſteps ſhall guide,
Chear thy hours, and guard thy ſide.

When the fatal trump ſhall ſound,
When th' immortals pour around.
Heav'n ſhall thy return atteſt,
Hail'd by myriads of the bleſs'd.

Little native of the ſkies,
Lovely penitent, ariſe,
Calm thy boſom, clear thy brow,
Virtue is thy ſiſter now.

More delightful are my woes,
'Than the rapture, pleaſure knows,

Richer far the weeds I bring,
Than the robes, that grace a king.

On my wars of ſhorteſt date,
Crowns of endleſs triumph wait,
On my cares a period bleſs'd,
On my toils, eternal reſt.

Come, with virtue at thy ſide,
Come, be ev'ry bar defy'd,
Till we gain our native ſhore,
Siſter, come, and turn no more.

FABLE XVI.

LOVE AND VANITY.

THE breezy morning breath'd perfume,
The wak'ning flow'rs unveil'd their bloom,
Up with the ſun, from ſhort repoſe,
Gay health, and luſty labour roſe,
The milkmaid carol'd at her pail,
And ſhepherds whiſtled o'er the dale;
When love, who led a rural life,
Remote from buſtle, ſtate, and ſtrife,
Forth from his thatch-roof'd cottage ſtray'd,
And ſtrol'd along the dewy glade.

A Nymph, who lightly tripp'd it by,
To quick attention turn'd his eye,
He mark'd the geſture of the Fair,
Her ſelf-ſufficient grace and air,

Her ſteps, that mincing, meant to pleaſe,
Her ſtudy'd negligence and eaſe;
And curious to enquire what meant
This thing of prettineſs, and paint,
Approaching ſpoke, and bow'd obſervant,
The Lady, ſlightly,——Sir, your ſervant,

Such beauty in ſo rude a place!
Fair one, you do the country grace;
At court, no doubt, the public care,
But Love has ſmall acquaintance there.

Yes, Sir, reply'd the flutt'ring dame,
This form confeſſes whence it came;
But dear variety, you know,
Can make us pride, and pomp forego.
My name is Vanity. I ſway
The utmoſt iſlands of the ſea;
Within my court all honour centers
I raiſe the meaneſt ſoul that enters,
Endow with latent gifts and graces,
And model fools for poſts and places.

As Vanity appoints at pleaſure,
The world receives its weight, and meaſure:

Hence all the grand concerns of life,
Joys, cares, plagues, paſſions, peace and ſtrife.

Reflect how far my pow'r prevails,
When I ſtep in, where nature fails,
And ev'ry breach of ſenſe repairing,
Am bounteous ſtill, where heav'n is ſparing.

But chief in all their arts, and airs,
Their playing, painting, pouts, and pray'rs,
Their various habits, and complexions,
Fits, frolicks, foibles, and perfections,
Their robing, curling, and adorning,
From noon to night, from night to morning,
From ſix to ſixty, ſick or ſound,
I rule the female world around,
Hold there a moment, Cupid cry'd,
Nor boaſt dominion quite ſo wide,
Was there no province to invade,
But that by love and meekneſs ſway'd?
All other empire I reſign,
But be the ſphere of beauty mine.

For in the downy lawn of reſt,
That opens on a woman's breaſt,

Attended by my peaceful train,
I chuſe to live, and chuſe to reign.

Far-ſighted faith I bring along,
And truth, above an army ſtrong,
And chaſtity, of icy mold,
Within the burning tropics cold,
And lowlineſs, to whoſe mild brow,
The pow'r and pride of nations bow,
And modeſty, with down caſt eye,
That lends the morn her virgin dye,
And innocence, array'd in light,
And honour, as a tow'r upright;
With ſweetly winning graces, more
Than poets ever dreamt of yore,
In unaffected conduct free,
All ſmiling ſiſters, three times three,
And roſy peace the cherub bleſs'd,
That nightly ſings us all to reſt.

Hence, from the bud of nature's prime,
From the firſt ſtep of infant time,
Woman, the world's appointed light,
Has ſkirted ev'ry ſhade with white;

Has ſtood for imitation high,
To ev'ry heart and ev'ry eye;
From antient deeds of fair renown,
Has brought her bright memorials down,
To time affix'd perpetual youth,
And form'd each tale of love and truth.

Upon a new Promethean plan,
She molds the eſſence of a man,
Tempers his maſs, his genius fires,
And as a better ſoul inſpires.

The rude ſhe ſoftens, warms the cold,
Exalts the meek, and checks the bold,
Calls ſloth from his ſupine repoſe,
Within the coward's boſom glows,
Of pride unplumes the lofty creſt,
Bids baſhful merit ſtand confeſs'd,
And like coarſe metal from the mines,
Collects, irradiates, and refines.
The gentle ſcience, ſhe imparts,
All manners ſmooths informs all hearts;
From her ſweet influence are felt,
Paſſions that pleaſe, and thoughts that melt;

To ſtormy rage ſhe bids controul,
And ſinks ſerenely on the ſoul,
Softens Ducalion's flinty race,
And tunes the warring world to peace.

Thus arm'd to all that's light and vain,
And freed from thy fantaſtick chain,
She fills the ſphere, by heav'n aſſign'd,
And rul'd by me, o'er-rules mankind.

He ſpoke. The Nymph impatient ſtood,
And laughing, thus her ſpeech renew'd.

And pray, Sir, may I be ſo bold,
To hope your pretty tale is told,
And next demand without a cavil,
What new Utopia do you travel?——
Upon my word theſe high-flown fancies
Shew depth of learning—in romances.
Why, what unfaſhion'd ſtuff you tell us,
Of buckram dames, and tiptoe fellows!
Go, child! and when you're grown maturer,
You'll ſhoot your next opinion ſurer.

O ſuch a pretty knack at painting!
And all for ſoft'ning, and for ſainting!
Gueſs now, who can, a ſingle feature,
Thro' the whole piece of female nature!
Then mark! my looſer hand may fit
The lines too coarſe for love to hit.

'Tis ſaid, that woman prone to changing,
Thro' all the rounds of folly ranging,
On life's uncertain ocean riding,
No reaſon? rule, nor rudder guiding,
Is like the comet's wandring light,
Eccentric, ominous, and bright.
Tractleſs, and ſhifting as the wind,
A ſea, whoſe fathom none can find,
A moon, ſtill changing, and revolving,
A riddle, paſt all human ſolving,
A bliſs, a plague, a heav'n, a hell,
A——ſomething, that no man can tell.

Now learn a ſecret from a friend,
But keep your council, and attend.

Tho' in their tempers thought ſo diſtant,
Nor with their ſex, nor ſelves conſiſtent,

'Tis but the diff'rence of a name,
And ev'ry woman is the ſame.
For as the world, however vary'd,
And thro' unnumber'd changes carry'd,
Of elemental modes and forms,
Clouds, meteors, colours, calms, and ſtorms,
Tho' in a thouſand ſuits array'd,
Is of one ſubject matter made;
So, Sir, a woman's conſtitution,
The world's enigma, finds ſolution.
And let her form be what you will
I am the ſubject eſſence ſtill.

With the firſt ſpark of female ſenſe,
The ſpeck of being, I commence,
Within the womb make freſh advances,
And dictate future qualms and fancies;
Thence in the growing form expand,
With childhood travel hand in hand,
And give a taſte of all their joys,
In gewgaws, rattles, pomp, and noiſe.

And now, familiar, and unaw'd,
I ſend the flutt'ring ſoul abroad;

Prais'd for her ſhape, her air, her mien,
The little goddeſs, and the queen,
Takes at her infant ſhrine oblation,
And drinks ſweet draughts of adulation.

Now blooming, tall, erect, and fair,
To dreſs, becomes her darling care;
The realms of beauty then I bound,
I ſwell the hoop's enchanted round,
Shrink in the waiſt's deſcending ſize,
Heav'd in the ſnowy boſom, riſe,
High on the floating lappet ſail,
Or curl'd in treſſes kiſs the gale.
Then to her glaſs, I lead the fair,
And ſhew the lovely idol there,
Where, ſtruck as by divine emotion,
She bows with moſt ſincere devotion,
And numb'ring ev'ry beauty o'er,
In ſecret bids the world adore.

Then all for parking, and parading,
Coquetting, dancing, maſquerading;
For balls, plays, courts, and crouds what paſſion;
And churches, ſometimes————if the faſhion;

For woman's ſenſe of right and wrong,
Is rul'd by the almighty throng,
Still turns to each meander tame,
And ſwims the ſtraw of ev'ry ſtream.
Her ſoul intrinſic worth rejects,
Accompliſh'd only in defects,
Such excellence is her ambition,
Folly, her wiſeſt acquiſition,
And ev'n from pity, and diſdain,
She'll cull ſome reaſon to be vain.

Thus, Sir, from ev'ry form, and feature,
The wealth, and wants of female nature,
And ev'n from vice, which you'd admire,
I gather fewel to my fire,
And on the very baſe of ſhame,
Erect my monument of fame.

Let me another truth attempt,
Of which your godſhip has not dreamt.

Thoſe ſhining virtues, which you muſter,
Whence think you they derive their luſtre?
From native honour, and devotion?
O yes, a mighty likely notion!

Truſt me, from titled dames to ſpinners,
'Tis I make ſaints, whoe'er makes ſinners;
'Tis I inſtruct them to withdraw,
And hold preſumptuous man in awe;
For female worth as I inſpire,
In juſt degrees, ſtill mounts the higher,
And virtue, ſo extremely nice,
Demands long toil, and mighty price,
Like Sampſon's pillars, fix'd elate,
I bear the ſex's tott'ring ſtate,
Sap theſe, and in a moment's ſpace,
Down ſinks the fabric to its baſe.

Alike from titles, and from toys,
I ſpring, the fount of female joys,
In every widow, wife, and miſs,
The ſole artificer of bliſs.
For them each tropic I explore;
I cleave the ſand of ev'ry ſhore;
To them uniting Indias ſail,
Sabæa breathes her fartheſt gale;
For them the bullion I refine,
Dig ſenſe, and virtue from the mine,

And from the bowels of invention,
Spin out the various arts you mention.

Nor bliſs alone my pow'rs beſtow,
They hold the ſov'reign balm of woe;
Beyond the ſtoic's boaſted art,
I ſooth the heavings of the heart;
To pain give ſplendor, and relief,
And gild the pallid face of grief.

Alike the palace, and the plain
Admit the glories of my reign;
Thro' ev'ry age, in ev'ry nation,
Taſte, talents, tempers, ſtate, and ſtation,
Whate'er a woman ſays, I ſay;
Whate'er a womun ſpends, I pay;
Alike I fill, and empty bags,
Flutter, in finery, and rags,
With light coquets thro' folly range,
And with the prude diſdain to change.

And now you'd think, 'twixt you and I,
That things were ripe for a reply——
But ſoft, and while I'm in the mood,
Kindly permit me to conclude,

Their utmoſt mazes to unravel,
And touch the fartheſt ſtep they travel.

When ev'ry pleaſure's run a-ground,
And folly tir'd thro' many a round,
The nymph, conceiving diſcontent hence,
May ripen to an hour's repentance,
And vapours ſhed in pious moiſture,
Diſmiſs her to a church, or cloyſter;
Then on I lead her, with devotion,
Conſpicuous in her dreſs and motion,
Inſpire the heav'nly-breathing air,
Roll up the lucid eye in pray'r,
Soften the voice, and in the face
Look melting harmony and grace.

Thus far extends my friendly pow'r,
Nor quits her in her lateſt hour;
The couch of decent pain I ſpread,
In form recline her languid head,
Her thoughts I methodize in death,
And part not with her parting breath;
Then do I ſet, in order bright,
A length of funeral pomp to ſight,

The glitt'ring tapers, and attire,
The plumes that whiten o'er her bier;
And laſt, preſenting to her eye
Angelic fineries on high,
To ſcenes of painted bliſs I waft her,
And form the heav'n ſhe hopes hereafter.

In truth, rejoin'd love's gentle God,
You've gone a tedious length of road,
And ſtrange, in all the toilſome way,
No houſe of kind refreſhment lay,
No nymph, whoſe virtues might have tempted,
To hold her from her ſex exempted.

For one, we'll never quarrel, man;
Take her, and keep her if you can;
And pleas'd I yield to your petition,
Since every fair, by ſuch permiſſion,
Will hold herſelf the one ſelected,
And ſo my ſyſtem ſtands protected.

O deaf to virtue, deaf to glory,
To truths divinely vouch'd in ſtory!
The Godhead in his zeal return'd,
And kindling at her malice burn'd.

Then ſweetly rais'd his voice, and told
Of heav'nly nymphs, rever'd of old;
Hypſipyle, who ſav'd her ſire;
And Portia's love, approv'd by fire;
Alike Penelope was quoted,
Nor laurel'd Daphne paſs'd unnoted,
Nor Laodamia's fatal garter,
Nor fam'd Lucretia, honour's martyr,
Alceſte's voluntary ſteel,
And Catherine, ſmiling on the wheel.

But who can hope to plant conviction,
Where cavil grows on contradiction?
Some ſhe evades or diſavows,
Demurs to all, and none allows;
A kind of antient thing, call'd fables!
And thus the Goddeſs turn'd the tables.

Now both in argument grew high,
And choler flaſh'd from either eye;
Nor wonder each refus'd to yield,
The conqueſt of ſo fair a field.

When happily arriv'd in view,
A Goddeſs, whom our grandames knew,

Of aſpect grave, and ſober gaite,
Majeſtic, awful, and ſedate,
As heav'n's autnmnal eve ſerene,
Where not a cloud o'ercaſts the ſcene;
Once Prudence call'd, a matron fam'd,
And in old Rome, Cornelia nam'd.

Quick at a venture, both agree
To leave their ſtrife to her decree.

And now by each the facts were ſtated,
In form, and manner as related;
The caſe was ſhort. They crav'd opinion,
Which held o'er females chief dominion;
When thus the Goddeſs, anſwering mild,
Firſt ſhook her gracious head, and ſmil'd.

Alas! how willing to comply,
Yet how unfit a judge am I!
In times of golden date, 'tis true,
I ſhar'd the fickle ſex with you,
But from their preſence long precluded,
Or held as one whoſe form intruded,
Full fifty annual ſuns can tell,
Prudence has bid the ſex farewell.

In this dilemma what to do
Or who to think of, neither knew;
For both, ſtill biaſs'd in opinion,
And arrogant of ſole dominion,
Were forc'd to hold the caſe compounded,
Or leave the quarrel where they found it.

When in the nick, a rural fair,
Of inexperienc'd gait and air,
Who ne'er had croſs'd the neighb'ring lake,
Nor ſeen the world beyond a wake,
With cambrick coif, and kerchief clean,
Tript lightly by them o'er the green.

Now, now! cry'd love's triumphant Child,
And at approaching conqueſt ſmil'd,
If Vanity will once be guided,
Our diff'rence ſoon may be decided;
Behold yon wench, a fit occaſion
To try your force of gay perſuaſion.
Go you, wbile I retire aloof,
Go, put thoſe boaſted pow'rs to proof;
And if your prevalence of art
Tranſcends my yet unerring dart,

I give the fav'rite conteſt o'er,
And ne'er will boaſt my empire more.

At once, ſo ſaid, and ſo conſented;
And well our Goddeſs ſeem'd contented;
Nor pauſing, made a moment's ſtand,
But tript, and took the girl in hand.

Mean while the Godhead, unalarm'd,
As one to each occaſion arm'd,
Forth from his quiver cull'd a dart,
That erſt had wounded many a heart;
Then bending, drew it to the head;
The bowſtring twang'd, the arrow fled,
And, to her ſecret ſoul addreſs'd,
Transfix'd the whiteneſs of her breaſt.

But here the Dame, whoſe guardian care,
Had to a moment watch'd the fair,
At once her pocket mirror drew,
And held the wonder full in view;
As quickly, rang'd in order bright,
A thouſand beauties ruſh to ſight,
A world of charms, till now unknown,
A world, reveal d to her alone;

Enraptur'd ſtands the love-ſick maid,
Suſpended o'er the darling ſhade,
Here only fixes to admire,
And centers every fond deſire.

FINIS.

Her Write His Name

Old Kensington *and* The Story of Elizabeth
Anne Isabella Thackeray
With a new introduction by Esther Schwartz-McKinzie
ISBN 1 85506 388 3 : 496pp : 1873 & 1876 editions : £17.75

Shells from the Sands of Time
Rosina Bulwer Lytton
With a new introduction by Marie Mulvey Roberts
ISBN 1 85506 386 7 : 272pp : 1876 edition : £14.75

Platonics
Ethel Arnold
With a new introduction by Phyllis Wachter
ISBN 1 85506 389 1 : 160pp : 1894 edition : £13.75

The Continental Journals 1798-1820
Dorothy Wordsworth
With a new introduction by Helen Boden
ISBN 1 85506 385 9 : 472pp : New edition : £17.75

Her Life in Letters
Alice James
Edited with a new introduction by Linda Anderson
ISBN 1 85506 387 5 : 320pp : New : £15.75

Also available as a 5 volume set : ISBN 1 8556 384 0
Special set price : £70.00

Subversive Women

The Art of Ingeniously Tormenting
Jane Collier
With a new introduction by Judith Hawley
ISBN 1 8556 246 1 : 292pp : 1757 edition : £14.75

Appeal of One Half the Human Race, Women, Against the Pretensions of the Other Half, Men, to Retain them in Political, and thence in Civil and Domestic, Slavery
William Thompson and Anna Wheeler
With a new introduction by the Rt Hon. Michael Foot and Marie Mulvey Roberts
ISBN 1 85506 247 X : 256pp : 1825 edition : £14.75

A Blighted Life: A True Story
Rosina Bulwer Lytton
With a new introduction by Marie Mulvey Roberts
ISBN 1 85506 248 8 : 178pp : 1880 edition : £10.75

The Beth Book
Sarah Grand
With a new introduction by Sally Mitchell
ISBN 1 85506 249 6 : 560pp : 1897 edition : £18.75

The Journal of a Feminist
Elsie Clews Parsons
With a new introduction and notes by Margaret C. Jones
ISBN 1 85506 250 X : 142pp : New edition : £12.75

Also available as a 5 volume set : ISBN 1 85506 261 5
Special set price : £65.00

Vivien Jones
is a Senior Lecturer in the School of English at the University of Leeds. She is the editor of *Women in the Eighteenth Century: Constructions of Femininity* (Routledge, 1990), and has published books on Henry James and Jane Austen, and articles on women and writing in the eighteenth century. She is the editor of *Pride and Prejudice* for the new Penguin Classics edition of Austen's works.

Marie Mulvey Roberts is a Senior Lecturer in literary studies at the University of the West of England and is the author of *British Poets and Secret Societies* (1986), and *Gothic Immortals* (1990). From 1994 she has been the co-editor of a Journal: 'Women's Writing; the Elizabethan to the Victorian Period', and the General Editor for three series: *Subversive Women*, *For Her Own Good*, and *Her Write His Name*. The volumes she has co-edited include: *Sources of British Feminism* (1993), *Perspectives on the History of British Feminism* (1994), *Controversies in the History of British Feminism* (1995) and *Literature and Medicine during the Eighteenth Century* (1993). Among her single edited books are, *Out of the Night: Writings from Death Row* (1994), and editions of Rosina Bulwer Lytton's *A Blighted Life* (1994) and *Shells from the Sands of Time* (1995).

Cover designed by Dan Broughton